'Effective programmes of change are underpinn   of
which can be developed with the help of this boo   .'
Rod Sowden, board director at Centre for Chan   g
Successful Programmes, MD for Aspire Europe

'Business analysis is a crucial tool in the hunt for improved performance, and whenever you investigate performance, you have to talk with people. The quality of your interactions with those people has a massive impact on how successful you can be as an analyst, and NLP has a wonderful set of tools to help improve those interactions. Peter has done a great job of bringing the generic tools of NLP into a pragmatic framework to help with business analysis.'
Paul Matthews, NLP trainer, MD of People Alchemy, author of *Capability at Work: How to Solve the Performance Puzzle*

'At Hudson, we recognise that successful outcomes are underpinned by effective behaviours and skills which, in turn, are developed from leveraging the right mindset for the right context. This approach, tailored to the BA context, will help you to develop yours.'
Stuart Packham, Talent Solutions Director for Technology, Change and Digital Transformation, Hudson

'At PMI we are keen for the BA and PM to work better together, and have products in both of these areas. This book demonstrates the NLP approach and toolset for developing effective behaviours for realising benefits from change management. We are pleased to endorse it.'
Yohan Abrahams, President of the United Kingdom Chapter of the Project Management Institute

'As the role of BA is growing to be more and more strategic, effective use of soft skills and stakeholder management will distinguish great BAs in the near future. The approaches proposed in this book definitely benefit developing these required skills.'
Marc-Andre Langlais, Senior Business Engagement Manager, Canadian National

'Peter is an impressive coach with an extensive professional experience. His long experience as an NLP practitioner allows him to initiate amazing transformational experience.'
Nadir Belarbi, CIO L'Oreal Canada

'In the PMO world, we recognise tools like NLP in developing soft skills necessary to engage the business.'
Lindsay Scott, Founder of The PMO Conference and PMO Flashmob

'It was refreshing to be on a course that focussed on attitudes and behaviours rather than on processes. I saw a number of 'light bulb' moments from the cohort and positive changes in attitude and behaviour from my co-workers immediately after the course.'
Jenny Lanaway, Resource Manager, Tsys

'Delivery is a combination of toolset and mindset. Currently the toolset box is overflowing and cluttered. On the other hand the mindset box is alarmingly empty.'
Steve Wake, Chairman of the Association for Project Management

'Businesses are made of people. Peter Parkes combines his extensive knowledge of NLP and the world of business to bring you an essential toolkit.'
Ewan Mochrie, NLP Master Trainer & MD of Inspire 360 Limited

'The book is essential for everyone who is involved in business change. Peter Parkes emphasises the need for self awareness and soft skills to deal with internal and external stakeholders.'
Soheir Ghallab, Chair, Business Change Specialist Group; BCS, The Chartered Institute for IT

'In order to work in an agile environment, modern BAs need to develop corresponding agile mindsets and behaviours.'
Brian Wernham, author of *Agile Project Management for Government*, 2012

'Peter Parkes, one of our associates, showed that NLP can provide a structured approach (dare I say, a method) to inter-personal and intra-personal techniques in a way that process and task oriented people can relate to and apply.'
Andy Murray, lead author of PRINCE2 (2009 refresh) and partner of global consultancy firm RSM

NLP FOR BUSINESS ANALYSTS

BCS, THE CHARTERED INSTITUTE FOR IT

BCS, The Chartered Institute for IT champions the global IT profession and the interests of individuals engaged in that profession for the benefit of all. We promote wider social and economic progress through the advancement of information technology, science and practice. We bring together industry, academics, practitioners and government to share knowledge, promote new thinking, inform the design of new curricula, shape public policy and inform the public.

Our vision is to be a world-class organisation for IT. Our 70,000 strong membership includes practitioners, businesses, academics and students in the UK and internationally. We deliver a range of professional development tools for practitioners and employees. A leading IT qualification body, we offer a range of widely recognised qualifications.

Further Information
BCS, The Chartered Institute for IT,
First Floor, Block D,
North Star House, North Star Avenue,
Swindon, SN2 1FA, United Kingdom.
T +44 (0) 1793 417 424
F +44 (0) 1793 417 444
www.bcs.org/contact

http://shop.bcs.org/

NLP FOR BUSINESS ANALYSTS
Developing agile mindset and behaviours

Peter Parkes

Published by BCS Learning & Development Ltd, a wholly owned subsidiary of BCS, The Chartered Institute for IT, First Floor, Block D, North Star House, North Star Avenue, Swindon, SN2 1FA, UK.
www.bcs.org

ISBN: 978-1-78017-281-1
PDF ISBN: 978-1-78017-282-8
ePUB ISBN: 978-1-78017-283-5
Kindle ISBN: 978-1-78017-284-2

Ebook available

British Cataloguing in Publication Data.
A CIP catalogue record for this book is available at the British Library.

Disclaimer:
The views expressed in this book are of the author(s) and do not necessarily reflect the views of the Institute or BCS Learning & Development Ltd except where explicitly stated as such. Although every care has been taken by the author(s) and BCS Learning & Development Ltd in the preparation of the publication, no warranty is given by the author(s) or BCS Learning & Development Ltd as publisher as to the accuracy or completeness of the information contained within it and neither the author(s) nor BCS Learning & Development Ltd shall be responsible or liable for any loss or damage whatsoever arising by virtue of such information or any instructions or advice contained within this publication or by any of the aforementioned.

BCS books are available at special quantity discounts to use as premiums and sale promotions, or for use in corporate training programs. Please visit our Contact us page at www.bcs.org/contact

Typeset by Lapiz Digital Services, Chennai, India.

CONTENTS

LIST OF FIGURES

ABOUT THE AUTHOR

Dr Peter Parkes progressed from a degree in mathematics and computing and an executive MBA up to Head of IT and CIO roles via delivery of technology-enabled transformational change in sectors from financial services to local government.

He is a member of the International Institute for Business Analysis (IIBA) and the Project Management Institute (PMI), is a Chartered IT Professional (CITP) and an associate consultant with the Society of IT Management (SocITM). Through continuous professional development, he became a Fellow of BCS The Chartered Institute for IT, the Association for Project Management, the Chartered Management Institute and the Institute of Directors. Since his first training in NLP in the mid-nineties, he has become an NLP Master Practitioner, a coach and internationally certified trainer who has delivered pragmatic workshops, training and group coaching around the world, often in association with professional bodies. He is currently supporting national infrastructure programs to develop requirements, deliver successful outcomes and realise business benefits.

FOREWORD

Business Analysis is about more than just gathering requirements and documenting them. It is built on effective communication with people at all levels, balancing different viewpoints and priorities. It is about working with people to negotiate valuable changes for the good of the organisation, present and future. Amongst other things, it is about flexing to the environment, understanding the multiple stakeholder perspectives and acting as a mediator between different world-views. To be a successful Business Analyst requires a high degree of emotionally intelligence in the workplace.

The behavioural competencies needed by the Business Analyst are now recognised by BCS's SFIA framework and IIBA's Body of Knowledge. Indeed, half of all of the points for award of 'Expert BA' are allocated to soft skills.

This book, using the structured approach and toolset of NLP, can help you with many aspects of business analysis, from surfacing requirements to building rapport with stakeholders and resolving conflict, and is extensively cross referenced to established competency frameworks.

It is written by an experienced practitioner, covering real world situations with a wealth of stories and anecdotes to embed learning.

If you want to develop yourself to become an expert BA with effective soft skills and beneficial behaviours, then this book is for you.

Dot Tudor CITP FBCS, author and chief examiner of 'AgileBA'

ACKNOWLEDGEMENTS

I would like to thank the following people:

BCS for commissioning this book, especially the head of publications at the time, Matthew Flynn, for his patience when we had to re-plan due to a series of life events arriving at my door during 2014.

For assisting with content, editorial and proof reading, Steve Smith, senior BA, Peter Durnford, Brian Wernham, Shelli Stone and Roy Cooper.

For discussions on agile methods in business analysis, Brian Wernham and Steve Messenger.

I am particularly grateful for contributions from business analyst (BA) colleagues and fellow NLP trainers: Richard Allen CBAP, currently principal BA in front office functions for one of the major banks, and Corrine Thomas, director of the IIBA's UK chapter and director of the BA Manager Forum.

Thanks also to various NLP trainers and associates who have helped me on my journey to date in addition to those above, especially Joe Orchard, Roy Cooper, Michael Beale, John Seymore, Ariel Essex, Paul Mathews, Chuck Spezzano and the grand wizard himself, Anthony Robbins.

I am honoured to have a foreword provided by Dot Tudor, Fellow of the BCS, who has worked to develop the International Business Analysis Diploma and Solution Development Diploma and is an accredited examination provider for these.

Most of all I would like to thank the numerous people who have entrusted professional development to me and helped me to gain a deeper understanding of the topic and myself along the way.

INTRODUCTION

IF YOU ALWAYS DO WHAT YOU ALWAYS DID THEN YOU WILL ALWAYS GET WHAT YOU ALWAYS GOT

Do you sometimes find during testing that the specification does not meet current needs? That schedules slip and projects overrun due to ever changing requirements? The solution you build captures the past rather than enables the future? Business representatives are reluctant to sign-off requirements? No one wants to take responsibility for benefits realisation? Projects might deliver assets, but often fail to realise business benefits? There is a focus on technology rather than capability? Processes around customer services seem broken? There is a lack of senior sponsorship, or even understanding of what that role entails? Post-mortems show that failure was avoidable and similar problems may be systemic?

Are you curious as to whether there is another way?

HOW NLP WILL HELP YOU AS A BA

I started my career as a chartered scientist and engineer, later becoming a Chartered IT Professional with BCS, and my view of the world was very much one of a 'hard' systems approach. A systems engineering approach is very effective, until you add people into the mix. Having spent far too many years seeing perfectly good systems fail to realise the benefits expected of them, I am convinced that **we all need to develop excellent 'soft skills' to facilitate change**.

Since becoming familiar with the Soft Systems approach originated by Peter Checkland[1] while studying under him for my MBA, I have completed hundreds of days of training courses and read hundreds of books, and from these have found the approach and toolset of NLP (neuro-linguistic programming) to be the most effective for developing soft skills. Learning and applying the techniques of NLP has helped me to deliver with more finesse and a lot less re-work. I am sure that it will help you in the same way should you choose to follow this route. So, if you want to be even more effective in your role then this book is for you.

---

1 Peter Checkland, Soft Systems Methodology (SSM) http://www.lancaster.ac.uk/lums/people/peter-checkland [accessed 22 June 2016].

I was particularly pleased that the new edition of the BCS publication *Business Analysis* retained an excellent table of technical and behavioural competencies for effective business analysts (BAs).[2] In Figure I.1 I have italicised all the technical competencies from Figure 2.1 covered in that book, leaving me a clear scope to focus on underpinning the behavioural competencies, emphasised in bold, in this one.

Figure I.1 Required competencies of a BA

Behavioural and personal qualities	Business knowledge	Techniques
Communication	*Finance and the economy*	**Project management**
Relationship building	*Business case development*	*Strategy analysis*
Influencing	*Domain knowledge*	**Stakeholder analysis and management**
Team-working	*Subject matter expertise*	
Political awareness	*Principles of IT*	**Investigation techniques**
Analytical skills and critical thinking	*Organisation structures and design*	*Requirements engineering*
		Business system modelling
Attention to detail	**Supplier management**	*Business process modelling*
Problem solving		*Data modelling*
Leadership		**Managing business change**
Self-belief		**Facilitation techniques**

The third edition of *A Guide to the Business Analysis Body of Knowledge* from the International Institute of Business Analysis (IIBA) has also evolved from coverage of mainly technical competencies and processes towards behaviours, which we will explore in more detail in Part 1.

To summarise, for you as a BA this book will:

- Strengthen your ability to connect with others and develop rapport.
- Help you to pick up and decode what is being communicated outside the obvious – words will give you an edge in everything from negotiation to leadership.
- Show you how to develop flexibility in behaviour to match context and requirements.
- Enable you to communicate more effectively and persuasively.
- Help you to facilitate, motivate and lead.

---

2 Figure 2.1 from Debra Paul, James Cadle and Donald Yeates, eds, 2014, *Business Analysis* 3rd edn, BCS.

- Give you an understanding of why you do things the way that you do, and what other choices are available.

- Help you to control the way you think, feel and act, even in stressful situations.

- Manage stress and build resilience.

- Help you to develop new skills.

- Enable you to model excellent behaviours from role models whom you meet.

STRUCTURE AND APPROACH OF THIS BOOK

This book is focused on the behavioural competencies required for effective business analysis.

The structure of the book follows an NLP approach itself. At the core of NLP is the pre-supposition that we all have unique world-views, and we communicate most effectively when we uncover overlap of these distinct worlds. Hence, in Part 1 I provide first an overview of the changing world of business analysis to get us onto the same page. Note that the IIBA *Body of Knowledge* only originated in 2003, so perspectives are still maturing in the world of business analysis, and we might expect some old hands to still be living in the world of systems engineering. Only after establishing a common understanding of what direction business analysis is likely to take in the future will I go on to Part 2, where I lay the foundations of NLP. In Part 3, I will bring the two worlds together and apply NLP to those behavioural competencies identified in the review in Part 1 (see Figure I.2).

Figure I.2 Bringing the worlds of business analysis and NLP together

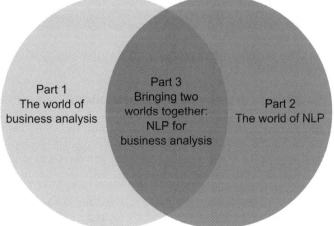

NLP is embedded in the book itself, so you might notice, for instance, that my style of writing sometimes varies from vague to precise, from raising curiosity to being directive, from telling stories to doing exercises, from using metaphor to providing processes. The first paragraph of this Introduction is a good example of using motivational 'away from' statements in an Eriksonian pattern, ending with the key learning initiator 'are you curious?'. NLP presupposes that learning new ideas is aided by a little discomfort and confusion to distract the conscious mind while the unconscious learns the new programs. The same key will not open every door, but keys are useful and every door can be opened.

> Perplexity is the beginning of knowledge.
>
> Kahlil Gibran, *The Voice of the Master*, 1998

I guest on a number of master's degree programs and deliver various training courses and master classes to very precise formats, which are well established in learning and development circles. Those formats work very well for transfer of knowledge and understanding. Standard training formats are not effective in transferring behavioural competencies though, leading most to say that they cannot be taught in the classroom. They might not be able to be taught, but they can be learned, using individual and group coaching formats. Hence, I do not follow a standard training format with this book, though I do use the book to support knowledge elements of workshops and group coaching.

One area where the written word can initiate change is through use of story and metaphor; you will see many examples in this book, ranging from simple quotes to stories of application.

> No man can reveal to you aught but that which already lies half asleep in the dawning of your knowledge.
>
> Kahlil Gibran, *The Prophet*, 1923

NAMING CONVENTIONS

In this book I will refer to a generic role of '**business analyst**', and we will look at the scope of that role in Part 1.2. In some organisations, parts of these responsibilities are broken down into separate roles with a variety of names, including change manager and account manager, but if you feel that you are responsible for working out solutions to problems and opportunities, and seeing them through development and testing to realise business benefits, then this book is for you.

I refer to the generic term '**projects**', though purists will recognise some of these concepts as applying more to programs of change. As a simple differentiator, projects can be thought of in terms of delivering assets or outputs, while programs focus on using these to achieve business outcomes and realise tangible business benefits.

In the past, human resources (HR) professionals have tended to draw a clear distinction between 'competences' and 'competencies'. The term 'competence' (competences) was used to describe what people need to do to perform a job and was concerned with effect and output rather than effort and input. '**Competency**' (competencies) described the behaviour that lies behind competent performance, such as critical thinking or analytical skills, and described what people bring to the job. However, in recent years, there has been growing awareness that job performance requires a mix of behaviour, attitude and action and hence the two terms are often used interchangeably. In line with the approach developed in a number of publications by the CIPD (Chartered Institute for Personnel and Development), including *Competency Frameworks in UK Organisations*,[3] I will use the term 'competency' throughout for consistency.

---

3 http://www.cipd.co.uk/hr-resources/factsheets/competence-competency-frameworks.aspx [accessed 22 June 2016].

PART 1. THE WORLD OF BUSINESS ANALYSIS

As described in the Introduction, this Part will focus exclusively on the evolving role of the BA. We will not look at application of NLP to behavioural competencies identified through the review in this chapter until Part 3, after we have laid the foundations of NLP in Part 2. If you think that you already know where business analysis is going, then you could go straight to Part 2 or 3.

Rather than merely develop the business case for a stronger focus on behavioural competencies, which I believe is already well established in the executive layer of most organisations, I go further and map the evolutionary direction of the profession. Not long ago, some looked on it as an administrative role of listing and analysing customer requirements. A few still do. The weight of evidence described here, however, points to it becoming an agent of change, underpinning survival in this age of agile organisations.

> In order to work in an agile environment, the modern BAs need to develop corresponding agile mindsets and behaviours.
>
> Brian Wernham, author of *Agile Project Management for Government*, 2012

I will review emerging trends, current thinking in the bodies of knowledge and the increasing focus on behaviours in competency frameworks. The increasing weighting of behavioural competencies in the growing raft of professional qualifications will become evident, and we will look at ways in which behavioural competencies, as against knowledge of processes, can be assessed. In doing so, I will demonstrate the equivalence to the emotional intelligence framework, which provides a much more stable and useable platform than often vague and disparate lists of behaviours developed independently.

1.1 BUSINESS ANALYSIS UNDERPINS EFFECTIVE DELIVERY OF CHANGE

> Research on why projects fail typically leads to a realisation that there were poor or incomplete requirements.
>
> Chuck Millhollan[1]

---

1 Chuck Millhollan, 2011, 'The Marriage of Professions: Business Analysis and Project Management Can Live Happily Together ... Forever', published as part of the Proceedings of the PMI Global Congress and available as a pdf download to members from PMI.

Successful business change is underpinned by competent analyses of problems and formulation of solutions. The role of the BA is key in that process, though often over-looked, with parts of the function falling to subject matter experts (SMEs), technical architects, project managers (PMs), change managers and account managers. Many holding the title of BA are still, at best, qualified through experience rather than formal training and development of supporting behavioural competencies. Is this lack of continuity and capability across the business analysis life-cycle part of the reason why so many projects still fail to realise their business case?

Having grown up with books such as *Reengineering the Corporation*,[2] and been involved as both victim and perpetrator in various organisational 'down-sizing' and 'right-sizing' initiatives,[3] historically for me the main focus of business analysis was organisational design and process re-engineering. Moving on to become involved with, and then lead, outsourcing programs driven by public–private partnerships (PPPs), the focus at the front-end during the bid process was due diligence on the 'as is' situation across the whole organisation, followed by financial modelling of options for 'to be', involving various degrees of organisational transformation. Thus, the focus remained on process effectiveness and then efficiency, even when we were putting in a raft of IT and customer service projects under Tony Blair's 'Transformational Government: Enabled by Technology'[4] and e-Government initiatives.[5] Training for BAs employed in my own company reflected this focus of trying to understand what the business was trying to achieve and then working out how to get there – the classic 'as is' to 'to be' approach.[6] In many instances, however, the scope of business analysis engagement may be restricted to the specification of systems, missing the foundation for realisation of business benefits.

It was not really until I started working in central government with very large systems going into test phases that I realised how poor our requirements gathering phase can sometimes be, with deficiencies often only manifesting themselves in the testing phase late in the life-cycle. As you may be aware, the cost of fixing stuff increases markedly as we progress through the life-cycle, with an order of magnitude cost increase for each stage often cited (see Figure 1.1).

More alarmingly, having worked as a Gateway™ Reviewer on high risk major projects for the UK government,[7] it is my experience that misunderstandings incorporated at the start of the project are often evident in reviews carried out late in the life-cycle. While presenting to the Association for Project Management (APM) annual conference in 2010, Sir Peter Gershon, former CEO of the Office of Government Commerce (OGC, now incorporated into the Cabinet Office), said that for some major projects it was fairly obvious at the outset that they were doomed to failure. There is probably a long list of projects in this category, and if you want to focus on failure then you might want to follow the

---

2 Michael Hammer and James Champy, 2001, *Reengineering the Corporation: A Manifesto for Business Revolution* 3rd edn, Nicholas Brealey Publishing.

3 Mike Sisco, 2015, *IT Organization: Right-size your Organization for Success* 2nd edn, Practical IT Manager GOLD Series Book 5, MDE Enterprises.

4 http://webarchive.nationalarchives.gov.uk/20130128101412/http://www.cabinetoffice.gov.uk/media/141734/transgov-strategy.pdf [accessed 22 June 2016].

5 http://researchbriefings.files.parliament.uk/documents/SN01202/SN01202.pdf [accessed 22 June 2016].

6 http://www.mbs.ac.uk/research/research-impact/impacts/change-management-local-councils.aspx [accessed 22 June 2016].

7 http://webarchive.nationalarchives.gov.uk/20100503135839/http:/www.ogc.gov.uk/what_is_ogc_gateway_review.asp [accessed 22 June 2016].

Figure 1.1 The ability to influence a project over time

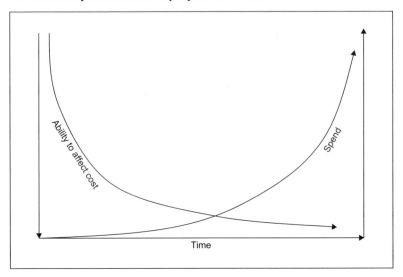

annual 'Chaos reports'.[8] More productively, you may want to think about carrying out a project autopsy before you start, using the 'pre-mortem' technique described in Section 3.8 of this book.

Throughout this book our focus will be on success rather than failure. Gerry Murphy, an assurance executive from the London Olympic Development Authority, said that they were able to have all the venues available well ahead of time because the Olympic governing body carried forward specifications for all venues and activities from one event to the next.[9] Thus, they were able to brief their delivery supply chain while their stakeholders were going through classic 'Form, Storm, Norm and Perform' stages.[10] Not only were the Olympics a great achievement for British athletes, they were evidence that we can do big projects really well when we understand the business goals and get the requirements right.

> What we have already learnt is that Britain is actually rather better at organising big projects than we often gave ourselves credit for.
>
> Business Secretary Vince Cable MP, *The Times* CEO Summit, June 2012

1.2 EVOLUTION OF THE ROLE OF THE BA

In this section we will look at the different definitions of BA and, perhaps more informatively, how definitions have evolved from a technical role towards a facilitator of change.

8 http://www.projectsmart.co.uk/docs/chaos-report.pdf [accessed 22 June 2016].
9 http://www.apm.org.uk/news/olympic-lessons-learned-public-sector-construction [accessed 22 June 2016].
10 Donald B. Egolf, 2001, *Forming Storming Norming Performing: Successful Communications in Groups and Teams*, iUniverse.

1.2.1 Evolution of definitions

In the BCS publication *IT-enabled Business Change*,[11] Sharm Manwani reproduces the definition of the role of BA from the website of the OGC:

> Business Analysts are responsible for identifying and documenting the functional and non-functional requirements for meeting business need. They should have a good understanding of the business area and be able to identify opportunities for effective use of IT.

Perhaps not intentionally, this somewhat reflects a common narrow view of BAs – they are there only to document requirements as a kind of scribe and add little further value.

The IIBA defined the role of a BA in the second edition of their *Body of Knowledge* (BABOK® v2)[12] as:

> Business Analysis is the set of *tasks and techniques* used to work as a liaison amongst stakeholders in order to understand the structure, policies, and operations of an organisation, and to recommend solutions that enable the organisation to achieve its goals.

This definition encompasses the concept of understanding and solving today's problems and enabling tomorrow's opportunities. I also like the link to strategic goals. I am not so keen on the narrowing of definition to 'a set of tasks and techniques', especially as the BABOK® v2 goes on to describe a useful set of supporting behavioural characteristics, encompassing even trust and ethics. During consultation on v3, a broader definition emerged which I believe encompasses the behavioural aspects of the role in terms of outcomes.

> Business analysis is the practice of enabling change in an enterprise by defining needs and recommending solutions that deliver value to stakeholders. Business analysis ultimately helps organizations to understand the needs of the enterprise and why they want to create change, design possible solutions, and describe how those solutions can deliver value.

This is the vision for business analysis that I will be developing in this book and in associated training and coaching.

BABOK® v2 went on to say that:

> The BA is responsible for eliciting the actual needs of the stakeholders, not simply their expressed desires. In many cases, the BA will also work to facilitate communication between organisational units. In particular, BAs often play a central role in aligning the needs of the business units with the capabilities delivered by IT, and may serve as a 'translator' between groups.

---

11 Sharm Manwani, 2008, *IT-enabled Business Change: Successful Management*, BCS.
12 *A Guide to the Business Analysis Body of Knowledge® (BABOK® Guide)* v2 http://www.iiba.org/babok-guide/babok-guide-v2.aspx [accessed 22 June 2016].

I like this emphasis on elicitation, facilitation and communication, which complements the process orientation of the guide. You will find excerpts from these definitions in corresponding sections in Part 3.

> The use of the term 'translator' reminds me of when I worked in the nuclear industry and the then chairman, Sir John Guinness, asked me what I did. I replied that I regarded myself as a translator. When he asked if I was fluent in Japanese, our biggest market, I replied, 'No, I speak fluent Geek and also MBA, and find that I add value interpreting our strategy to our "back-room" boys and our capabilities to the guys upstairs.' It earned me a spell carrying his briefcase and facilitating a move 'upstairs' myself.

Although I am firmly in favour of dedicated trained and experienced BAs having continuity across the business change life-cycle, we should remember that these activities are sometimes carried out piecemeal and may be spread across several roles. Again from IIBA's BABOK® v2:

> A business analyst is any person who performs business analysis activities, no matter their job title or organizational role. Other common job titles for people that perform business analysis include business systems analyst, systems analyst, requirements engineer, process analyst, product manager, product owner, enterprise analyst, business architect, and management consultant. A business analyst can also be any other person who performs the Tasks described in the BABOK® Guide, including those who also perform related disciplines such as project management, business process management, software development, quality assurance, and interaction design.

The Skills Framework for the Information Age[13] (SFIA) describes business analysis as:

> The methodical investigation, analysis, review and documentation of all or part of a business in terms of business functions and processes, the information used and the data on which the information is based. The definition of requirements for improving processes and systems, reducing their costs, enhancing their sustainability, and the quantification of potential business benefits. The creation of viable specifications and acceptance criteria in preparation for the construction of information and communication systems.

I have worked with people carrying out these activities in roles designated as: due diligence (during acquisition and outsourcing); business process re-engineering (BPR); business change; business transformation and engagement and account managers. The BA is often the de facto PM during the early stages of a project, especially where a business case needs to be created, approved and funded before a dedicated PM and team can be mobilised. During my time with 'Big 4' consulting firms, although we usually carried a title from the PM family, I thought we created most value when we undertook business analysis type activities, particularly when using the well versed script, 'Where are you now? Where do you want to be? Let's look at your capabilities and options for getting there.'

---

13 www.sfia-online.org [accessed 22 June 2016].

1.2.2 Scope of business analysis

Not all work carried out by BAs is formalised as projects, particularly in support of operations and process efficiency, and much of it might not be initiated by a formal business case. However, I like to apply the discipline of business change and consider it in terms of projects/programs.

Having been involved in a lot of project recovery as well as assurance, it is my view that projects generally go off track during feasibility and initiation stages, after which it is almost impossible to fully rescue the business case. Hence it is very important to have clarity on who is doing what, and more importantly, who is not doing what.

> That which starts out badly rarely improves.
>   Sir Peter Gershon, former CEO of the OGC, now part of the Cabinet Office

I like to think of the scope of change as depicted in Figure 1.2, and hence the scope of the BA role should address these four elements. In *Managing Successful Programs*,[14] use of similar perspectives of POTI (Process, Organisation, Technology and Information) are recommended to analyse and describe 'as is' and 'to be' states. I accommodate both views by combining 'processes and supporting technology' and incorporating 'information flows', which encompasses the wider scope of information governance and assurance. Technology and process are well covered by a range of books and knowledge-based training, so our focus in subsequent sections will be on people skills and organisational context.

Figure 1.2 Four aspects of business change

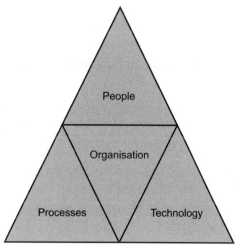

---

14 *Managing Successful Programs*, 2011, TSO publications.

Fundamentally, BAs bridge the gap between the business opportunity or problem and implementation of the solution. Along the way, they might be engaged to:

- Elicit information about the problem situation or opportunity created by changes in the market or available technology.
- Draft the goals and measures of success.
- Develop requirements.
- Gain an understanding of possible options.
- Test technical and practical suitability.
- Develop success criteria and a test strategy.
- Map 'as is' systems and processes.
- Scope resources required.
- Develop an outline business case.
- Identify, map and engage stakeholders.
- Present and sell the preferred option.
- Help to mobilise the project team.
- Work with any PM to ensure that the solution is moving towards business outcome.
- Recommend phasing and a release strategy.
- Monitor quality of testing.
- Confirm the business is ready.
- Hold hands along the way.
- Monitor realisation of benefits from the business case.

1.2.3 Five trends affecting the role of business analysis

Today's organisations exist in a climate where change is ubiquitous. The many dynamic and contradictory drivers for change include innovations in technology, working practices (including outsourcing and partnerships), mergers, increasing demands from regulation and, for the public sector, delivery of policy driven by change political parties and/or ministers. Whatever the organisation, wherever it is located, however it is structured, the rate of change is increasing. 'Introduction' to *Managing Successful Programmes Pocketbook*[15]

As a segue into this section, I give an example of where the pace of change rendered analysis of requirements obsolete.

---

15 *Managing Successful Programmes Pocketbook*, 2007 TSO publications.

TECHNOLOGICAL ADVANCES FORCE A RE-DESIGN AND RE-WORK ON MEGA-PROJECT

The multi-billion pound London Heathrow Terminal 5 project was caught out by development of radio frequency identification (RFID).

It made good business sense to implement RFID to track the millions of bags during luggage handling. The problem was that the steel supports for the building design under construction acted as a shielding Faraday cage and blocked signals. They decided to go into re-design and re-work. Hence, in Heathrow Terminal 5 you will now find a huge hangar-like open structure re-designed to enable wide-scale use of wireless and radio frequency technology.

A recent BCS survey on IT trends[16] did not throw up any new concerns compared with previous years, though the order changed a little. The top three headline management issues for leaders were: business transformation and organisational change; strategy and planning; and operational efficiencies. Business analysis has a key part to play in delivering all of these.

Unsurprisingly, the report rated near-term trends as: mobile computing; information security; and cloud computing. Longer term trends on a three- to five-year time horizon were: data security; cloud computing; and 'big data'. Clearly, security risks are not going to go away and cloud computing is not yet mature. The marketing term 'big data' has now taken a firm hold, with even the UK government getting in on the act and announcing an initiative for 'big data' amongst the headlines for the 2014 annual budget.[17]

Where are we with resources and skills to support these trends? A near universal agreement was found in lack of resources, with 90 per cent of respondents feeling that they had significant capacity and capability issues. Note that capability gaps, particularly in soft skills, were considered to be more severe than capacity gaps.

Gaps in skills fell into the hemispheres of technical know-how and 'people skills'. Technical gaps were, as would be expected, around emergent trends cited above, particularly data management and security for Bring Your Own Devices (BYOD), including use of social media to address corporate goals.

Given that IT leaders noted a 'lack of basic computing knowledge' in executive boards, leading to the belief that IT-enabled change is solved by merely buying new infrastructure, it is no surprise that essential skills included a greater understanding of the business and an appreciation of what was practical from what was possible within the organisational context. Given this separation in world-views, it is no surprise, then, that a specific skills gap was identified around communicating ideas and getting buy-in. Business analysis was specifically mentioned, alongside the ability to deal with ambiguity and to work fast in a flexible way (the rise of agile methods will be specifically discussed in the next section). Despite IT's continuing efforts to redress the geeky image, one IT director in the survey captured the essence of the problem:

---

16 *ITNOW* Spring 2014; BCS's third CIO survey 'What digital leaders say...', pp 52–4. A full report is available at http://www.bcs.org
17 https://www.gov.uk/government/news/73-million-to-improve-access-to-data-and-drive-innovation [accessed 20 June 2016].

There is still a lack of people-people – those that can work with the business and create solutions that can engage.

and that is what this book focuses on.

Developing an agile mindset

> Agile is more about having an agile mindset than a toolset or method.
> Steve Messenger, Chairman of the Agile DSDM Consortium

Agile became a mainstream trend from around 2010 when central government in the UK and the US tried to distance themselves from large expensive failures,[18] though they were not initially too successful in that.[19] Several methods abound for agile, but I particularly like the thrust of the Agile Manifesto, which places the emphasis on behaviours rather than method.[20]

> We are uncovering better ways of developing software by doing it and helping others do it. Through this work we have come to value:
>
> • Individuals and interactions over processes and tools
>
> • Working software over comprehensive documentation
>
> • Customer collaboration over contract negotiation
>
> • Responding to change over following a plan.
>
> That is, while there is value in the items on the right, we value the items on the left more.[21]

Recent publications from the Agile DSDM Consortium[22] include *Agile Business Analysis*,[23] which introduces methods and tools commonly taught in business schools. It is worth noting that BCS also have a publication covering agile methods for BAs, *Agile and Business Analysis* by Debra Paul and Lynda Girvan.[24]

Now that agile is mainstream, formal best practice groups within APM are looking at governance of agile projects and assurance of agile projects. The Governance group is developing guidance for agile using agile principles, including publishing drafts after each 'sprint'.[25] The Assurance group is focusing on how to assure agile behaviours across project teams (we look at some of these behaviours in Section 3.4.1).

> Delivery is a combination of toolset and mindset. Currently the toolset box is overflowing and cluttered. On the other hand the mindset box is alarmingly empty.
> Steve Wake, Chairman of the Association for Project Management

18 Brian Wernham, 2012, *Agile Project Management for Government*, Maitland and Strong.
19 http://www.computerweekly.com/news/2240187478/Why-agile-development-failed-for-Universal-Credit [accessed 22 June 2016].
20 http://www.dsdm.org/ [accessed 22 June 2016].
21 http://www.agilemanifesto.org/ [accessed 22 June 2016].
22 Agile DSDM Consortium http://www.dsdm.org/ [accessed 22 June 2016].
23 Dot Tudor, 2015, *Agile Business Analysis Handbook*, Agile DSDM Consortium.
24 Debra Paul and Lynda Girvan, 2016, *Agile and Business Analysis: Practical Guidance for IT Professionals*, BCS.
25 http://www.apm.org.uk/news/development-apm-agile-governance-guide#.VBTMTvldWSo [accessed 22 June 2016].

BCS has run a specific interest group on agile methods for many years.[26] The standard for agile in IT service management dates back to 2010,[27] and more recently BCS announced qualifications in agile methods at foundation and practitioner level in partnership with APM Group, who were the licencing body for PRINCE2™ (PRojects IN a Controlled Environment).[28] Guidance on PRINCE™ and agile was re-launched in 2015.[29]

> When we started the public consultation for the update to PRINCE2, we were overwhelmed by requests to include the behavioural aspects in the method. We did not include them, but instead chose to sign-post the critical importance of them. Peter Parkes, one of our associates, showed that NLP can provide a structured approach (dare I say, a method) to inter-personal and intra-personal techniques in a way that process and task oriented people can relate to and apply. I found it incredibly complementary to PRINCE2.
>
> Andy Murray, lead author of PRINCE2 (2009 refresh) and partner of global consultancy firm RSM

Program thinking and benefits management

Increasing adoption of an agile approach encourages us to question the fundamentals of what we are delivering and how value can be realised. Benefits realisation mapping was added to the second edition of BCS's *Business Analysis*. This provides us with the ammunition to link to organisational strategy and push back on scope creep and ever changing requirements.

Functional testing, while important from a systems perspective, is not as important to the end user as realising the benefit they were expecting from the system, so there will be increasing focus on understanding where value can be created. This requires a different approach to users than simply harvesting 'requirements' and expecting them to sign-off, but rather a deeper understanding of their map of the world and interpretation of how systems and tools can surface hidden needs and exceed their expectations (see Figure 1.3).[30]

The UK Cabinet Office has developed qualifications specifically for program management,[31] the Project Management Institute (PMI) has also developed a specific qualification, Program Management Professional,[32] and the APM has a very active best practice group.[33] In the latest edition of BoK, the APM has restructured its body of knowledge to separate out aspects of portfolio, program and project for each knowledge area.

I write extensively on delivering through programs of change in Section 3.18.

---

26 http://www.bcs.org/category/16392 [accessed 23 June 2016].

27 Dorothy J Tudor, 2010, *Agile Project and Service Management: Delivering IT Services using ITIL, PRINCE2 and DSDM Atern*, OGC/TSO.

28 http://certifications.bcs.org/category/17491 [accessed 23 June 2016].

29 Axelos, 2015, *PRINCE2 Agile*, TSO.

30 Prof Keith Goffin, January 2011, 'Creating breakthrough products from hidden needs', *The European Business Review*, pp 10–11.

31 Rod Sowden, 2011, *Managing Successful Programmes*, OGC/TSO.

32 http://www.pmi.org/certification/program-management-professional-pgmp.aspx [accessed 23 June 2016].

33 https://www.apm.org.uk/group/apm-program-management-specific-interest-group [accessed 23 June 2016].

Figure 1.3 For programs, the focus requires more refined 'people skills'

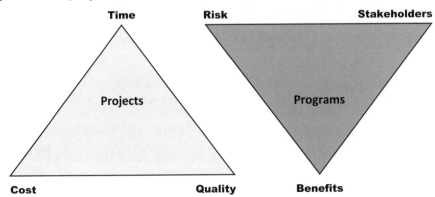

Mega-projects – complex or just complicated requirements?

> Projects do not generally fail for novel reasons, but for the same boringly repetitive ones.
>
> Sir Peter Gershon addressing the APM annual conference in London, 2010

With major investments in infrastructure, and military platforms being increasingly technology-based, managing complexity and mega-projects has been a theme of many publications and conferences.[34] In terms of delivery, complexity, which infers emergent behaviour and inherent un-predictability, often gets confused with just plain compli-cated, which can be managed through work break-down. (For fans of the film series *Terminator*, consciousness arising from Skynet was a fictional emergent property.)

While assuring a major IT project for a client, the contractor confided in me: 'When we put a million lines of new code on to twenty million pounds of hardware with numerous interfaces into other lines of business, sometimes we are not really able to predict what will happen.' The world's most advanced fighter aircraft has tens of millions of lines of code controlling hundreds of millions of dollars of hardware – little wonder that testing and debugging is years behind.

ADVANCING CUSTOMER EXPECTATIONS RENDER DESIGN OUT-DATED

As part of the learning legacy project from the 2012 London Olympic games,[35] telecoms partner BT gave several examples of how technology had moved so fast that

---

34 A review of mega-projects is available via the APM website, including https://www.apm.org.uk/news/governing-mega-projects-towards-public-value-management [accessed 23 June 2016].
35 http://www.apm.org.uk/learninglegacy [accessed 23 June 2016].

it rendered their best laid plans and future-proofing substantially short of demand. They might have used iPads for all of their mobile monitoring and control, except that the iPad had not even been invented when they went into high level design!

When sizing up requirements for data BT took their worst case scenario and then applied a factor of 10. However, someone from Apple then came along and gave 100,000 spectators the expectation that they could simultaneously stream live high definition video of the poster girl of the Olympics, Jessica Ennis, crossing the line to win her gold medal.

As Donald Rumsfeld famously stated, we can be aware of known unknowns and still be left with unknown unknowns. From our perspective of business analysis, the question is: are they truly un-knowable, or did we just not do the work to investigate thoroughly before embarking on delivery? I believe they are largely knowable, predictable and, more importantly, avoidable if we use the right techniques to explore our stakeholders' maps of the world.

The rise of the enterprise portfolio office and centres of excellence for business analysis

As project management has matured in general, I have seen a steady rise in organisations progressing from project support offices, through program offices, to enterprise portfolio offices. Guidance on the role of various forms of P3Os – that is, portfolio, program and project offices – can be found in several recent publications, including PMI's publication on portfolio management,[36] and a refresh of the P3O guide itself.[37] The P3O guide has an appendix describing a 'service model' for P3Os, which includes centre of excellence functions. Incorporation of a business analysis capability within an enterprise portfolio office not only leads to a centre of excellence, but also makes it pragmatic to maintain BA engagement through the life-cycle. Short-term benefits arise from linking testing and implementation back to user needs and design, but a BA with the right competencies and an understanding of the technology, needs and business users can also greatly simplify implementation and adoption.

There is a positive relationship between the length of time a PMO has been established and successful project performance.
> PriceWaterhouseCoopers annual report Insights and Trends:
> Current Program and Project Management Practices, 2015

A 2015 survey presented by international training organisation ESI,[38] illustrated that the least mature areas in P3Os were alignment to organisational strategy and soft skill training. I spoke at the same conference in London on development of soft skills in P3Os using NLP.

In the PMO world, we recognise tools like NLP in developing soft skills necessary to engage the business.
> Lindsay Scott, Founder of The PMO Conference and PMO Flashmob

36 https://www.pwc.com/en_US/us/people-management/assets/program_project_management_survey.pdf [accessed 23 June 2016].
37 Eileen Roden, 2013, *Portfolio, Program and Project Offices*, TSO.
38 http://www.esi-intl.com/about-us/press-releases/esi-international-releases-its-global-state-of-the-pmo-survey-2015 [accessed 23 June 2016].

BAs and PMs working better together

In the last few years there have been a number of papers,[39] conference presentations[40] and workshops aimed at helping the PM and BA to appreciate how they can work better together so that the sum is greater than the parts. The key to realising the full potential of each partner's acumen and focus is a mutual understanding of how each contributes to managing stakeholder expectations and managing requirements. The general competencies are complementary but with a different emphasis, which will be explored in relation to each other in Section 3.27.

Figure 1.4 BA and PM 'better together' (adapted from Maritato, 2012)

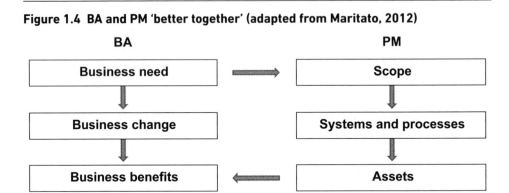

Outside business-as-usual, most changes are implemented through structured projects, and the BA is required to work in close partnership with any appointed PM. In the early stages of the project life-cycle, during development of the business case and scoping of the project, the BA is likely to take a lead role, acting as the de facto PM prior to funding and appointment of a dedicated PM resource. A BA might also remain within the project team and take on key responsibilities, particularly around configuration management, testing, business readiness and implementation. Given these overlaps, it is little surprise that hybrid training qualifications are now emerging in business analysis for PMs, with the US-based Project Management Institute (PMI) piloting a business analysis qualification for PMs.

I elaborate further on effective behaviours for collaboration between BAs and PMs in Section 3.27.3.

---

39 Michele Maritato, 2012, 'Project Management and Business Analysis: The Dynamic Duo', Proceedings of PMI EMEA Congress, 7–9 May, Marseilles, France http://marketplace.pmi.org/Pages/ProductDetail.aspx?GMProduct=00101371701 [accessed 23 June 2016]. http://www.pmi.org/learning/partnership-project-managers-business-analysts-9865 [accessed 23 June 2016].
40 C Millhollan, 2011, 'The Marriage of Professions: Business Analysis and Project Management can live happily together … forever', Proceedings of PMI Global Congress, Dallas, TX, and available as pdf download to members from PMI.

1.3 THE MAKING OF AN EFFECTIVE BA

> In the 90s we were recruited for our knowledge. In the noughties we were promoted for the skills we had developed. Now, our career depends on our behaviours.
>
> Christine Connelly[41]

Historically, most people calling themselves BAs learned on the job and had little formal training, let alone professional qualifications. Indeed, the IIBA itself was only formed in 2003.[42] Thankfully, many are now engaged with the support and development network offered by professional bodies and are seeking recognition through an expanding stable of qualifications.

In this section we will look at the evolving range of qualifications for the BA and the behavioural competencies which underpin them.

1.3.1 Qualification routes for BAs

BCS offers a range of qualifications in business analysis, change management and consultancy at three levels:

1. foundation certificates in business analysis and IT-enabled business change;
2. practitioner certificates; and
3. higher qualifications including the **diploma in business analysis** and the certificate in information systems consultancy practices.

These qualifications can contribute to the Chartered IT Professional (CITP) qualification aligned to the SFIA framework,[43] which ultimately leads to fellowship level for those progressing to senior roles who can demonstrate suitable breadth and depth of experience.

IIBA created the Certified Business Analysis Professional™ (CBAP®) and Certificate of Competency in Business Analysis (CCBA®) to demonstrate a level of knowledge and skill through the application process and examination.[44] The CBAP may also be used towards BCS's diploma in business analysis.

Only since 2009 has a forum for managers of BAs existed to share ideas on development of the capability.[45] The BA Manager Forum has established capabilities required of an 'Expert BA', developed the assessment process and achieved endorsement of the award from BCS and the Chartered Management Institute.[46]

The US-based PMI, better known for its stable of qualifications in the project management space, piloted the PMI Professional Business Analyst qualification in May 2014.[47] The driver and focus appears to be on requirements management, and will be supported by a practice guide.

---

41 Address to BCS 'Ten most influential CIOs', from Christine Connelly, then CIO of the NHS, April 2011.
42 http://www.iiba.org [accessed 23 June 2016].
43 http://www.bcs.org/category/10972 [accessed 23 June 2016].
44 http://www.iiba.org/Certification-Recognition/CBAP-Designation.aspx [accessed 23 June 2016].
45 http://www.bamanagerforum.org [accessed 23 June 2016].
46 http://www.bamanagerforum.org/the-expert-ba-award/ [accessed 23 June 2016].
47 http://www.pmi.org/Certification/PMI-Professional-in-Business-Analysis-PMI-PBA.aspx [accessed 23 June 2016].

The International Requirements Engineering Board (IREB), headquartered in Germany, was founded in 2006 and established the Certified Professional for Requirements Engineering (CPRE) certification concept. This is based on a three-tier model, with more than 20,000 people reported to have taken the basic level examination in the first 10 years. Although headquartered in Germany by like-minded systems engineering professionals, its scope and breadth is expanding through a global partnership framework.

Demarcation between BAs and change managers is blurred. The Change Management Body of Knowledge (CMBoK), introduced only in 2012, is the product of work done by the Australian-based Change Management Institute and APMG, an examining institute and former licence owner for OGC's suite of products encompassing project management method PRINCE2™ and service delivery method ITIL™ (Information Technology Infrastructure Library).[48] They run the 'Accredited Change Manager' qualification based on their BoK and competency model.[49] BCS operates a special interest group (SIG) on change management,[50] and APM launched a change management SIG in 2013.[51] The UK-based Centre for Change Management offers a range of modules designed to complement traditional qualifications in project management.[52]

We have noted the benefit of consultancy skills in business analysis and vice versa. Another 'CMI', the UK-based Chartered Management Institute,[53] encompasses the Institute of Consulting[54] and both have routes to chartered practitioner status. As noted above, the Chartered Management Institute sits alongside BCS and IIBA in the 'Expert BA' awards. Having risen through both the CMI and IC to Fellowship status, I can attest to their relevance, not only in introducing analysis techniques but also for layering on influencing skills and tools for organisational development.

1.3.2 Skills frameworks, competency models and bodies of knowledge underpinning qualifications and assessment

> While it is useful to have a good technical background, it is not essential to manage an IT project. It is more important to have other skills and characteristics.
>
> Hughes *et al.*[55]

Qualifications are usually assessed against a skills framework. As noted in Section 1.2 on evolution of the business analysis role, some of these frameworks are narrowly focused on technical competencies, while others, described below, have evolved to encompass behavioural competencies. As effective behaviours are the focus of this book, I will draw out the behavioural competencies explicitly recognised within these sources.

---

48 https://www.axelos.com/best-practice-solutions/itil [accessed 23 June 2016].
49 http://www.change-management-institute.com/accreditation [accessed 23 June 2016].
50 http://www.bcs.org/category/12139 [accessed 23 June 2016].
51 http://www.apm.org.uk/group/enabling-change-sig [accessed 23 June 2016].
52 http://www.c4cm.co.uk [accessed 23 June 2016].
53 http://www.managers.org.uk/ [accessed 23 June 2016].
54 http://www.iconsulting.org.uk/training_and_qualifications/cmc [accessed 23 June 2016].
55 Bob Hughes, Roger Ireland, Brian West, et al., 2012, *Project Management for IT-related Projects*, BCS.

The European eCompetence Framework

This is described as a common European framework for all information and communications technology (ICT) professionals in all industry sectors, which describes competencies across a life-cycle of Plan – Build – Run – Enable – Manage.[56] While giving good technical coverage, the 40 competencies described do not encompass any behavioural aspects so we will not explore it any further.

The Skills Framework for the Information Age (SFIA)

The SFIA[57] is used worldwide in all sectors of industry and government as the preferred framework for defining skills required of IT professionals. It is used by more mature recruitment companies looking to demonstrate skills of candidates for senior roles up to CIO.[58] It is owned by the SFIA Foundation, a not-for-profit organisation whose members are:

- BCS, The Chartered Institute for IT;
- Tech Partnership (formerly e-skills UK);
- The Institute of Engineering and Technology (IET);
- The Institute of Management Information Systems (IMIS);
- The IT Service Management Forum (itSMF).

Whereas SFIA is designed to be tailored to organisational needs, the more detailed SFIAplus[59] should be treated as a standard that enables organisations to classify, benchmark and develop their IT skills. The BA skill set in SFIA is aligned to the 'business change' category.

BCS Business Analysis

Figure 2.1 in the third edition of *Business Analysis*[60] illustrates the competencies of a BA (see Figure 1.6). The competencies marked in italics are covered in that book, and associated training courses, leaving all those marked in bold to be covered in this book. Since behavioural competencies are difficult to teach in the classroom, the scope and level of BCS's business analysis qualifications are currently limited to method and knowledge. Hence this book and associated training is complementary in addressing the supporting behavioural aspects of the BA role.

IIBA's *Body of Knowledge*

As well as describing technical competencies similar to those above, BABOK® v2 includes underlying competencies (chapter numbers in brackets):

- Behavioural characteristics (8.2): including trust(worthiness) and ethics. We will cover ethics specifically in Section 3.32. Trustworthiness is being increasingly recognised as underpinning authentic leadership.[61]

---

56 http://www.ecompetences.eu/ [accessed 23 June 2016].
57 http://www.sfia-online.org/ [accessed 23 June 2016].
58 http://uk.hudson.com/3d-it-skills-assessment [accessed 23 June 2016].
59 http://www.bcs.org/category/17784 [accessed 23 June 2016].
60 Figure 2.1 from Debra Paul, James Cadle and Donald Yeates, eds, 2014, *Business Analysis* 3rd edn, BCS. Technical competencies are italicised, leaving the behavioural competencies for us to focus on.
61 http://www.forbes.com/sites/kevinkruse/2013/05/12/what-is-authentic-leadership/#4e90bf432ddd [accessed 23 June 2016].

Figure 1.5 The Skills Framework for the Information Age (SFIA™)

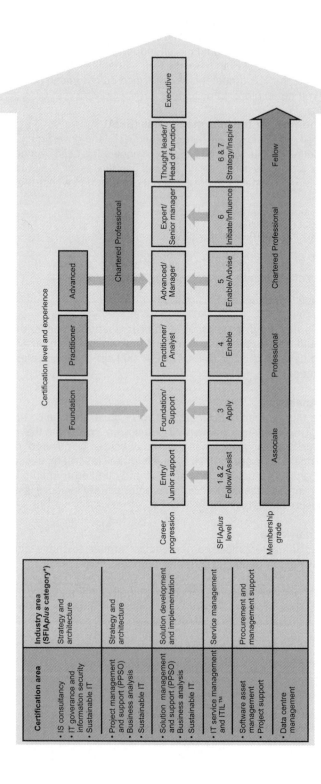

Figure 1.6 Required competencies of a BA

Behavioural and personal qualities	Business knowledge	Techniques
Communication	*Finance and the economy*	**Project management**
Relationship building	*Business case development*	*Strategy analysis*
Influencing	*Domain knowledge*	**Stakeholder analysis and management**
Team-working	*Subject matter expertise*	**Investigation techniques**
Political awareness	*Principles of IT*	*Requirements engineering*
Analytical skills and critical thinking	*Organisation structures and design*	*Business system modelling*
Attention to detail	**Supplier management**	*Business process modelling*
Problem solving		*Data modelling*
Leadership		**Managing business change**
Self-belief		**Facilitation techniques**

- Communication skills (8.4): encompassing listening, 'understanding how an audience perceives the BA' (the meta-position in NLP terms), understanding of the objective of the communication, the message itself ('speech acts' in NLP), and the most appropriate media and format of the communication. Under 'Teaching' (8.4.2) we are also advised to consider the sensory preferences of the learner, as to whether they are mainly visual, kinaesthetic or aural. In Part 3.4 I expand these to include 'audio digital (AD)', which can be considered to be data and logic oriented. While this preference is estimated at around only 2% of the general population, the filters we install around personal and professional selection mean that there is massive over-representation in the business analysis profession. Just as well, as in my opinion the BABOK is void of language or content on the three previous sensory preferences, but would be quite appealing to those of us with an AD orientation. Note that other preferences for learning are not included,[62] but Kolb is equally important and we cover that in Section 3.21.1.

- Interaction skills (8.5): including helping the organisation reach agreement, which we will cover in Part 3, as well as facilitation style of leadership. Teamwork (8.5.3) is included, and we will cover high performance teams in Section 3.26. Management of conflict is included within teamwork, and we will cover that in some depth in Section 3.25.

---

62 http://en.wikipedia.org/wiki/Learning_styles [accessed 23 June 2016].

PMI Professional in Business Analysis

The US-based PMI launched a pilot business analysis qualification in May 2014 which will be supported by a guide.[63] The current online examination guide includes an appendix of 40 skills. These are mainly process- and tool-based, and references to soft skills refer to the process and tools approach to these; for example, 'negotiation tools'. Soft skills elements in the list include:

- communications;
- conflict management;
- elicitation tools;
- leadership principles and tools;
- negotiation tools;
- political and cultural awareness;
- problem-solving tools.

We will cover some behavioural elements of elicitation in Section 3.28 and describe a model for creativity and problem solving in Section 3.14. Cultural awareness is covered in Section 3.6. The other four elements mirror terms in IIBA's BoK, which are described in the section above.

Change management practitioner competencies

A good example of competencies is found in the Australian Change Management body of knowledge developed in 2008,[64] as it encompasses definitions and indicative behaviours for each skill. The skills included are:

- strategic thinking;
- facilitating change;
- facilitating meetings and workshops;
- thinking and judging (note that this is one of the Myers-Briggs type indicators[65]);
- influencing others;
- coaching for change;
- project management;
- communication;
- professional development;
- learning and development;
- communication;
- self-management.

---

63 http://www.pmi.org/Certification/PMI-Professional-in-Business-Analysis-PMI-PBA.aspx [accessed 23 June 2016].
64 http://www.change-management-institute.com [accessed 23 June 2016].
65 http://www.myersbriggs.org [accessed 23 June 2016].

This list is obviously focused on the soft skills required to promote organisational change and is well covered in Part 3 of this book. Note particularly 'self-management', which is one of the four components of the emotional intelligence (EI) framework described in Section 1.4 and covered in detail in Part 3 alongside its precursor of self-awareness.

Expert BA

The white paper defining the Expert Business Analyst award,[66] a partnership between BCS, the Chartered Management Institute and the BA Forum, states that professional BAs need to demonstrate competency in three areas:

1. Personal skills relating to behaviours and attitude.
2. Professional skills relating to techniques and approaches applied within business analysis work.
3. Knowledge relating to business in general and their specialist domain in particular.

It is vital that all BAs have this holistic basis for their skills given the range and variety of work they may be required to carry out. The diagram in Figure 1.7 shows the suggested weightings for these competencies for the expert BA.

Figure 1.7 Expert BA competency requirements

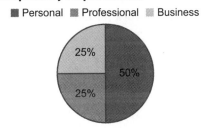

The personal skills assessed comprise:

Core skill	Specialist skill
stakeholder relationship management	negotiation and conflict
leadership and influencing	mentoring and coaching
creative problem analysis and resolution	presentational skills

All of these aspects are covered in Part 3.

---

66 http://certifications.bcs.org/category/17851 [accessed 23 June 2016].

1.4 CAPTURING BEHAVIOURAL COMPETENCIES IN AN EMOTIONAL INTELLIGENCE FRAMEWORK FOR THE BA

The view from the 'C-level' is that, rather than academic theory, soft skills and emotional intelligence can be the difference between success and failure.[67]

As you will have noticed in the review of publications above, there is no obvious consistency in terms used for effective behaviour across the various guides. For this reason, I map cited behaviours from all of the above sources onto the well-established EI framework to provide common terminology and, more importantly, a platform for evaluating and developing them.

1.4.1 Introducing the emotional intelligence framework

When Daniel Goleman's first book on emotional intelligence entered the public domain it captured what people knew, but had not articulated up to that point; namely, that there are factors other than IQ which have more influence on success by many measures, including both career success and fulfilment in life in general (see Figure 1.8). These have been refined over the years and settled down to a consistent set and standard terminology.

Figure 1.8 Daniel Goleman's framework for emotional competencies[68]

	Self (personal competency)	Other (social competency)
Recognition	Self-awareness	Social awareness
	Emotional self-awareness	Empathy
	Accurate self-assessment	Organisational awareness
	Self-confidence	Service
Regulation	Self-management	Relationship management
	Emotional self-control	Inspirational leadership
	Transparency	Influence
	Adaptability	Developing others
	Achievement	Change catalyst
	Initiative	Conflict management
	Optimism	Building bonds
		Teamwork and collaboration

---

67 Chris McLean, Head of Fujitsu PPM Academy, to letters page, *Project* magazine, June 2011.
68 Daniel Goleman, 1996, *Emotional Intelligence: Why it Can Matter More Than IQ*, Bloomsbury.

Today, I hope that everyone realises that EI is essential, but the original books only told you what it was and how important is was. Some measurement frameworks evolved,[69] but a majority probably assumed that it was static like IQ. The most attractive feature of NLP for me is that it is very effective in changing behaviours and modelling skills to improve your emotional quotient (EQ).

1.4.2 How behavioural competencies for BAs fit on to the EI framework

When one looks at the competency frameworks for BAs, although several of the components of EI are captured in fairly generic terms, some, remarkably, are not. The most striking element of this list absent from BA competency frameworks is 'self-awareness'. It was a discussion with the head of capability for one of the largest management consultancies in the IT sector that prompted me to write on this subject because, when we were discussing training and development, he said that the one competency which he wished he could improve in his people was self-awareness. I address it early on in Part 3 as, without this, personal development is likely to be limited.

> Knowledge of the self is the mother of all knowledge. So it is incumbent on me to know my self, to know it completely, to know its minutiae, its characteristics, its subtleties, and its very atoms.
>
> Kahlil Gibran

In Figure 1.9 I show the competencies identified by the various BA organisations in Part 1.3.2 on the EI framework:

In Part 3 we will apply NLP tools and techniques against these various competencies and also the wider scope of the EI framework.

We have found that training using NLP-type methods is the only effective way of measurably increasing the components of EI, from self-awareness, through self-management and social awareness to social influence.

> It was refreshing to be on a course that focussed on attitudes and behaviours rather than on processes. I saw a number of 'light bulb' moments from the cohort and positive changes in attitude and behaviour from my co-workers immediately after the course.
>
> Jenny Lanaway, Resource Manager, Tsys

We have now started to offer global standards in EI measurement approved by the founder of the EI movement, Daniel Goleman. Should they wish to use it as a measure of effectiveness, individuals and organisations can opt for assessment before and after training and group coaching to augment the qualitative measures evidenced on every feedback sheet.[70]

---

69 P. Carter, 2009, *Test Your EQ*, Kogan Page.
70 See NLP4BA.com.

Figure 1.9 BA competencies on the EI framework

	Self (personal competency)	Other (social competency)
Recognition	Self-awareness	Social awareness
	Understanding how others see us	Listening
		Cultural awareness
		Political awareness
		Problem analysis and solution
Regulation	Self-management	Relationship management
	Ethics	Relationship building
	Trustworthiness	Influencing
	Self-belief	Facilitation
	Critical thinking	Negotiation
	Creativity	Management of conflict
	Personal development	Coaching
		Mentoring
		Teamwork
		Learning and development
		Presentation skills
		Communication
		Leadership

1.4.3 Star performance builds on emotional intelligence

> Research shows that EI accounts for more than 85 per cent of star performance in top leaders.
>
> Hay Group research on emotional intelligence 2012[71]

The significance of EI increases with job difficulty. A top performer in a complex role can be 100 per cent more productive than an average performer. Competency research in over 200 organisations worldwide attributes one-third of this difference to technical

---

71 Hay Group research 2012 on emotional intelligence https://atrium.haygroup.com/downloads/marketingps/ww/PS_WW_Emotional_intelligence_leadership_prescription_for_tough_times_final.pdf [accessed 23 June 2016].

and cognitive ability, and two-thirds to EI (Hay Group research). Note the similarity to the independently derived split in the BA competency model in Figure 1.9. Are we on to something here?

Figure 1.10 Star performance builds on emotional intelligence rather than technical ability

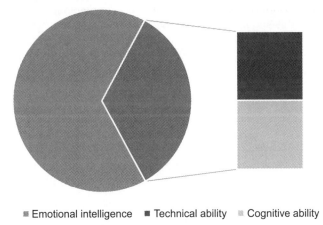

■ Emotional intelligence   ■ Technical ability   ▨ Cognitive ability

Some people hold the view that someone is probably good at something, such as leadership or customer focus, or not, and you just have to select those who show aptitude (see Figure 1.10). This is probably based on the fact that it is difficult to change attitude and behaviours and to learn new skills using conventional classroom training. As Craig Rollason quotes in the introduction to the section on competencies in *Business Analysis*:

> It is often said that it is easier to give a person with good behavioural skills the techniques they need to do the job rather than to graft behavioural skills on to a good technician.

1.5 ASSESSING AND DEVELOPING BEHAVIOURAL COMPETENCIES

> The only true wisdom is knowing that you know nothing.
>
> Socrates

Competencies emerged in the 1980s as a way of modelling effective performance and are now an accepted part of human resource management. A competency refers to how a task is achieved. The competency-based approach focuses on the individual's skills, knowledge, attitudes and behaviours rather than on their qualifications and experience.[72] It is measured by observing behaviour at work, using examples of how effective

---

72 S. Whiddett and S. Hollyforde, 2003, *A Practical Guide to Competences*, Chartered Institute of Personnel and Development (CIPD).

individuals behave to achieve their high levels of performance. Competencies are built up over time and are not innate.[73]

1.5.1 Assessing your level of competency

BCS has a specific publication on competency and assessment.[74] Even for those of you fortunate enough to be reasonably competent in those areas that make effective BAs, it is a requirement of the profession that we all undertake continuous professional development. Ultimately, this should lead to improvement in capability through to expert level against those competencies deemed most appropriate for the specific role. The table in Figure 1.11 shows a standard approach to levels of competency with descriptions.[75]

Figure 1.11 Levels of competency

Level	Description
Stage 1 Foundation	Can demonstrate basic skills that contribute to the activity under direct supervision of competent practitioners.
Stage 2 Intermediate	Can demonstrate acceptable performance in the activity, but requires some supervision and guidance.
Stage 3 Proficient	Can demonstrate competent performance in the activity to specific criteria without direct supervision.
Stage 4 Advanced	Can demonstrate skilled activity with advanced theoretical knowledge and understanding, based on current research/ best practice and any relevant policies, procedures and guidelines.

> Ignorance more frequently begets confidence than does knowledge.
>
> Charles Darwin

Research repeatedly shows that most of us think that we are smarter/better than we actually are.[76] This is said to be because 'ability' itself includes the meta-ability of being able to assess that ability (see Figure 1.12).

---

73 R. Boyatzis, 1982, *The Competent Manager: A Model for Effective Performance*, Wiley & Sons.
74 John Holt and Simon A. Perry, 2011, *A Pragmatic Guide to Competency: Tools, Frameworks and Assessment*, BCS.
75 www.alchemyformanagers.co.uk [accessed 23 June 2016] – access subscription required.
76 J. Kruger and J. Dunning, 1999, 'Unskilled and unaware of it: How difficulties in recognising one's own incompetence leads to inflated assessments', *Journal of Personal and Social Psychology*, 77(6), 121.

Figure 1.12 People's false perceptions of their own ability

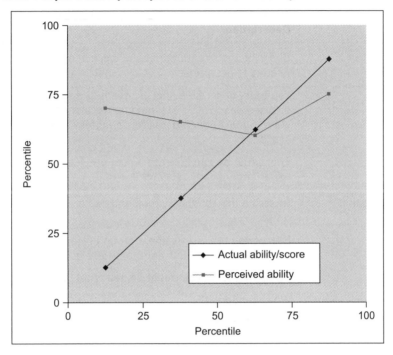

> The fool who knows he is a fool is for that reason wise. The fool who thinks himself wise is the greatest fool of all.
>
> Shakyamuni

Asking people if they are good at soft skills, or even business analysis, is a bit like asking if they are good at driving – we probably all think that we are better than others perceive us to be. Hence, it is necessary to have a structured and evidence-based approach to assessing behavioural competencies.

The STAR technique is widely used in assessment (see Figure 1.13). We return to the STAR technique in Part 3.12.1 to show how it can be developed further to tell very succinct stories as well as to demonstrate competency.

BCS assesses its senior membership level, that is, Fellow, against the SFIA.[77] This is centred around leadership competencies which would normally be at level four of a five stage model. In Section 3.9 I focus on development of leadership competencies.

---

77 SFIA – Skills Framework for the Information Age http:// www.sfia.org.uk [accessed 23 June 2016].

Figure 1.13 The STAR technique for assessing behavioural competencies

Level	Description
Situation or task	Describe the situation that you were in or the task that you needed to accomplish.
	You must describe a specific event or situation, not a generalised description of what you have done in the past. Be sure to give enough detail for the interviewer to understand.
	This situation can be from a previous job, from a volunteer experience, or any relevant event.
Action you took	Describe the action you took and be sure to keep the focus on you.
	Even if you are discussing a group project or effort, describe what you did, not the efforts of the team.
	Do not tell what you might do, tell what you did.
Results you achieved	What happened?
	How did the event end?
	What did you accomplish?
	What did you learn?

1.5.2 Developing your level of competency

In relation to overall competency, there is a widely agreed but little used chart of progress through the professions. People still overestimate their own abilities, and it should be noted that the knowledge axis on the chart below would be in terms of thousands of hours of study at high difficulty, similar to post-graduate qualifications at the top end, not a few tens of hours on standard week-long training courses (see Figure 1.14).[78]

The experience axis is 10 years and beyond at the high levels. This does not mean 10 years doing the same job, which is more like one year times 10. Usually this experience is only gained by moving through different types of assignment, roles and probably organisations. Even better is to experience different sectors and industries.

As your competency increases there needs to be a change in focus from traditional classroom-based training, through reflection on structured experience, to individual and role-based coaching (see Figure 1.15).

---

78 http://gladwell.com/outliers/the-10000-hour-rule/ [accessed 23 June 2016].

Figure 1.14 Competency increases with knowledge and experience

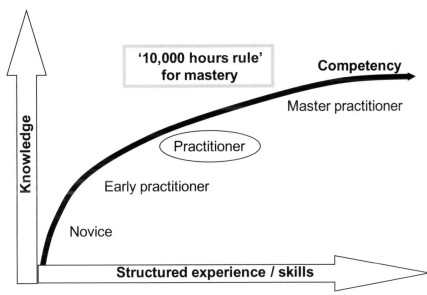

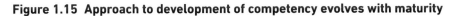

Figure 1.15 Approach to development of competency evolves with maturity

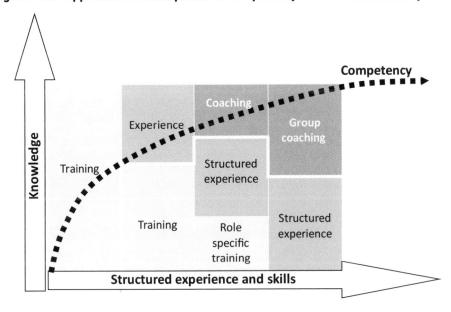

For behavioural change, coaching is much more effective. Coaching can be conducted in groups with similar objectives,[79] which helps to develop high performance teams at the same time, as described in Part 3.26.

1.6 SUMMARY OF PART 1

In this first Part we have looked at the evolving map of the BA's world, and requirements to meet the challenges.

We started off by exploring how the business world and the systems being delivered into it are becoming more complex as a result of factors including rapidly advancing technology, increasing scale, a fragmented supply chain often encompassing international capacity and mature customer expectations. Perhaps not surprisingly, the failure rate has not diminished. An agile approach helps, but more helpful is an agile mindset.

We have seen that the role of the BA is fundamental to understanding problems and opportunities, interpretation of requirements, formulation of solutions, smooth passage through testing, acceptance by operations and realisation of benefits by end users.

A review of professional organisations, bodies of knowledge, competency frameworks and qualification routes illustrated that the role of the BA is evolving from formalisation of the technical tools and techniques to a focus on underpinning attitudes, behaviours and skills displayed by effective role models. We provided an overview of different professional development routes and qualifications.

We showed that behavioural competencies developed by different bodies can be readily encompassed into the well-established framework for emotional intelligence. From there it was practical to illustrate how behavioural competencies can be assessed, and how developmental routes for these are different from the approach for technical competencies.

In Part 3 we will apply various NLP tools and techniques to the behavioural competencies identified here to illustrate how they can be developed. In the meantime, let us move on to explore the world of NLP in Part 2.

---

79 Manfred F. R. Kets de Vries, 2005, 'Leadership group coaching in action: The Zen of creating high performance teams', *Academy of Management Executives*, 19(1).

PART 2. THE WORLD OF NLP

2.1 INTRODUCTION

One of the reasons that this chapter is included in the book, rather than just launching into the applications of NLP for you as a BA, is that, being a complete system, there are some aspects of NLP that underpin any and every activity that we use it for. In this chapter we establish the foundations of NLP, including its origins, principles, presuppositions and generic tools and techniques which underpin more specific applications. It will provide you with sufficient understanding to try out all of the applications to the role of BA described in Part 3.

Originating from the fields of linguistics and cybernetics, and through the modelling of leading therapists, NLP quickly found application in counselling and personal change. As an understanding of the mind–body connection, it has also expanded rapidly into health applications and led to growth in coaching for leading sports professionals and athletes. Introduction into the field of management was relatively late, after modelling of successful business leaders at Fiat. The body of knowledge around NLP is now large, but I will focus on those aspects directly applicable to development of behaviours and skills for effective BAs.

We will start by looking at what NLP can do for BAs, which is extensive, before looking at what it is and its scientific origins. The four pillars of NLP will introduce the underlying requirements for effecting NLP techniques: outcome thinking, sensory acuity, building rapport and behavioural flexibility. Without these basic elements NLP will not work. Underpinning all of these is ethics, or ecology as it is referred to in NLP.

The concept of everyone having different world-views is central to the NLP communications model. The way these world-views are formed by filtering information, and coded using representational systems and sub-modalities, is shown to give us an opening into people's beliefs systems. But without rapport there can be no effective communication, and ways of quickly establishing rapport by meeting someone on their map of the world, for example by aligning meta-programs, are introduced here before being fully developed in Part 3.

Being able to communicate with the unconscious mind, both by being able to interpret it through the meta-model for deep structure of language, and communicate to it via metaphor and hypnotic language, will be discussed.

It may sound a bit technical, especially with the over-fondness for the term 'meta', but the subject is not intellectually difficult. It just takes application and practice, of which there will be plenty in the context of business analysis in Part 3.

If you already have a good grounding in NLP and just want to look at the application to business analysis, then jump straight to Part 3, but please note that some elements, such as meta-programs, are not usually introduced until Master Practitioner level or beyond.

2.2 ABOUT NLP

> We take the very best of what people do, synthesise it down, make it learnable and share it with each other – and that is what the real future of what NLP will be and its gonna stay that way!
>
> Richard Bandler, co-founder of NLP

NLP has evolved through a number of routes and means different things to different people. Here I will define it within the context of my assumed audience and the way we will be applying it.

2.2.1 What is NLP?

> NLP is an attitude and a methodology, not the trail of techniques it leaves behind.
>
> Richard Bandler

NLP has been described as a user's manual for the brain and the study of human excellence.

It can be described as the science of how the brain codes learning and experience. The memories of our subjective experience have specific structures, and NLP can be used to elicit that structure and replicate it through modelling, thus providing a mechanism for transferring so-called tacit skills and behaviours.

Where learned behaviours are no longer effective in some contexts, NLP can be used to alter the structure of the subjective experience, changing meaning, and to generate alternative behaviours. Some other definitions of NLP include:

- A form of applied psychology.
- A means of achieving more for yourself and being more fulfilled in your personal and professional lives.
- The difference that makes the difference.
- A means of achieving peak performance.

It has been described as a system, a methodology and a set of processes. To me though, NLP is an approach.

2.2.2 What can NLP do for me as a BA?

If you don't want to change anything then NLP has nothing to offer you.

Anthony Robbins

Once you adopt the approach of NLP and start to learn some of the tools that it offers, it will help your development enormously. As mentioned in the Introduction to this book, for a BA NLP will:

- Give you an understanding of why you do what you do, and what other choices are available.

- Help you to pick up and decode what is being communicated outside the obvious – words will give you an edge in everything from negotiation to leadership.

- Strengthen your ability to connect with others and develop rapport quickly and easily.

- Enable you to communicate more effectively and persuasively.

- Manage stress and build resilience.

- Help you to control the way you think, feel and act.

- Show you how to develop flexibility in behaviour to match the context and requirements.

- Help you to motivate and lead.

- Help you to develop new skills.

- Enable you to model excellent behaviours from role models that you meet.

2.2.3 Where did NLP come from – the science behind the approach

Richard Bandler, a PhD computer scientist, and John Grinder, a professor of neuro-linguistics, are recognised as the founders of NLP in the early 1970s.[1] To me, everything in science has a predecessor, and so you can trace the ancestors of NLP back a long way. I feel that it is important to establish this pedigree to demonstrate that NLP is a science.

Formally, Alfred Korzybski's work on general semantics is credited with coining the phrase 'neuro-linguistic' back in the early 1930s.[2] His work has breadth beyond NLP, and his maxim, 'The map is not the territory', is widely quoted in the world at large. Basically, he was one of the first people to formally make the distinction that words are only an approximation of what they represent.

The TOTE model (test, operate, test, exit [experimental cycle]), extensively used for modelling (see Exercise 3.4 in Section 3.4.3), originated from the work of George Miller and

---

1 John Grinder and Richard Bandler, 1975, *The Structure of Magic I: A Book About Language and Therapy*, Science and Behaviour Books.
2 Alfred Korzybski, 1994, *Science and Sanity* (first published 1933), Institute of General Semantics,

co-workers in the late 1950s.[3] Since Miller is also credited with the famous 'magic number of 7, plus or minus 2', his work was also very influential on NLP's view of filtering of stimuli from the real world to create an impoverished map of reality.[4]

Gregory Bateson's work from the 1950s led to the integration of systems theory and cybernetics, which underpin much of the intellectual basis of NLP. Bateson also introduced many of the key players to each other.

The idea that people have different 'parts' of their personality was introduced in the 1960s by Eric Berne, and is widely known through transactional analyses.[5] Theory on negotiations using the form of relationships of personalities of 'adult', 'parent' and 'child' originate from this work. The metaphor of parts of personality is widely used in NLP for resolution of inner conflict.

Fritz Perls was one of the first to use the idea of representational systems in therapy. Gestalt therapy, that is, the treatment of groups of events as a whole, was introduced from his work.[6] In the early 1970s Richard Bandler and John Grinder started to integrate the work of their predecessors and use it to model successful therapists. The first of these was Virginia Satir on family therapy.[7] Their seminal work *The Structure of Magic* identified the coding of experience and showed how it could be replicated and altered to model and modify behaviours.[8]

Modelling of therapist Milton Erickson had a huge influence on NLP, resulting in incorporation of hypnotic techniques and development of the meta-model for language which we explore under effective communications.[9]

These constituents, and many more, went into the melange that Bandler and Grinder created. They are still active, and have been joined by many peers. Of these, Robert Dilts and Tad James have probably been most active, particularly on the introduction of timeline therapies and neurological levels, which I personally make a lot of use of.

Many people were introduced to NLP, particularly in the USA, by Anthony Robbins and his evangelical approach to personal development.[10] He is still hugely popular in print and live performances, attracting several thousand to worldwide venues, often culminating in people overcoming limiting beliefs to do 'the fire walk' (I have the T-shirt).

Not mentioned in accounts of origins of NLP are at least two names that I use during training on the topic. There is not a Nobel prize for psychology, but two psychologists did manage to be awarded in allied fields.

---

3 K. Pribham, G. Miller and E. Gallanter, 1960 *Plans and the Structure of Behaviour*, Prentice Hall.
4 George Miller, 1956, 'The magic number seven, plus or minus two', *Psychological Review*, 63, 81–97.
5 Eric Berne, 1961, *Transactional Analysis in Psychotherapy*, Souvenir Press.
6 Fritz Perls, 1969, *GestaltTherapy Verbatim*, Real People Press.
7 Virginia Satir, Richard Bandler and John Grinder, 1976, *Changing with Families*, Science and Behaviour Books.
8 John Grinder and Richard Bandler, 1975, *The Structure of Magic I: A Book About Language and Therapy*, Science and Behaviour Books.
9 John Grinder and Richard Bandler, 1975, *Patterns of the Hypnotic Techniques of Milton H. Erickson, 1 & 2*, Meta Publications.
10 Anthony Robbins, 1987, *Unlimited Power*, Harper Collins.

Many of us were taught about Pavlov and his conditioning of dogs to the ringing of a bell at meal times during basic biology.[11] It seems quite quaint now to think that someone would win a great prize for such an obvious concept as establishing responses to sensory anchors, especially when most of us find it so easy to use music, images and smells to transport us back in time or cheer us up. But of course the concept of anchoring has become pervasive through marketing now, where fonts (Coca-Cola) and colours (IBM) have been trademarked and are instantly recognisable. Few are familiar with another discovery made by Pavlov. After the cellar where he conducted his experiments was flooded, the surviving dogs failed to salivate on hearing the ringing bell to indicate food. He said: 'It is as if their brains were washed by the water.' Hence, he was the discoverer of 'brain washing' as a technique to erase behavioural conditioning. Why do I include Pavlov here? We make extensive use of anchoring in NLP to manage our state – remember, one of the four quadrants of the EI framework is 'state management'. Perhaps even more importantly, Pavlov illustrated that we can install new behaviours and also un-install and download versions with improved functionality. You will be pleased to read that you can do this without 'water-boarding'.

The second Lauriat managed to get a bestseller onto the book shelves in the last few years and has been featured in BBC *Panorama* specials, TED talks and extensively cited by popular authors. Since the 1970s, Daniel Kahneman and his colleague, Amos Tversky, had been in the background, publishing fantastic observations supported by extensive academic evidence that I would shy away from claiming under an NLP banner. Their work on Priming and Framing to effect decision making is, however, now widely adopted in negotiation and marketing and I make use of them in this book and associated training. It was their related work on how we consistently make mistakes in decision making, and consequently how our decisions can be manipulated, that earned a Nobel prize. Again it seems obvious in retrospect that there was a flaw in the belief that economics of boom and bust was rational, but they opened up a whole new field of behavioural economics.

Figure 2.1 Evolution of NLP

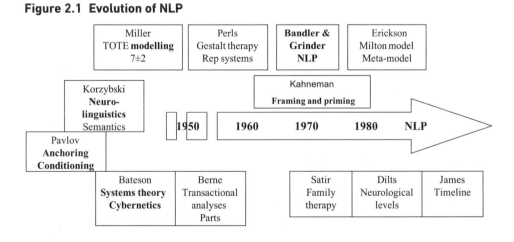

---

11 http://www.simplypsychology.org/pavlov.html [accessed 29 June 2016].

NLP is now a rich picture, and you can take its learnings and development in any direction you choose (see Figure 2.1). The only limitations are your own beliefs, and NLP can help you to change those, if you choose to.

2.2.4 How to learn NLP

NLP is experiential. Just like learning a musical instrument, you have to practice it a lot to become proficient (see Figure 2.2). This book will, however, open your eyes to new ways of seeing, hearing, feeling and analysing the world and make further practice compelling.

This book gives you practical examples to show how it can be used to achieve results. From there, having decided to embark on personal improvement, I recommend some formal training and supervised practice. You do not need to advertise that you are 'doing NLP', as it is only modelling natural processes anyway, and when done elegantly should be invisible. The only visible part will be the way that you start to exhibit more flexible behaviour, build better relationships and communicate more effectively.

Figure 2.2 NLP requires practice as well as knowledge

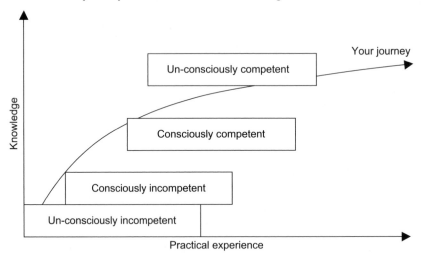

The fact that you have picked up this book and read this far means that you are well on that journey.

2.3 THE FOUR PILLARS OF NLP

> The scientific man does not aim at an immediate result ... His duty is to lay the foundation for those who are to come, and point the way.
>
> Nikola Tesla

One of the reasons that this chapter is included in the book, rather than just launching into applications, is that, being a complete system, there are some aspects of NLP that underpin any and every activity that we use it for. Many tools and techniques have been modelled and developed over four decades, but initially these pillars were all the founders had to work from. They still hold true today (see Figure 2.3).

Figure 2.3 The four pillars of NLP

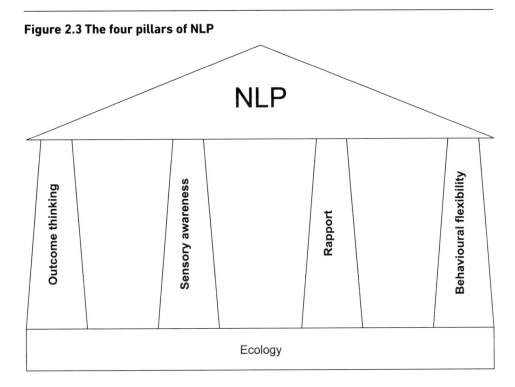

With NLP, like all good projects, we start with the **outcome** in mind.

In NLP we develop **sensory awareness**, not only to tell us what is going on in a situation, but also to give us feedback on the effectiveness or otherwise of our own actions. All processes in NLP should be based on sensory evidence and not guess-work.

Rapport underpins not only NLP, but all of our relationships. Without first establishing rapport, no NLP technique will work. For counselling work, resistance in a client is a clear sign of lack of rapport. (This should be picked up through sensory awareness, as above.)

Behavioural flexibility is required by NLP – if what you are doing is not working, then try something else.

I have shown these pillars resting on a base of **ecology**, which in the context of NLP is related to ethics and the appropriateness of actions to all parties. If what we are attempting is not ethical for all parties, then it will fail and re-bound.

You will find these pillars of NLP cropping up time and again throughout the rest of the book.

2.4 PRESUPPOSITIONS OF NLP

Presupposition: a thing tacitly assumed beforehand at the beginning of a line of argument or course of action.

Oxford English Dictionary

Presuppositions, like beliefs, are things that are taken as true without further proof. As far as NLP is concerned, however, they are simple statements that have proven useful. In effect, they are the belief system of NLP. They originated from the contributing elements of NLP such as systems theory and cybernetics. Rather than deal with them as a group here, I have liberally doused relevant sections with them so that they appear in context, but for summary I present them in the form of a mind map (see Figure 2.4). (I adopted mind maps as they have the ability to satisfy both 'big picture' and 'detail' predispositions in one view, and are an excellent tool for co-creation by a team.)

While presenting on soft skills at a leadership conference in Berlin, I was delighted that a fellow speaker from the utility sector gave his whole talk based on the presuppositions of NLP with the title 'Ethical leadership'.

2.5 WORLD-VIEWS AND FILTERS

If a man is offered a fact which goes against his instincts, he will scrutinise it closely, and unless the evidence is overwhelming, he will refuse to believe it. If, on the other hand, he is offered something which affords a reason for acting in accordance to his instincts, he will accept it even on the slightest evidence. The origin of myths is explained in this way.

Bertrand Russell, philosopher and Fellow of the Royal Society

The basic premise of NLP, building on the early work on semantics by Korzybski, is that people make maps of the world, and these maps are mistaken for reality. In fact, these maps are only impoverished models that are influenced by a host of factors specific to the individual's previous experiences (see Figure 2.5).

Figure 2.4 The presuppositions of NLP

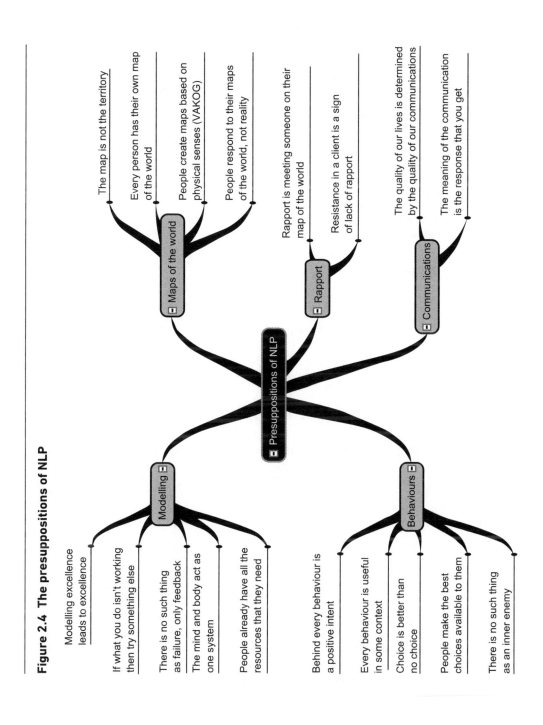

Modelling excellence
leads to excellence

If what you do isn't working
then try something else

There is no such thing
as failure, only feedback

The mind and body act as
one system

People already have all the
resources that they need

Behind every behaviour is
a positive intent

Every behaviour is useful
in some context

Choice is better than
no choice

People make the best
choices available to them

There is no such thing
as an inner enemy

The map is not the territory

Every person has their own map
of the world

People create maps based on
physical senses (VAKOG)

People respond to their maps
of the world, not reality

Rapport is meeting someone on their
map of the world

Resistance in a client is a sign
of lack of rapport

The quality of our lives is determined
by the quality of our communications

The meaning of the communication
is the response that you get

Maps of the world

Rapport

Communications

Presuppositions of NLP

Modelling

Behaviours

Figure 2.5 We react according to our map of the world, not reality

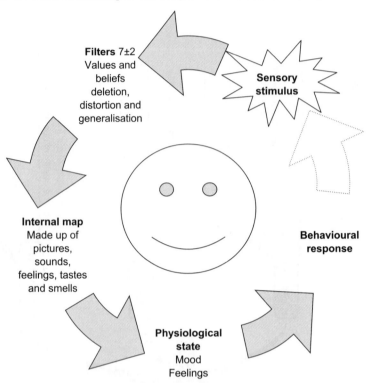

Filters 7±2
Values and
beliefs
deletion,
distortion and
generalisation

Sensory
stimulus

Internal map
Made up of
pictures,
sounds,
feelings, tastes
and smells

Behavioural
response

Physiological
state
Mood
Feelings

Aside from not realising that our 'reality', though seeming real, is a mere internal representation, most do not realise that other people's maps of reality are markedly different from our own. With a huge range of values and beliefs, and combinations of more than 60 behavioural meta-programs acting as filters, the chances of someone's perception matching ours is remote. From a Myers–Briggs Type Indicator I found that only two per cent of the population shared my preferences, and that is from only four pairs of alternatives. Sixty pairs of behavioural meta-programs produce the potential for at least two to the power of 60 alternatives, or enough to fill a hundred million earth-like planets full of individuals. Hence, the person sitting next to you is certainly different from you.

> Everyone has their own map of the world.
>
> NLP presupposition

Our map is also based on our interpretation of past experiences, most of which occurred during our formative years and were lost from our conscious recall. Gestalts, or groupings, of those memories, and our interpretation of them, act as a strong filter on our behaviours, especially in complex personal relationships.

The way individuals react to the same stimulus or situation is also dependent on their physiological state at the time – you do not react in the same way to events when you are happy as when you are sad or angry.

So, we all have different filters leading to us all having different maps of the world which we treat as the only reality (see Figure 2.6). Is it any wonder that we have break-downs in communications, let alone situations where people are willing to kill and die for what they 'know' is right?

> People react to their maps of the world, not reality.
>
> NLP presupposition

The NLP approach recognises that we all have different partial maps, and aims to discover the maps of others so that we can have a dialogue on some partial overlap of realities.

Figure 2.6 Our perspective influences what we observe

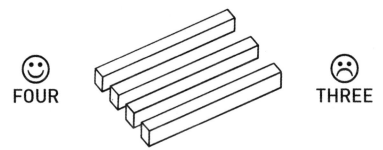

FOUR   THREE

Where behaviours are not appropriate in some contexts, we can use the tools of NLP to uncover how some of the filters, or emotional states, are producing those behaviours. If desired, we can also use NLP techniques to change internal representations, and hence meaning, such that we can adopt additional behaviours and have more choice.

Where we recognise excellent behaviours that could be useful to us, we can use NLP tools to explore the subject's map of the world and emulate their processes and behaviours.

Hence, you could think of NLP as a translational tool for communicating between the languages of different mental operating systems, and of comparing common representations that hold different meanings in different systems. This aspect of bridging the communication divide is developed further through practical examples in Part 3.

Rapport is meeting someone on their map of the world.

NLP presupposition

2.6 THE SUBCONSCIOUS MIND – WHO IS REALLY IN CHARGE?

A lot of moves are subconscious. I make them without realising my thought processes.

Magnus Carlson, youngest ever competitor in the World Chess
Championships and ranked world #1 in 2010 at the age of 18

Although we are by definition unconscious of our unconscious, we can have little doubt of its importance. Most obvious is the fact that this engine room runs our body for us, breathes for us, digests our food for us, and manages a biochemistry through hormone and enzyme secretion that the conscious brains of this planet have still to fully understand.

In NLP, we view the mind and body as a holistic system; what affects one part influences the other. Our physical state affects our emotions, and our mental state, which is largely subconscious, affects our behaviours. It seems obvious that peak performance depends on optimum physical, emotional and mental states, and NLP gives us specific tools for achieving these optimal states rather than being a victim of circumstance.

From an NLP perspective, the subconscious has many other roles. All of our senses are run by our subconscious, and all information from them is analysed, interpreted, filtered and edited before it ever comes into our conscious awareness. Indeed, modern thinking, supported by brain imaging techniques, suggests that free will itself might be an illusion.

All of our meta-programs, that is, learned behaviours, run in our subconscious. The accumulation of these form our beliefs, values and identity. Our experiences are filtered and interpreted by these meta-programs, beliefs and values. The subconscious interprets and groups events and gives them meaning. For traumatic experiences, the subconscious may repress memories from our conscious selves until a time when we have accumulated sufficient resources to deal with them. It will install involuntary phobias to protect us from perceived danger. Similarly, it will develop limiting beliefs to keep us in our comfort zone and away from risk.

Personal change is most readily achieved through the subconscious mind, whether that is to drop a bad habit, change a behaviour, re-interpret past events and meaning, remove a limiting belief or learn a new skill.

So, who is in charge, and wouldn't it be good to start a dialogue?

2.7 BELIEFS, VALUES AND IDENTITY

> Just as no one can be forced into belief, so no one can be forced into unbelief.
> Sigmund Freud

Beliefs are assumptions or presuppositions that you make about yourself and the world around you which you accept as true without evidence. Not only do we not question our own beliefs, but they are also largely invisible to us, and we only become aware of them when we encounter someone with opposed beliefs.

Where beliefs have an evaluation attached to them, such as good or bad, right or wrong, then we call them values. Values are unconsciously formed and held, but drive our behaviours. If you hand in a lost wallet, then it is probably because you value honesty. If you value friendship, then it will take precedence over things that you value less, such as money. When you get a strong emotional reaction from someone, it is usually because you have transgressed their values, or pressed their 'hot buttons'. Hence, if you do not understand someone's behaviour, then that is probably because you do not know their values, and they are probably different from yours.

Whenever we use a phrase such as 'I am a business analyst', then we are expressing identity. When aspects of our identity are challenged, it has a fundamental impact on us.

Where we become aware that our beliefs are no longer useful to us or limit our performance, we can use NLP to change them.

2.7.1 Origins of values and beliefs

As you may have realised, you do not get to choose your values. On reflection, isn't it a bit strange that the things that you might be willing to die for were not chosen by you? The learning machine that is your unconscious brain distilled a set of values for you that it thought would best preserve you in the environment that you grew up in from the role models that it had to draw on (see Figure 2.7). The fact that you are reading this means that it has done a pretty good job of preserving you and your ancestors so far.

Figure 2.7 Development of values and beliefs

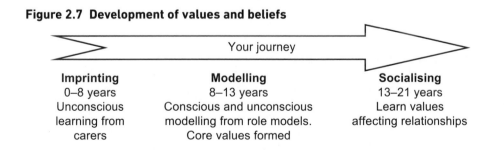

Imprinting	Modelling	Socialising
0–8 years	8–13 years	13–21 years
Unconscious learning from carers	Conscious and unconscious modelling from role models. Core values formed	Learn values affecting relationships

2.7.2 The belief cycle

> People become what they expect themselves to become.
>
> Mahatma Gandhi

If you believe that you are not good at gaining qualifications, then you are more likely to focus on all the past experiences where you have had difficulty, and subconsciously delete any good experiences. This makes you feel bad about your ability, which means that you are likely to perform badly or play safe by avoiding tests and exams. This means that you might not have many qualifications, therefore creating a self-fulfilling belief (see Figure 2.8).

Figure 2.8 The belief cycle

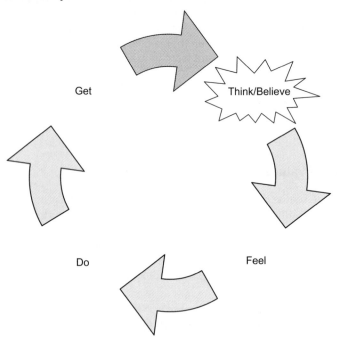

2.7.3 Limiting values and beliefs

Bizarrely, our education system is probably the biggest culprit in developing our limiting beliefs and expectation of failure. Are you a good singer and dancer? Most of you will not put your hands up, but you may have done so when you were five years old. Since you started school you may have had belief in yourself slowly but surely trained out by being judged in relation to others day after day. And yet, like walking, we learn best through failure – or test and feedback, as we like to reframe it to the positive in NLP.

There is no failure, only feedback.

NLP presupposition

Aside from the motivational aspects of values, they are fundamental to NLP in that they act as filters, affecting the way we interpret experience and judge things as good or bad. As such, they also give us maximum leverage for change – if you want to change a behaviour, then the surest way is to change an underlying belief. Beliefs are not fixed. Some people used to believe in Santa Claus. It is not too difficult to change limiting beliefs if you are motivated to do so, and it does not have to involve a sabbatical with the Moonies and a dose of brainwashing.

2.7.4 Hierarchy of neurological levels underpinning identity and purpose

Robert Dilts elaborated the earlier work of Bateson to establish a logical hierarchy of neurological levels (see Figure 2.9).[12] Who we believe we are is compounded from our values, beliefs, capabilities, behaviours and environment. If we say, 'I am a professional business analyst' (identity), then it is the result of having operated in that context, developed capabilities and competencies through appropriate behaviours and slowly built up certain beliefs about the right and wrong way of doing things.

Figure 2.9 Hierarchy of neurological levels (after Dilts)

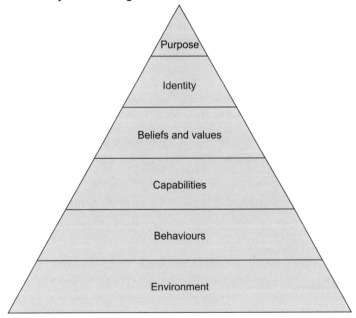

We use these neurological levels as the basis for establishing rapport in Section 3.20.3. It also underpins one of our strategies for modelling, covered in Section 3.10.

---

12 Robert Dilts, 1983, *Applications of NLP*, Meta Publications.

2.8 META-PROGRAMS AND BEHAVIOURS

> Knowing that we can control our own behaviour makes it more likely that we will.
> Peter Singer, philosopher and author of *Practical Ethics*

Use of the term 'program' when talking about the human mind originates from cybernetics, which likens the human brain to a biological computer. According to this mind-as-computer metaphor, the brain is constantly running a complex set of programs. A meta-program then, sitting 'meta' or above the program, is the rule that determines which model or set of instructions we run. Remember, one of the originators of NLP was a computer science major, while the other was a professor of linguistics. Some of the older generation may remember another NLP – natural language processing.

Does your glass feel half empty or half full; that is, are you an optimist or pessimist? Do you only want to hear about the big picture, or see the detail? Are you drawn towards opportunity, or do you run away from risk? These are some of the 60+ meta-programs identified to date. Whole books have been written on just some aspects of them, such as matching language to meta-programs.[13] Many of those useful to you in business analysis are contained in Figure 3.7 and described in Section 3.3 on self-awareness, where you are invited to assess your own preferences.

You will meet people with all variants and combinations of these 60+ meta-programs in your career. They see the world differently from you, have different motivational factors from you and need different evidence from you. Most of this is out of your hands, but being aware of these differences, being able to recognise them and being able to adjust your language to communicate effectively with them is in your hands. Being able to do so will give you a huge advantage in your career and life in general.

I find meta-programs extremely useful for gaining rapport, understanding behaviours and communicating effectively. Rather than discuss the detail of meta-programs in this background section, I have illustrated their application liberally throughout Part 3. How to match language to specific meta-programs in order to gain rapport is covered in Section 3.20.6, while the best options for meta-programs to help gain rapport are covered in Section 3.20.5 and Exercise 3.20. Motivational aspects of meta-programs are illustrated in Section 3.26.2.

Specific meta-programs discussed in detail in Part 3 in the context of business analysis include:

- in time/through time;
- big picture/detail;
- convincer pattern;
- dissociation;
- rule structure;
- stress response;

---

13 S. R. Charvet, 1995, *Words that Change Minds: Mastering the Language of Influence*, Kendall Hunt.

- same/difference;
- working style (independent/cooperative);
- task orientation (person/thing).

2.9 FRAMES AND REFRAMING

> The meaning of any experience depends on the frame that we put around it.
>
> Anthony Robbins

All of experience is subjective, and the way we frame something profoundly affects our interpretation of its meaning. If the frame changes then the meaning changes with it.[14] Jokes are a good example of how a twist of frame at the end transforms meaning.

In politics the expression 'set the frame, win the game', has evolved.[15] Whoever is successful in framing what the debate is about is fighting the political battle on home turf. Nowhere was this more successful than when Barrack Obama won his first term as president. At the time, the USA was in the middle of 'The war on terror', and Obama, a lawyer, was one of few presidents not to have had some military or intelligence services background. His adversary, John McCain, was a war veteran and hero. Obama's team popularised the reframe for the debate 'It's about the economy, stupid.' What did a war veteran know about economics? (Or a lawyer for that matter.) The rest is history.

Daniel Kahneman's research over the last 40 years has not only helped to establish a new discipline of behavioural economics, but also proven beyond doubt that the way we frame options decides what we choose.[16] Whether you choose to make use of it or not, understanding of it will help you to realise what is going on around you. As one student responded to me during a training course, 'I just realised I was *framed* this morning.'

Closer to home, if the frame for conversations about your projects is not constructive, consider reframing from discussions about time, cost and scope to benefits, outcomes and creation of strategic capabilities.

Figure 2.9 shows relevant frames as a hierarchy – they are often used in this way during personal change work to ensure that the change of behaviour is appropriate, real, suitable to the context and permanent.

Reframing is a powerful way of changing interpretation and affecting change and is covered extensively in Part 3, particularly in Section 3.23 on reframing difficult situations (outcome frame, context reframe, and 'as if' frame).

> I am more and more convinced that our happiness or unhappiness depends far more on the way we meet the events of life, than on the nature of those events themselves.
>
> Wilhelm von Humboldt

14 Richard Bandler and John Grinder, 1981, *Reframing*, Real People Press.
15 George Lakoff, 2011, *Don't Think of an Elephant! Know Your Values and Frame the Debate*, Chelsea Green Publishing Co.
16 Daniel Kahneman, 2012, *Thinking Fast and Slow*, Penguin.

Figure 2.10 Frames

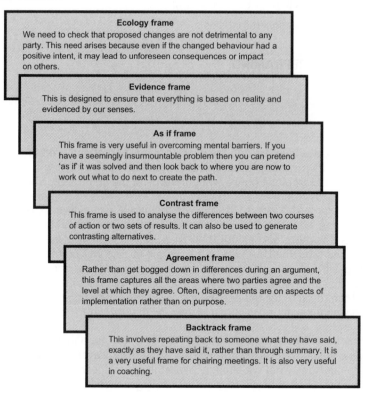

Ecology frame
We need to check that proposed changes are not detrimental to any party. This need arises because even if the changed behaviour had a positive intent, it may lead to unforeseen consequences or impact on others.

Evidence frame
This is designed to ensure that everything is based on reality and evidenced by our senses.

As if frame
This frame is very useful in overcoming mental barriers. If you have a seemingly insurmountable problem then you can pretend 'as if' it was solved and then look back to where you are now to work out what to do next to create the path.

Contrast frame
This frame is used to analyse the differences between two courses of action or two sets of results. It can also be used to generate contrasting alternatives.

Agreement frame
Rather than get bogged down in differences during an argument, this frame captures all the areas where two parties agree and the level at which they agree. Often, disagreements are on aspects of implementation rather than on purpose.

Backtrack frame
This involves repeating back to someone what they have said, exactly as they have said it, rather than through summary. It is a very useful frame for chairing meetings. It is also very useful in coaching.

2.10 REPRESENTATIONAL SYSTEMS AND OUR PRIMARY SENSES

> If the doors of perception were cleansed then everything would appear to man as it is, infinite. For man has closed himself up, till he sees all things thru' chinks of his cavern.
>
> William Blake, poet and thinker

In Section 1.3.2, where we reviewed IIBA's *BoK*, we read that workshop leaders should bear in mind individuals sensory preferences in order to tailor the way we relay information. This has been modelled into NLP. Indeed, for our trainings we consider for each topic how best to cover all of the sensory preferences and learning styles. This avoids delivering material which corresponds only to the trainer's preference.

As we think about the world around us, we do so using pictures, sounds, feelings, tastes and smells, and in NLP these are referred to as the representational systems. As we grow up we tend to unconsciously develop a preference for one of these senses, which is called our primary system. This may be due to spending a lot of time with music, or images, or in sport or dance, for example. Alternatively, we may adopt, or model, the primary system of someone close to us during our development through natural rapport building.

We unconsciously indicate which representational system we are using at any time by the words that we use. For example, which system would be indicated by:

- 'I like the sound of that.'
- 'I don't trust their offer, it smells like a trap.'
- 'The future is looking brighter.'
- 'Nothing beats the taste of success.'
- 'Run that by me one more time.'

Exercise 2.1 Determining your primary system through predicates
In the table at Figure 2.11, write down your own examples of words similar to those supplied in the Example predicates column as quickly as you can. You might choose to give yourself one minute on each box, or tackle all three together and jot them down as they spring to mind (this will depend on which meta-programs you run).

Figure 2.11 Testing your familiarity with sensory predicates

Primary system	Example predicates	Your examples
Visual	Clarify Clear-cut Focus Hindsight Take a dim view	
Auditory	Discuss Clear as a bell Outspoken Loud and clear Harmonise	
Kinaesthetic	Impact Get a load of this Walk through the proposal Foundation Stir up trouble	
Olfactory (smell)	Sweet smell of success There is something rotten about this	
Gustatory (taste)	Their offer leaves a bitter taste The acid test	

Most people are usually good at writing a lot of similar words in at least one of the boxes, though most have difficulty coming up with candidates for all of the boxes. This indicates which of the senses you use in everyday language, which in turn indicates which sense you filter the world through.

2.10.1 Matching predicates for rapport

Now that you have gained the understanding that the predicates people use are not random but, rather, linked to the way they filter information and store memories, after you have expanded your vocabulary to cover a wider set of predicates, you will be able to match those used by your audience in order to gain understanding and rapport more quickly.

Watch situations where a sponsor may say something like, 'Can you talk me through the main sound bites', to be met by the responder who replies with something like, 'I will show you the full report so that you can see as much detail as you like.' Do you think they valued the information that they received? How else might you respond?

When someone has a specific preference, then they are also likely to have this as their reference system, which means that someone with a kinaesthetic preference would want to 'feel right' inside. For visual preference the picture would have to 'look right', perhaps vivid or bright, and for auditory preference it would have to 'sound right'. See Figure 2.12 for examples of what a switched-on response might be once you start to hear what is not being said, namely, 'This is my preferred filter and anything not using it has a good chance of ending up on the cutting room floor.' Sound a bit extreme? In coaching, people often complain to me that they have proposed things in meetings but it has been ignored, only to have someone else say the same thing and the chairman latch on to it. They read all kinds of intent into it, but, usually, it has simply been filtered out by the subconscious and not even heard by the intended recipients' consciousness. To improve your chances of being heard, practice matching predicates. But first, of course, you have to listen for them.

What were the primary systems being used in the above examples?

Figure 2.12 Being heard through matching of predicates

Expressions of discomfort by client	Matching by respondent
I do not *feel very comfortable* presenting this.	What *support* would you like?
I don't like what I am *hearing*.	What would you like me to *say*?
I don't think you *see* my point of *view*.	*Show* me how you *see* it.
This doesn't *smell* right to me.	How can we *clear the air*?
Are there any *tastier* options?	One of them is really *sweet*.

2.10.2 Eye-accessing cues

We do not use eye-accessing cues within application in Part 3, but it is necessary to introduce them as, although they are not core to NLP, they are associated with it. A behavioural psychologist working in organisational design for projects commented to me that she can sometimes tell novice NLP practitioners as they stare at her eyes in an attempt to read something. As we discussed, this is a bit strange, really, as, if you miss all the other more obvious cues, you can just ask them what they mean or what they are thinking without the risk of looking like a weirdo. Basically, direction of gaze when accessing information can indicate which primary sense is being accessed, but do not stare, for the above reasons.

People look up, above the 'horizon', when they are processing visually and about level when dealing with sounds and voices. Eye movement to their left indicates that they are recalling something (right as you look at them). Movements to their right indicate that they are imagining something or mentally constructing something (see Figure 2.13). Hence, if you ask someone to remember something and they look to their right then it could indicate that they are fabricating a reply. It should be noted that eye movements are very rapid, and can be quite subtle, so it is easy to make mistakes unless well trained. Personally, I do not train them, though I do practice them and use them as a source of information to inform my questions.

Figure 2.13 Standard eye-accessing cues

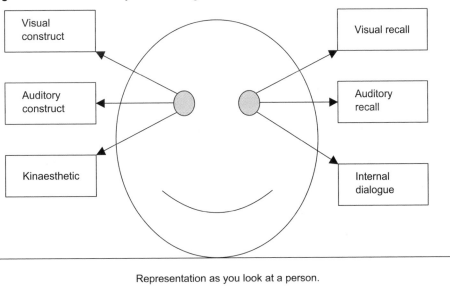

Visual construct		Visual recall
Auditory construct		Auditory recall
Kinaesthetic		Internal dialogue

Representation as you look at a person.

Eye movements down to their right are associated with feelings. Eye movements down to their left indicates that someone is listening to an internal dialogue. I assume that most of us have an internal voice, but some people have a strong preference for internal dialogue, over and above sight and sound, and can appear quite dissociated from their feelings. If you want to dissociate from feeling, for some reason, then try looking down to your left rather than right.

To practise eye-accessing cues, try asking questions like those illustrated in Figure 2.14. Of course, do not practise in a tricky situation, but, rather, somewhere more relaxed and neutral such as at a party.

Figure 2.14 Eliciting eye cues through questions

	Recall	Construct
Visual	What colour is your car?	What would your house look like painted red?
Auditory	What does you mother's voice sound like?	What would an elephant sound like playing a trumpet?
Kinaesthetic	What does it feel like to have your feet tickled?	
Auditory dialogue	Should PMs have to sit entrance exams to the profession and have designatory letters?	

Eye-accessing cues help to elicit 'strategies', that is, simple mental processes such as buying behaviour and decision making. (Strategy elicitation is not within the scope of this book, but is covered in depth in *Modelling with NLP*.[17])

2.10.3 Other cues to representational systems

Since the mind and body are one, the way we think also exerts its influence on our behaviours (see Figure 2.15). I find it much easier to pick up lead systems from more obvious signals in association with vocabulary.

How would you adapt your breathing, which also affects your voice tone and tempo, to match someone from one of the other two styles?

---

17 Robert Dilts, 1998, *Modelling with NLP*, Meta Publications.

Figure 2.15 Indicators of preferred representational systems

	Visual	Aural	Kinaesthetic
Breathing	Shallow and high in the chest	Even from mid-chest	Deep from the diaphragm
Voice	High pitched	Clear	Low and deep
Speech	Fast	Medium pace	Slow with pauses
Other signals	Usually very smart appearance	Often angle head to preferred ear	Usually dressed for comfort

2.11 SENSORY ACUITY, BODY LANGUAGE AND MIND READING

> The average human looks without seeing, listens without hearing, touches without feeling, eats without tasting, moves without physical awareness, inhales without awareness of odour or fragrance, and talks without thinking.
>
> Leonardo da Vinci

Social awareness is one of the quadrants of the emotional intelligence framework and underpins good listening and rapport, which in turn underpin high performance teams and leadership.

After most post-project reviews that I have attended, we end up with 'more communication' at the top of the flip chart. Some people may want more, but really I think that we are talking about more effective communication. It is not usually that there has been no communication, but rather that the message has not been received and understood across different stakeholder segments.

> The meaning of the communication is the response that you get.
>
> NLP presupposition

It is well established that the bulk of meaning is conveyed not by words themselves, but by subtleties of voice and body language.[18] The more we train ourselves to be sensitive to nuances, the more meaning we can accurately pick up.

> The quality of our lives is determined by the quality of our communications.
>
> NLP presupposition

When you go on a NLP practitioner course, you will undoubtedly spend several hours working on ways to develop sensory acuity; that is, the ability to recognise physical evidence linked to emotional states.

---

18 A. Mehrabian and M. Wiener, 1967, 'Decoding of Inconsistent Communications', *Journal of Personality and Social Psychology*, 6(1), 109–114.

> Let me not judge my neighbour until I have walked a mile in his moccasins.
> Native American proverb

We are all familiar with this saying, but how many of us actually do it? More likely we will imagine walking their journey, but in our own shoes, and noticing how we would do things differently, without understanding why they do what they do in the way that they do it. We are walking on our map of the world, not theirs.

One exercise widely used is called 'walking in someone else's moccasins'. Basically, you pair up and observe each other; for example, walking in a park. You then try to emulate the nuances of stance and gait repeatedly. With practice, the general mood of the other person can be 'read' by emulating them in close detail. Anthony Robbins demonstrates extremes of this with the audience in his 'Unleash the power within' road-show,[19] where half the audience report that they have successfully 'guessed' what the person is thinking about after being physically manipulated into an exact mirror.[20] I use a variant of this 'mind read' technique myself where I try to accurately model the posture and breathing of someone when I am trying to get a deeper understanding of what they are feeling. If you can avoid looking like a mimic, it is also a very fast route to deep rapport.

Television 'mentalist' Derren Brown says that he uses sensory acuity to 'mind read' his audience, noticing minute leakage from thoughts to muscle, especially being able to guess names and words people are thinking about from tiny unvoiced movements in the throat.[21] Of course, as a mentalist, many of his results are achieved by misdirection of the audience after subtly priming his subject with the answer he wants them to give.

For matching and mirroring, discussed in Section 2.14 on rapport, you will need to be very accurate in your reading of slight changes in other people's posture. Personally, I like to match breathing, which, when shallow as when seated and resting, can be barely noticeable. Matching breathing will also put you at a similar energy level. Some would-be Anthony Robbins NLP practitioners seem to want to be high energy motivators most of the time. This can work with a large audience, as it is easier to get the audience into rapport with you than to try to get into rapport with numerous different states, but I find it more effective to make the effort to match the individual client and small groups.

We have already talked about the eye-accessing cues in Section 2.10 on representational systems. The ability to spot these fleeting, sometimes subtle, eye movements takes a lot of practice, especially doing it without staring into people's eyes as though you just escaped from a secure mental unit.

Matching of tone and tempo are not so difficult, but it takes intent and practice to do so.

Whatever you believe, being more observant will help you to work out what is going on. For personal change work on others, being able to recognise tiny shifts in physiology is essential as all outcomes must be evidence based rather than mind reading / guesswork.

---

19 Anthony Robbins' 'Unleash the power within' events https://www.tonyrobbins.com/events/unleash-the-power-within/ [accessed 29 June 2016].
20 Anthony Robbins, 1992, *Awaken the Giant Within*, Simon & Schuster.
21 Derren Brown, 2006, *Tricks of the Mind*, Channel 4 Books.

You can practise your own sensory acuity by, well, practising it. Pick a regular time and use it to be more aware. On your commute to work, for example, you could use 5–10 minutes each day to run through your senses and make a mental note of what you pick up. What can you see, big things first and then details of things that catch your eye? What sounds beneath the clatter of rails and iPods? Each day you will notice more layers even for a common scene. As you practise more it will become less conscious and you will find yourself noticing more detail as a matter of course. The rest is elementary, my dear Watson.

One definition of NLP is an attitude of curiosity, and that is nowhere truer than in developing your sensory acuity. Perhaps Sherlock Holmes was a trailblazer for NLP and sensory acuity?

2.12 SUB-MODALITIES – THE CODING OF OUR MEMORIES

One of the presuppositions of NLP is that experience has structure, and the sub-modalities used to store the experience are part of that subconscious structure.[22]

We covered the primary senses under representational systems in Section 2.10. Each of these basic five senses, or modalities, stores memory with sub-modalities, examples of which are shown in the table at Figure 2.16.

Figure 2.16 Sub-modality check-list

Visual representations	Auditory representations
Dull/bright	Stereo/mono
Colour/black and white	Volume (loud/soft)
Near/far	Pitch (High/low)
Clear/blurred	Tempo (Fast/slow)
Associated/dissociated	Near/far
Moving/still	Rhythm
Location of image	Melody
Size of image	Clear/muffled
	Whose voice?
Kinaesthetic representations	**Auditory digital representations**
Hot/cold	About self or other
Heavy/light	Simple or complex
Rough/smooth	Constant or intermittent
Strong/weak	Volume
Dry/wet	Location of voice
Static/moving	Pitch
Large area/small area	Whose voice?
Internal or external	

22 R. Bandler and W. MacDonald, 1988, *An Insider's Guide to Sub-Modalities*, Meta Publications.

Exercise 2.2 Experiencing sub-modalities
The best way to understand sub-modalities is to practise experiencing them.

- Think of a time when you were happy, perhaps a recent holiday or event.
- Close your eyes and try to associate with the experience and re-live it.
- What do you see? Use the table of sub-modalities in Figure 2.16 to help to extract the sub-modalities for vision. Is it bright? Does the check-list have colour? Is it vivid? Moving?
- What can you hear? Are there voices? Near or far? Deep or high pitched?
- What do you feel? Where do you feel it? Dull or intense?
- What can you smell and taste?
- Write it all down.

It has been found in practice that the impact and meaning of a memory is affected more by the sub-modalities used to code it than the actual content. Changing sub-modalities changes the feelings associated with your memory of the experience. The 'episodic', or factual elements of the memory remain the same but the emotional content changes. Remembering that in the brain, sounds, images and feelings are stored in different physical parts, which are blended together in some subconscious editing suite before being represented to our conscious mind, we are in effect over-writing and corrupting the original memory while it is plastic during recall. This approach is widely used for curing phobias and changing beliefs, but can be used for less dramatic changes.

Exercise 2.3 Exploring the sub-modalities of good and bad memories
Although this exercise is best facilitated, try repeating the exercise above for good work events and also for bad experiences and poor work experiences.

Now, compare the sub-modalities used for each of the four examples. What are the common sub-modalities for the good experiences, what are the common ones for the bad experiences and what are the key differences between good and bad experiences for you?

By swapping over the way you store these memories through sub-modalities you can change your subjective experience of them. This is the basis behind phobia cures, which can neutralise debilitating fears.[23]

Changing sub-modalities is used in Section 3.2.4 for changing limiting beliefs and 3.11.2 for taking away the power of our inner voice, which can sometimes be our worst critic.

---

23 I. McDermott and W. Jago, 2001, *Brief NLP Therapy*, Brief Therapies series, Sage Publications.

Figure 2.17 Differences in sub-modalities for good and for bad experiences

Sub-modalities of happy experience	Sub-modalities of bad experience
Sights Sounds Feelings Thoughts Smells and tastes	
Sub-modalities of good work event	**Sub-modalities of poor work event**
Common sub-modalities for good experiences	**Common sub-modalities for bad experiences**

2.13 ANCHORING OF RESOURCEFUL STATES

Anchoring is the association of mental states and memories with sensory stimulus. When the alarm bell went off at school it elicited a response from us just as that bell did for Pavlov's dogs. As we grew up, new anchors were installed, many against our will – for example, by advertising campaigns. Other anchors or associations are more subtle and outside our consciousness unless we dig for them.

2.13.1 Conditioning

Conditioning of behaviours goes a lot further than simple responses. If you travel through the streets of India, you may be shocked that full grown elephants are expected to remain tethered and controlled by thin pieces of rope or even string. Elephants have a leg tethered by rope from a very early age while they are small and relatively weak in order to condition them so that a rope means they are immobile. Long after they have the resources to break free, they remain constrained by this limiting belief – and all discovered by village people long before Pavlov got his Nobel prize. What limiting beliefs have been conditioned into you, and what are the anchors for them? What flimsy pieces of string stop you going where you want to go?

2.13.2 Installing anchors

Before we go into exercises for anchors, there are several parameters to bear in mind to make them most effective:

- Anchors have to be **unique**. During training it is easiest to use kinaesthetic anchors. Touching points on the wrist is common. Anchors on the hands can be contaminated through regular handshaking and use of the hands. In setting my own anchors I use, for example, pressing my thumb and forefinger together or pinching my ear lobe. (When I used them in martial arts I would press my tongue against the roof of my mouth for resourceful states when fighting.)

- Anchors have to be **timely**. You need to activate the anchor at the same time that you elicit the emotion that you want to anchor. Start a second before the peak intensity of the emotion and exert peak pressure to coincide with full association. An anchor should be triggered for less than five seconds otherwise it might become contaminated with secondary emotions.

- Anchors have to be **consistent**. You need to be able to replicate the exact trigger in terms of position and pressure if you are using a kinaesthetic anchor.

As you become more practised in using anchors, you may start to use the context as the anchor, such as standing at a podium to present.

2.13.3 Choosing your mood

Wouldn't it be great to always be able to choose our mood, and select the best resources for the task in front of us? Well, with NLP and practice you can.

> We have all the resources within us to achieve what we want.
>
> NLP presupposition

While I was leading a transformation program in local government, outside normal hours I also offered some individual counselling for those personally affected by changes. One of our staff from the PMO asked for some help with a job interview as she became very nervous in such situations. Bearing in mind the presupposition above, I looked for a resource within her to use in the exercise below.

I asked if she had ever been in a situation where some people may have been very nervous when she managed to stay calm. 'Oh yes,' she replied, 'I used to be an international gymnast.' This lady had managed to remain calm and composed as she was about to do a back flip on a 10 centimetre bar, but was experiencing nerves going for a secretary's job in her own department. An extreme example of a common occurrence. We had the resources we needed. She came back after her interview some days later with a big smile on her face. I asked if she had got the job. 'No, but I was pleased that I remained really calm and was in control of myself for a change.'

Are there types of situations where you really want to perform or would like to overcome anxiety? Exercise 2.4 will help you to practise accessing resourceful states at will, rather than being a victim of the prehistoric hormones that can hijack our senses.

Exercise 2.4 Anchoring positive resources

1. Identify a problem or situation where you would like additional resources. An example might be when you are presenting to a group of strangers.
2. Think of a resource that might help you in the situation. For example, you may want extra confidence when you are presenting.
3. Now, think of situations where you have experienced this resource. Think laterally. Do you have a hobby where you feel very confident? Did you have an achievement that made you feel really confident?
4. Now, shake off this state by thinking of something completely different, for example, the smell of your favourite food. This step is called 'breaking state'.
5. Identify three types of anchor that you could use for this resource. For example, one might be kinaesthetic like pulling your right ear, one might be visual, such as looking at a projector, and one might be a word, such as 'confidence'.
6. Recall the situation where you had this resource. Fully associate with the feelings, images, sounds and memories of this experience and, while you do, trigger your anchors.
7. Break state by, for example, thinking about the sound of a fire engine.
8. Now, fire your anchors and re-live the associated experience of confidence. How vivid was it?
9. Repeat with other examples of experiencing this state until your anchors trigger an experience as vivid as when they actually occurred.
10. Think of a time when you might need this resourceful state.
11. Imagine the situation.
12. Now fire your anchors and experience this state of confidence.
13. You now have additional resources to perform at your peak.

2.13.4 Do not shoot the messenger

Have you ever wondered why the kings of old used to kill the bearer of bad news? Perhaps they became a visual anchor for the emotion (and hence it was wise to send a messenger instead of delivering bad news in person). We can become associated with negative emotions in others by accident. If someone has received some bad news or experienced a bad event, then do not stand in front of them, especially if it is a regular occurrence; for example, repeatedly reviewing all the risks and issues with key stakeholders. Keep the focus on something inanimate, such as the log itself or a flip chart, and do not put yourself directly into their field of view. (Another good reason not to sit directly opposite someone unless they are in a particularly friendly mood.)

2.13.5 More about anchors

An exercise known as 'circle of excellence', where we stack up several positive resources for a challenging task, is illustrated in Section 3.29.2 on state management. There are several techniques on variations of anchoring, including chaining anchors, sliding anchors and collapsing anchors, which I have not included as they are refinements and are better done with facilitation. Anchoring of resources is part of the process of changing personal history and timeline therapy, which are outside the scope of this book.[24] Phobias are extreme forms of anchors; for example, severe reaction to even an image of a snake, but can be removed through NLP.[25]

2.14 RAPPORT – THE GATEWAY TO BETTER COMMUNICATION

> Rapport: a close and harmonious relationship in which the people or groups concerned understand each other's feelings or ideas and communicate well.
> *Oxford English Dictionary*

Rapport is one of the pillars of NLP, as without it you would not be able to lead, communicate or negotiate. It is natural, and the best leaders all exhibit it. Through NLP, it can be learned.

While you would naturally tend to spend the bulk of your time with people who are more or less like yourself, the world of work is filled with people who are even more different from you than they would at first seem. In order to deliver transformation, you will need to learn to get on with a wide variety of people in order to influence their behaviours. Do not worry, this does not mean that you are going to have to start liking your boss or the guy from accounts and go down the pub with them, but you do need to foster an atmosphere of trust, mutual respect and understanding of each other's worlds and ways. NLP provides processes to help you achieve rapport at will.

Practical approaches to building rapport are illustrated in Part 3, particularly Section 3.15 on stakeholder management and 3.26.2 on motivating the project team.

2.14.1 Matching, mirroring and mimicking

Neurological levels were introduced in Section 2.7. Ideally, by finding out about the person that we are trying to relate to, we should be building bridges with identity, values and beliefs. Practical ways of doing this are illustrated in Section 3.20 on rapport with stakeholders. Before we manage to do that, however, we must initially develop some rapport in order for them to trust us enough to give us their time and reveal something about themselves.

If you watch people, it is not difficult to notice from their body language who gets on and who does not. People who get on are 'in synch', and flow together. Their body language, though not identical, is complementary. People who are not getting on seem awkward

---

24 T. James, 1989, *Timeline Therapy and the Basis of Personality*, Meta Publications.
25 I. McDermott and W. Jago, 2001, *Brief NLP Therapy*, Brief Therapies series, Sage Publications.

with each other. Recall, for example, images of ex-Prime Minister Tony Blair in awkward stance next to his Chancellor, Gordon Brown. Compare those with a confident Blair at ease with President George Bush junior. People immediately believed newspaper stories of animosity between Blair and Brown, and a special relationship between Blair and Bush, because their eyes told them as much.

When done elegantly, matching and mirroring can get you to a point of open communication much quicker than awkwardness and fumbling. Deliberately matching someone requires sensory acuity to notice details of the other person, not only the inclination of their torso and limbs, but also their gestures, energy, breathing, pace and tone. Experience of crude matching and mirroring, on the other hand, is what puts some people off NLP. This is what we call mimicking, and like the person in the playground who used to copy everything that you said, it can be very annoying. It definitely does not build trust or rapport.

Mirroring is where you literally act like a mirror to their posture. It happens naturally when you are in rapport. When you accurately mirror someone's body language it is surprisingly easy to get into tune with their thoughts. It is not at all subtle, however, so most people use matching, where you pick some elements and match those. Matching of the torso is quite unobtrusive.

If people remain standing, then you probably want to do the same, and if people take their jackets off, then you probably want to match. For a very important meeting with a blue chip company, I visited their offices the day before to get a feel for their HQ and how people were dressed so that I could blend in on arrival the next day. No need to take it too far, but turning up in jeans to a room full of pinstripe suits, or vice versa, is not a great start, though it can be rescued by applying some of the other approaches below.

2.14.2 Matching through energy and pace

Irrespective of people's posture, and whether you are sitting and they are standing, they will have a natural energy and pace to them. This is particularly true if they are under the influence of a strong mood such as anger or excitement. To give your message the best chance of being heard, you should match their pace and energy. Personally, I am primarily visually oriented and my pace is fast. When I talk to someone who is kinaesthetically oriented it can feel like I am watching a slow motion film, so to adjust the energy and pace I drop my breathing from my chest to my diaphragm and look down to my right to associate with my body and feelings, which naturally slows my pace and drops the tone of my voice. We now have a much better chance of having a meaningful conversation, rather than just talking at each other on different frequencies.

2.14.3 Pacing and leading

At one time I thought that, when people were angry or excited, the answer was to stay calm, but this risks mismatching them and failing to communicate. Instead it is better to match their energy until you have established a measure of rapport. Once you have an effective dialogue going on, you can start to set the pace and slowly lead them back to a less excited state.

One client arrived at the hotel foyer across from her office and she was highly energetic from a meeting she had just left. Rather than just sit her down and commence, I took a few minutes to 'walk around to the coffee shop', using the opportunity to match and then pace her steps until I had her in a calmer state and more likely to be in rapport with her thoughts and feelings before we commenced proper. She realised what had happened and asked how I remembered to do everything. The answer is that I was not consciously aware of what I had done, as pacing and leading has become ingrained in me and was operating at an unconscious level of competency through repeated practise. Am I performing a 'parlour trick', as someone commented on the group discussion, or am I 'what we repeatedly do'?

Successful change management, in effect, uses pacing and leading at an organisational level. First you must show people that you are listening and trying to understand their view. Once they feel as though they are valued and being listened to, then you can start to introduce some of your drivers and ask them what impact these might have. Only then do you look for accommodations and start to co-construct a solution. Once an agreed amount of change has been achieved, often called a meta-state, you go into another round of matching before agreeing the next set of outcomes. As you work with, and pace, the organisation, they become acclimatised to the new culture of continuous change. (But please do not consult with them on changes that you have already decided in a closed room – better to just implement these rather than insulting their intelligence by pretending to listen and then doing what you were going to do anyway.)

Managing change is covered in depth in Part 3, and co-constructing solutions is covered in Section 3.15.

2.14.4 Matching through language

Although most information about personal interaction is predicated by body language and tone, beyond this we must get our actual message through. Many of us fail at this hurdle because we do not match our language to our audience. Most effect is achieved by matching predicates to our audience's lead representational system, as illustrated in Section 2.10. Practical examples of matching to individuals' meta-programs is covered at length in Section 3.20 on stakeholder management.

2.14.5 Noticing and using mismatching

Have you ever found yourself at a party being bored to tears by someone who was very enthusiastic about some topic and wonder how they failed to notice your complete lack of interest? Do you know anyone at work who bores the pants off everyone, droning on while everyone else tunes them out and doodles in their notebooks? How can they not notice all the negative body language and absence of any type of rapport? When we are absorbed in what we are talking about, we sometimes get lost in the story, especially for visual types, and drop out of the moment into a mini storytelling trance. At such times we are just not self-aware, let alone socially aware and monitoring our impact on others.

In such circumstances you need to mismatch in a strong way, by adopting very different body language, energy, tone and movements. Having your hand on the door handle just will not do, as they will fail to notice. (Read Section 2.11 on sensory acuity for more ways to notice if you ever bore your audience.)

For less extreme cases, for example when you have to be somewhere else for another meeting, a single change of body posture or tone should be enough to break rapport and signal the end of the conversation.

2.15 SURFACE AND DEEP STRUCTURE OF LANGUAGE USING THE META-MODEL

> Wisdom is not in words; wisdom is meaning within words.
>
> Kahlil Gibran

The meta-model is the heart of NLP. It was the first model developed when the founders of NLP, Richard Bandler and John Grinder, modelled successful therapists Virginia Satir[26] and Fritz Perls. They observed that certain types of question had a therapeutic effect. These were summarised into 12 language patterns in the first NLP book, *The Structure of Magic* in 1975.[27]

Basically, below the surface structure of the words that we hear, which is the grammar element, is a deep structure of our coding of meaning. The meaning is distorted by our internal filters through deletion, distortion and generalisation. The deep structure or meaning can be re-interpreted from our words, as was done successfully by leading therapists, by applying the meta-model. Hence, the meta-model is a coding of successful language patterns that help to uncover deeper meaning and, in the process, reveal the internal filters, or world-view, of the subject.

On the face of it, the meta-model can at first appear to be an academic study; but, as you start to use it, you will realise how pervasive these filters are, and when you realise that these statements are not random, but reflect actual beliefs, you will understand the power that understanding of the meta-model can give you. Milton Erickson made a career out of it, and helped many people to return to wellness.

Have you ever had a run-in with a project sponsor and come away believing that '(all) sponsors don't tell you anything'?

The table in Figure 2.18 illustrates the 12 patterns of deletion and distortion revealed by the meta-model.

Check your own language – which of these patterns regularly fall out of your mouth?

Obviously, you would not reel off a series of these challenges as written and expect to remain in rapport. Hear them in your head and follow the conversation, only intervening when you really do need to check meaning. Practise listening in to your next project board or team meeting and keep a score of meta-model distortions by type. Try to frame appropriate questions to challenge.

---

26 Virginia Satir, Richard Bandler and John Grinder, 1976, *Changing with Families*, Science and Behaviour Books.
27 John Grinder and Richard Bandler, 1975, *The Structure of Magic I: A Book About Language and Therapy*, Science and Behaviour Books.

Figure 2.18 The 12 patterns of the meta-model

Pattern	Example	Response
Simple deletion An important object has been left out of the statement	'I am disappointed'	'Disappointed about what?'
Comparative deletion A comparison is implicit	'It's better to go along with things'	'Better than what?'
Lack of referential index Subject or object isn't specified	'People won't support me'	'Who won't support you?'
Unspecified verbs Verb is not adequately defined	'I explain things badly'	'How do you explain things badly?'
Cause and effect A causal relationship is implied	'The supplier drives me crazy'	'How do they drive you crazy?'
Mind reading Inference of intent from behaviour	'The sponsor thinks that I am incompetent'	'How do you know that?'
Complex equivalents A relationship is implied	'I didn't pass my PMP exam – I am a complete failure'	'How does a test make you a failure?'
Lost performatives Opinion presented as fact	'Its not right to have to work overtime to complete the project on time'	'Not right according to whom?'
Nominalisations Verbs expressed as nouns	'There is not enough communication'	'What communication aren't you getting?'
Universal quantifiers Broad generalisations, e.g. every, always, never, no-one	'His reports are never on time'	'Never?'
Modal operators of necessity and possibility Statements that limit behaviour	'I cant delegate'	'What would happen if you did?'
Presuppositions An implied belief	'If they respected me they would behave differently'	'How do you know that they don't respect you?'

When people employ hypnosis, they reverse this clarification procedure and introduce generalisation, distortion and deletion to confuse the conscious brain in order to directly access the subconscious mind.[28] If you listen to politicians speaking, including those that play office politics, you will hear deliberate meta-model violations. There you can expect many vague 'motherhood and apple pie' messages that are interpreted by individuals into their own maps of the world without challenging any of their beliefs. We tend to think we have similar beliefs, until we later realise what behaviours underpin their vague statements. Listening to an election rallying speech by a famous US president, I heard all 12 meta-model violations deliberately used in the first 10 minutes; and the audience looked mesmerised! We employ the meta-model in the language of leadership in Section 3.12.2.

To avoid being confused into a waking trance by people using this type of monologue, concentrate on the meta-model violations and insert your own clarification questions to stay focused. The meta-model is extremely useful as a listening skill, and is covered in Section 3.22.3 on being a better listener. We use the meta-model for clarification in the negotiation process in Section 3.24. We practice using the meta-model to ask better questions in Section 3.16.4.

2.16 TIMELINES

> Yesterday is but today's memory, and tomorrow is today's dream.
>
> Kahlil Gibran

We spoke about different maps of the world in Section 2.5. One might think that time, being linear and measurable, is fairly constant. In fact, the way we code memories in time is arbitrary, and the meaning of time to individuals is as individual as they are.

Do you know anyone who is so 'in the moment' that they miss appointments, meetings and deadlines more often than not? What about people who seem to live in the past, and constantly hark back to how things used to be, and how things were done differently? And what about those who seem to live only for tomorrow, constantly planning for the future with little heed of the past or association with the present? Time means different things to each of us.

2.16.1 Meta-program for time – in time and through time

People who are good at managing to time generally have a 'through time' bias for this meta-program; that is, are largely dissociated and objective. You might think that this would be ideal in projects. For building relationships, and general communication, however, it is better to be 'in time'; that is, living in the moment. Hence you will need to develop flexibility, or at least recognise what tasks require which behaviour, and flex or delegate appropriately.

---

28 Richard Bandler and John Grinder, 1975, *Patterns of the Hypnotic Techniques of Milton H. Erickson*, Meta Publications.

An exercise for elicitation of your timeline is described in Section 3.7, alongside an exercise for developing flexibility in your approach to time. People attending associated workshops regard being able to flex your orientation to time as one of the top three benefits. Do we sometimes rush around too much for our own good?

2.16.2 Gestalt memories and timeline therapy

Gestalt: an organized whole that is perceived as more than the sum of its parts.
Oxford English Dictionary

When we code experiences, we tend to do this as an association with similar memories in a gestalt. Thus, when we experience a situation that our filters decide belongs to a gestalt then it triggers all the associated memories at the same time.[29] Hence, we sometimes completely overreact to some situations, because in fact we are reacting to a long history of situations that our subconscious has associated for us. 'The (extra) straw that broke the camel's back' would be an appropriate metaphor. Sometimes, these associations can be tenuous in the light of day. Not only that, but the associations are often long forgotten and hidden from our conscious awareness. As you may have realised, the triggers for these gestalts are mood dependent. One of the first people to be modelled by the founders of NLP was the psychotherapist Fritz Perls, founder of the school of gestalt therapy.

There is a whole discipline of timeline therapy, developed originally by Tad James,[30] which is extremely powerful for changing behaviours by revisiting the earliest incident that created the gestalt and re-interpreting its meaning in order to diminish the associated emotion. Timeline therapy is particularly useful when dealing with traumatic experiences and suppressed memories. These techniques use the metaphor of timeline regression. As they are mainly associated with therapy, I do not cover them in the scope of this book, but I personally make extensive use them for behaviour change in myself and in others. Off-line in one-on-one coaching, we have found them rapid and effective in changing deeply held beliefs about events in the past still affecting the present moment.

It is never too late to have had a happy childhood.

Anthony Robbins

2.17 MODELLING OF EXCELLENCE

People are natural modellers, and most of our early life learning is from implicit modelling. But as we get older we seem to develop an aversion to trying new things, perhaps out of a subconscious fear of 'failure'. This trait would not have served us well when learning to walk and talk by modelling those around us, where we learned from our 'failures'. To model and learn you have to be involved in the process – you could never learn to play the piano or football by reading a manual. Modelling is already extensively

---

29 Fritz Perls, 1969, *Gestalt Therapy Verbatim*, Real People Press.
30 Tad James, 1989, *Timeline Therapy and the Basis of Personality*, Meta Publications.

used in top level sports.[31] Fran Tarkenton, NFL Hall of Fame quarterback, said: 'Most of my learning has come from modelling other people and what they do.' Similarly, Dale Carnegie set out to 'model' excellence, and Covey sought to identify 'the difference that makes the difference'. Here, we present a more structured NLP approach.

2.17.1 NLP and modelling

> If one person can do something then anyone can learn to do it.
>
> NLP presupposition

Another NLP presupposition is that 'experience has structure'. It is the latter that NLP focuses on; namely, uncovering the deep structure or meaning so that others can learn to do it. It led to the first treatise on NLP, *The Structure of Magic*.[32]

NLP was originally developed by John Grinder and Richard Bandler by modelling the shared cognitive, linguistic and behaviour patterns of exceptional psychotherapists such as Fritz Perls (gestalt therapy), Virginia Satir (family therapy), and Milton Erickson (hypnotherapy). Modelling of techniques used by these eminent counsellors explains why there remains a strong focus on counselling and use of hypnotherapy, though we do not cover those aspects in this book.

What is now taught in this book and on NLP courses is largely a collection of models of excellent skills and behaviours. The first NLP model was the meta-model for language. The second NLP model was representational systems. The third NLP model was the Milton model (after the hypnotic language patterns of Milton Erickson).[33] An example of modelling of a simple skill is illustrated in Section 3.10.1.

2.18 SUMMARY OF PART 2

In this Part we learned that NLP is an approach with a long pedigree of familiar ideas and concepts than can help BAs communicate more effectively and develop flexibility in behaviour to match different contexts.

We learned about the pillars of NLP: outcome thinking, sensory acuity, rapport and behavioural flexibility, which are required to support any NLP technique, and the fact that everything is underpinned by ecology of the human system as a whole.

The established concept of different 'world-views' was explored, and the way in which our world is filtered by our prior experiences, beliefs and values was introduced. Coding of memories, and hence beliefs, via the representational system of our primary senses

---

31 I. Woosnam, H. Alder and K. Morris, 1997, *Masterstroke: Use the Power of Your Mind to Improve Your Golf with NLP*, Piatkus Books.
32 John Grinder and Richard Bandler, 1975, *The Structure of Magic I: A Book About Language and Therapy*, Science and Behaviour Books.
33 Richard Bandler and John Grinder, 1975, *Patterns of the Hypnotic Techniques of Milton H. Erickson*, Meta Publications.

was shown to be dependent on the sub-modalities of those senses – the qualities of brightness, colour, sounds and feelings. The NLP technique of changing beliefs, including limiting beliefs, by changing the way that we code our memories was illustrated, enabling us to develop more flexible behaviour.

We introduced meta-programs to help explain our individual thinking patterns. Although meta-programs are not usually introduced until Master Practitioner level, I make extensive use of them as a working tool in Part 3, and in training courses, as effective BAs must develop flexibility in behaviours to suit different contexts and tasks.

The meta-model, which describes the deep structure of the meaning of language, was introduced. Although appearing quite academic at first sight, it is a powerful tool to assist listening skills and identify hidden meaning. The origin of the meta-model in hypnosis and therapy was explained. It is developed further in Part 3 as a tool to elicit requirements and separate needs from wants.

Of great importance in projects, timelines were discussed. Despite time being linear, our experience of time is not, and the concept of gestalt memory and re-interpretation of meaning was explained. More practically, a way of moving from being time focused to situation focused was introduced, as BAs must switch between orientations depending on the situation and task.

You now have all the background and underpinning tools which you need to understand and carry out the exercises in Part 3. These exercises will help you to communicate even more effectively and develop flexible behaviour that can be used in all aspects of business analysis. As you will have realised by now, they apply in all aspects of your life.

PART 3. BRINGING THE TWO WORLDS TOGETHER – PUTTING NLP INTO PRACTICE FOR BUSINESS ANALYSIS

3.1 INTRODUCTION TO PART 3

In this final Part, we get to apply the essence of NLP, established in Part 2, to the behavioural competencies required for effective delivery, established in our review of the role of BAs in Part 1. In my experience, NLP is the most effective toolset for effecting personal change and developing soft skills. Study and practice of these tools and techniques, ideally with coaching and practical training support, will help you to become even more agile in your behaviours, approach and mindset.

The soft skills described in the following sections are not only very important to BAs, but are transferable to other domains including most aspects of your personal life. Of the top 14 most searched topics in People Alchemy for Managers,[1] 13 are included in this set.

Change management is on that list, and one of the top three headline management issues for leaders in a 2014 BCS survey on IT trends[2] was business transformation and organisational change. As I was coaching on transformational change while drafting this book, and it was apparent that a lack of awareness of breadth and depth in change management contributes to high failure rates, I have included a large section on transformational change to give an overview of successful behaviours and tools (see Section 3.18).

It may have come as a surprise to many while reading Section 2.6, that our conscious mind is not actually in charge of what we do. I think of it as the user interface to the complex biological computer that sits behind. I wasted many years trying to intellectualise myself into changing. What we will be changing with the tools and techniques in this Part are behaviours/meta-programs long embedded in the subconscious mind. Many of us working as coaches and counsellors spend a large proportion of our time and effort distracting and disengaging the conscious mind in order to get direct access to the subconscious where we can facilitate change. Hence, when practising exercises like these, disengage your brain – do not think, just do!

> Knowing is not enough, we must apply. Willing is not enough, we must do.
>
> Bruce Lee

---

1 People Alchemy for Managers http://www.peoplealchemy.co.uk [accessed 29 June 2016].
2 BCS's 3rd CIO survey, 'What digital leaders say...', *ITNOW* Spring 2014, pp 52–54. A full report is available at http://www.bcs.org [accessed 29 June 2016].

3.2 ADOPTING AN ATTITUDE OF CONTINUOUS PROFESSIONAL DEVELOPMENT

> Be a yardstick of quality. Some people aren't used to an environment where excellence is expected.
>
> Steve Jobs, Apple founder and Zen Buddhist

Continuous professional development was specifically mentioned in several competency frameworks for BAs reviewed in Section 1.4.2. In this section we will explore what that means, over and above attending talks and seminars.

In Part 1 I mapped the behavioural competencies for effective BAs onto the EI framework. In subsequent sections, I will demonstrate that NLP can be used to develop all aspects of EI, including those supporting effective business analysis.

3.2.1 Increase your emotional intelligence

> EQ, far more than IQ, ordains success, and it can be trained.
>
> Victor Serebriakoff, honorary international president of MENSA, in the Foreword to *Self-scoring Emotional Intelligence Tests*[3]

Around 1995, while completing an executive MBA, I came across a newly published book on EI.[4] I read the book with great interest and, like Victor Serebriakoff and probably most of the millions of others who read this bestseller, I became convinced that EI was the best indicator of future levels of success in the real world. This has been borne out by many studies, including the lifetime tracking of America's most intelligent kids through school and their careers. That study concluded that, above the modest intelligence equivalent to a good college degree, your career progression is strongly dependent on your EQ rather than your IQ. This is probably true of your life satisfaction too.

In Malcolm Gladwell's bestselling book, *Outliers: The Story of Success*,[5] he illustrated quite convincingly that success in any sphere is mostly down to EQ and structured practice. Indeed, it was this book which established the '10,000 hours rule' of experience and structured practice required to achieve mastery in any discipline (see Figure 3.1). Do you think this is true for business analysis?

Gladwell illustrates this theory with a story about Christopher Langan, assessed as the world's most intelligent person with an estimated IQ of 200, the maximum on standard scales. (For comparison, Einstein had an IQ of 'only' 150.) Yet he could not complete his college studies, hold down a job or a relationship. Gladwell parallels this with the story of Oppenheimer, the scientist put in charge of perhaps the biggest and most complex of mega-projects, the Manhattan project to develop the atomic bomb. Oppenheimer was

---

3 Mark Daniel, 2000, *Self-scoring Emotional Intelligence Tests*, Sterling Publishing.
4 Daniel Goleman, 1995, *Emotional Intelligence: Why it Can Matter More than IQ*, Bantam Books.
5 Malcolm Gladwell, 2009, *Outliers: The Story of Success*, Penguin.

no saint, and was caught poisoning his professor and thus putting him in hospital. Yet he was able to talk his way out of any situation and influence those around him with great success (see Figure 3.2).

Figure 3.1 Many hours of experience and structured practice are necessary to develop behavioural competencies

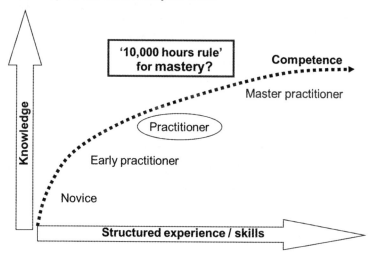

Figure 3.2 EQ and IQ are orthogonal

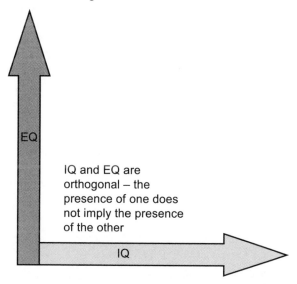

Gladwell concluded that practical intelligence includes 'knowing what to say, to whom, knowing when to say it, and knowing how to say it for maximum effect. It is procedural.' Do you think that ability would be useful to you and those around you?

The last clause, 'It is procedural', is particularly significant. When I finished reading that first book on EI I was convinced of my need for development in this area. Unfortunately, as I turned the last page, I realised that the author was merely noting its impact, and had no practical method of improving it. In fact, the general consensus at the time was, like IQ, EQ was more or less fixed. Fortunately, they were wrong, at least about EQ.

In this book I outline a very effective approach of developing all the areas of the EI framework. The following sections illustrate techniques for developing your self-awareness, managing your emotional state, helping you to be more aware of what is going on around you including other people's drivers and levers, and how to influence others through your use of language, all of which will help you to be a more effective BA. These aspects are mapped out in Figure 3.3.

Figure 3.3 Skills for knowing and managing self and others

	Self (Personal Competence)	**Other (Social Competence)**
Recognition	Self-awareness Feedback Self-coaching Presenting yourself Self-confidence	Sensory acuity Listening Rapport
Regulation	State management Goal setting Continuous development Handling stress Flexibility Big picture/detail Time management Modelling	Reframe Conflict management Negotiation Motivation Feedback

Of course, as we set out, we need to do this in an agile way, cycling through capability levels and embedding new behaviours. As described in Section 1.4, we can even baseline EQ using established methods and demonstrate quantifiable improvements (see Figure 3.4).

> There are no limits. There are only plateaus, and you must not stay there, you must go beyond them.
>
> Bruce Lee

Figure 3.4 Emotional intelligence can be improved through a structured approach

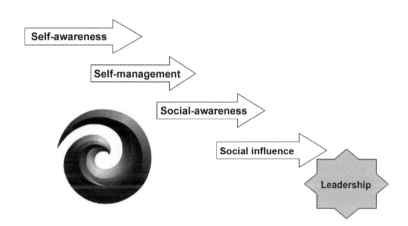

3.2.2 'Sharpen your tools'

> Perfection is not attainable, but if we chase perfection we can catch excellence.
>
> Vince Lombardi, American football player and coach

In Covey's book, *The 7 Habits of Highly Effective People,*[6] his last habit was what he refers to as 'sharpening the saw'. I put it as my first behaviour because if we cannot motivate ourselves towards personal improvement then the rest of the book is wasted reading. I relate it by paraphrasing his story:

> A man walks to work and notices another man sawing a tree. On the way home he sees that the man is still sawing the same tree. He suggests, 'Have you thought of sharpening your saw?' The man replies, 'I don't have time to sharpen my saw, I am too busy sawing this tree!'

In my professional life, I often see people who are too busy with the day job to invest in making the day job easier, that is, by developing themselves in parallel through new skills and tools. What proportion of your time do you spend 'sharpening your tools'?

In my work with the professional bodies, we spent a lot of voluntary effort bringing in a wide range of quality presenters to pass on their substantial experience, but statistics across professional bodies show that engagement with members is consistently below 10 per cent. So, some 90 per cent are always too busy sawing the tree. Bearing in mind that membership of professional bodies is low in the first place where it is not a de facto standard, this means that only a small percentage are actively seeking ongoing

---

6 S. R. Covey, 1989, *The 7 Habits of Highly Effective People*, Simon & Schuster.

development. But do not worry, you picked up the book and so are in the few who want to sharpen the saw. NLP is sometimes called the search for 'the difference that makes the difference', so here is the opportunity to really sharpen your saw!

3.2.3 You are the project

We should not judge people by their peak of excellence; but by the distance they have travelled from the point where they started.

Henry Ward Beecher, former US congressman and social reformer

Having spent so much time in change management, I often think of myself as a change management project. As with many change management projects, it is a journey rather than a destination, with many 'meta-states' along the way where we pause to consolidate improvements, having achieved our outcomes for the current phase.

Figure 3.5 The DIY change project

What you get by achieving your goals is not as important as what you become by achieving your goals.

Zig Ziglar

The more naive recruitment agencies ask for BAs who have worked on exactly the same type of project in exactly the same sector, using the same solution vendor, and so on. In NLP we refer to the sameness / difference preference meta-program. People preferring sameness make good operational managers but are not so good at facilitating change. People sometimes say they have 10 years' experience, but in reality they may have been doing more or less the same thing for 10 years and learned little since their first year.

To develop your potential, seek out challenges and stretch your zone of comfort. It is not necessary to change sector or even employer to get variety, just seek out novelty and set yourself personal development objectives at the start of every assignment.

Active engagement with professional bodies and communities of practice help enormously to structure your development and provide resources and mentoring.

3.2.4 Believing in yourself and removing limiting beliefs

There is a difference between wishing for a thing and being ready to accept it. No one is ready for a thing until they believe they can acquire it. The state of mind must be belief, not mere hope or wish. Open-mindedness is essential for belief.

Napoleon Hill, author of *The Law of Success*

Dale Carnegie said: 'In order to get the most out of this book, you need to develop a deep, driving desire to master the principles of human relations.'[7] That is good advice, but how do we develop a deep desire? Reading that statement on the page will not change our identity, beliefs, motivating values, behaviours or meta-programs. So how do we develop that motivation and take away our limiting beliefs?

Beliefs are not fixed, but are plastic and fluid. If we choose to, we can change them at will.

If your mind can conceive it, and your heart can believe it, you can achieve it.

Reverend Jesse Jackson

In Section 2.7 we discussed beliefs. These are usually buried deep in our psyche and we are not aware of them ourselves. They are often evident to others via our language and behaviours. Expressions like 'I am bad at exams', 'I am not good with stakeholders', or 'I will never be a good business analyst', do not just fall out of our mouths, but actually represent deeply held beliefs. We all have these types of thoughts in our psyche to a greater or lesser extent at some time or other.

Exercise 3.1 Changing limiting beliefs

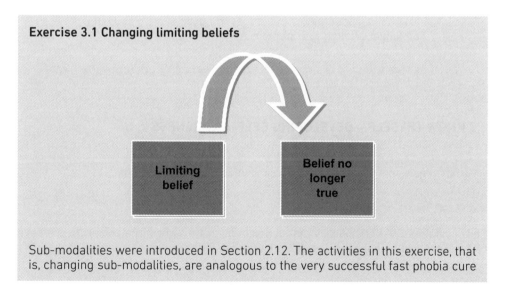

Sub-modalities were introduced in Section 2.12. The activities in this exercise, that is, changing sub-modalities, are analogous to the very successful fast phobia cure

---

7 Dale Carnegie, 1936, *How to Win Friends and Influence People*, Simon & Schuster.

that many of you may have seen on TV carried out by the likes of Paul McKenna. This very visible demonstration of belief change was also the professional starting point for NLP guru Anthony Robbins.[8] The exercise is based on the NLP presupposition that we can change the meaning of memories by changing the way we store them and the way that they are represented.[9]

1. Think of a recent scenario where the outcome has not been satisfactory. What were you believing about yourself that created the outcome that you got?
2. Think of the limiting belief that you would like to change.
   a. Close your eyes. Create a picture as you think about it.
   b. Explore all the sub-modalities (pictures, sounds, feelings).
3. Open your eyes and note down the sub-modalities of the limiting belief (a check-list is shown in Figure 2.14).
4. Think of a belief that you once held, but that is no longer true for you.
   a. Close your eyes and bring up a picture of this belief. Concentrate until it is vivid.
   b. Explore all the sub-modalities (pictures, sounds, feelings).
5. Open your eyes and note down the sub-modalities within this belief.
6. Work out which sub-modalities are different, and make a note of what needs to be changed.
7. Close your eyes and bring back the picture of the limiting belief.
   a. Change the sub-modalities (from 3 and 4) in turn by making the changes to the picture.
8. Open your eyes.
9. Now think about the old belief that you used to have and notice how it is no longer limiting your behaviour.

If you believe you can, or believe you cannot, you are probably right. Henry Ford

3.3 KNOW THYSELF – DEVELOPING SELF-AWARENESS

He who knows others is wise; he who knows himself is enlightened.

Lao Tzu

Self-awareness was specifically mentioned in the review of competencies for effective BAs in Section 1.4 under the description 'understanding how others see us'.

---

8 Anthony Robbins, 1987, *Unlimited Power*, Harper Collins.
9 Robert Dilts, 1990, *Changing Belief Systems with Neuro-Linguistic Programming*, Meta Publications.

Self-awareness means understanding ourselves and our emotions and is the fundamental step to gaining emotional intelligence. Unless we have deliberately studied them, we are mostly unaware of most of our own core behaviours/meta-programs, or the fact that people have markedly different ones from ourselves, as we usually develop them subconsciously at an early age.

> 'Know thyself', said Socrates. But how many of us do? 'Know thyself? If I knew myself I would run away', said Von Goethe.

Here are a few descriptions from various texts which relate to self-awareness:

- reflective, that is, learning from experience;
- open to candid feedback;
- open to new ideas and perspectives;
- aware of our strengths and weaknesses;
- knowing our limitations, and knowing when and how to ask for help;
- able to admit mistakes;
- able to laugh at ourselves (before others do it for us).

In my straw poll of stakeholders, self-awareness was rated the number one characteristic for effective delivery. Hence it sits here, before any other aspect of personal development. If you do not appreciate it yourself, know that people who pay for your services do appreciate it. So do not run away.

> I visited the head of capability at one of the big global consultancies several years ago and, rather than attempt to sell myself, I used a tried-and-tested consultancy technique. Since something had already got me through the door, they had obviously seen something they liked, so I asked, 'What is it about me that you see of value to you?' (Incidentally, this is a very good technique for convincing a potential client, as they will not resist their own assertions, whereas there will always be resistance to you making your own claims – a sort of one-up on the principle of using third-party advocates and references.) They replied, 'You are very self-aware, and I want to develop that into my people.'

3.3.1 To see ourselves as others do

The technique of JoHari Windows[10] is used to help organisations form a fuller picture of themselves. We can also apply it to ourselves.

---

10 C. Handy, 2000, *21 Ideas for Managers*, Jossey-Bass.

Figure 3.6 JoHari Windows

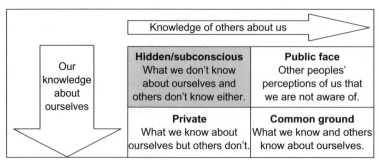

In one of the four boxes in Figure 3.6, we have what we and others agree about ourselves, that is, largely factual. Then we have the stuff that only we know about ourselves, some of which we may want to keep private. Then we have the more interesting area of what people know or think about us, but we do not know or realise ourselves. This would be what our stakeholders know or think, but want to keep to themselves, or just that we have not got around to asking them. Companies spend a fortune on market research to find out what people think about them and their products. You may think that a company should know everything about its own products, but most realise that 'the only reality is perception'. Companies also spend a fortune on consultancy, many to confirm what their own employees could have told them. Why?

> Oh wad some power the giftie gie us
> To see oursels as others see us!
> It wad fra monie and blunder free us
> An foolish notion.
>
> Robert Burns

Aren't we supposed to get feedback from our managers? How many managers loathe the annual ritual of giving feedback for fear of causing a scene, and often resort to selecting the middle performance marking and writing something mundane. Why? Because they assume that we do not know how we come across. Is it not much better to get into the routine of seeking feedback at the end of each piece of work rather than waiting for the dreaded annual review?

I was fortunate enough to be in a large multinational that adopted 360 degree appraisals for senior staff. This is where you ask peers, subordinates, managers and customers to give feedback via a standard process/tool and the results are fed back in a structured form. The results can be most illuminating, especially if you treat the exercise as a development opportunity and choose people to respond that you have had misunderstandings with, rather than only people you get on with in order to engineer a flattering score. (Hence it is a bad idea to link 360 appraisals with performance pay, as it ceases to be a development tool, which was its original purpose.)

There are many other tools that can help us to understand ourselves which all have value, including: Myers-Briggs Type Indicator (MBTI),[11] occupational personality questionnaire (OPQ), de Bono's Thinking Hats,[12] and so on. There are also a number that are useful to understand our natural role in teams, including Belbin.[13]

When I was interviewed as a program manager for a Swiss airline company, part of the interview was with an occupational psychologist, which I was told was routine in Switzerland for senior posts. They ran a number of tests, and I agreed with the results of all of them. Most surprisingly, the handwriting expert was able to give a very detailed analysis of my inner workings that I agreed entirely with. Interestingly, I never went through any of these types of personality or behavioural tests when I went to high level clearance in the nuclear sector.

3.3.2 Behaviours as meta-programs

What does NLP have to contribute to all of these different types of assessment? Fundamentally, tests such as Myers–Briggs are assessing some groupings of behaviours/meta-programs. More than 60 meta-programs have been identified from composite behaviours.[14] The basis of meta-programs was introduced in Section 2.8, but to recap a few points:

- Meta-programs are one of the sets of filters that we use to create our world-view and deeply affect how we interpret things, for example, whether the glass is half empty or half full.

- They are systematic and habitual, not random.

- They can be context specific; that is, different in work or in the home environment.

Exercise 3.2 Meta-programs for business analysis
In Figure 3.7 is a selection of the most relevant meta-programs to BAs. Although shown in pairs, they are analogue rather than binary. Think about your work context and score yourself – which end are you closer to? Remember, like MBTI, there is no right or wrong, just an understanding of your natural inclination; and, unlike the earlier story, it is possible to develop flexibility in your meta-programs if you choose to, as demonstrated later.

Having considered what our preferred meta-programs are, and what the alternatives are, we can use this information to develop more flexible behaviour.

---

11 Isabel Myers with Peter Myers, 1980, *Gifts Differing: Understanding Personality Type*, Davies-Black Publishing.
12 Edward de Bono, 1990, *Six Thinking Hats: An Essential Approach to Business Management*, Penguin.
13 R. Meredith Belbin, 1991, *Management Teams: Why They Succeed or Fail*, Butterworth.
14 Charvet meta-programs https://www.successstrategies.com/ [accessed 30 June 2016].

Figure 3.7 Scoring your meta-programs

---

1 → 10

Proactive
Initiates action.

Reactive
Analyses first then follows the
lead from others.

Towards
Focused on goals.
Motivated by achievement.

Away from
Focuses on problems to be
avoided.

Internal
Has internal standards.
Takes criticism as
information only.

External
Gets reference externally.
Likes direction.

Match
Notices points of similarity.

Mismatch
Notices differences.

General
Likes to take a 'helicopter view'
and gets bored with detail.

Specific
Likes to work with detailed
information and examples.

Options
Likes to generate choices.
Good at developing alternatives.

Procedures
Good at generating logical flows.
Likes to have processes docu-

mented.

Associated
Feelings and relationships are
important.

Dissociated
Detached from feelings.
Works with information.
Task oriented.

In time
Lives in the moment.
Creative but poor with
deadlines.

Through time
Good at keeping track of time
and managing deadlines.

Self/Introvert
Need to be alone to recharge
batteries. Few relationships
with deep connections.
Interested in a few topics
but to great detail.

Other/Extrovert
Relaxes in the company of others.
Has a lot of surface relationships.
Knows about a lot of things,
not in detail.

Sameness
Likes things to be the same.
Doesn't like surprises.

Difference
Likes challenge.
Looks for opportunities to try
new things.

(Continued)

Figure 3.7 (Continued)

1 → 10

Independent
Wants to work alone.
Wants sole accountability.

Cooperative
Wants to work as part of a team.
Likes shared responsibility.

Person
Oriented towards people and
focuses on feelings and
thoughts.
People are the task.

Thing
Focused on tasks, systems,
ideas, tools.
Getting the job done.

3.4 DEVELOPING AGILITY IN APPROACH AND STYLE

It is not the strongest of the species that survives, nor the most intelligent. It is the one that is the most adaptable to change.

Charles Darwin

Speaking to colleagues about the trend towards agile development, we concur that, although some people, perhaps more detail, process and logic/AD oriented, are promoting defined methods for agile, it is more about having an agile mindset, as per the Agile Manifesto.[15]

In discussions with other coaches while developing the contents of this book, we reflected on what the most useful behaviours would be for effective BAs. We concluded that it was not particularly any part of the role, but, rather, the attitude and approach to the role itself.

If we could wave our magic wand, we would help BAs to recognise context and flex to the big picture at will from a natural bias towards detail. The main advantage of this would be when presenting to executive audiences. We cover techniques for 'chunking up' to big picture in Section 3.5.

Building on this would be practising adoption of the other person's perspective. This is a true life skill and occupies much of the territory of the third quadrant of the EI framework on social intelligence. Not only are there benefits in understanding the other person, but also in being able to relate to them more effectively. We will practice tools for adopting the other person's perspective in Section 3.24.3.

---

15 http://agilemanifesto.org/principles.html [accessed 30 June 2016].

These two aspects together also help us to shift the focus from asset or process to business benefit, which is now included in the scope of BA competency frameworks. As in the current IIBA definition of the role of an effective BA, you need to act as a translator between the business and the delivery capability. To do this you must become fluent in both positions and adept at flexing between the different world-views, behaviours and language patterns. IIBA's definition of the role of business analysis in v3 goes even further:

> Business analysis is the practice of enabling change in an enterprise by defining needs and recommending solutions that deliver value to stakeholders. Business analysis ultimately helps organisations to understand the needs of the enterprise and why they want to create change, design possible solutions, and describe how those solutions can deliver value.[16]

When you 'help the organisation to understand', and 'describe how solutions can deliver value', you should provide the translation to their map of the world.

3.4.1 How to assure an agile approach by looking at behaviours

When I was a board member of the professional body, my remit was to sponsor and develop best practice groups, and we launched one on Assurance in 2006. Some excellent work has come out of the group since then, but the growing popularity of agile methods poses some problems for traditional thinkers. For a waterfall approach, assurance is quite straightforward in that you develop a specification and then deliver to it against an agreed plan and budget. For agile, however, the timescale is fixed, our resource pool is assumed fixed, but our scope is variable, and we do not have a forward plan showing all of the activities and when they are supposed to happen. So, how can you and your client have confidence in an agile approach?

Exercise 3.3 Assuring agile behaviours which underpin success
Given that luminaries in the agile world concur that agile is more about mindset than toolset, it follows that, for assurance to be forward looking and provide a measure of confidence in delivery, we should focus on behaviours. So, which behaviours do you think are important to the success of an agile approach? I have started the table in Figure 3.8 from statements in the Agile Manifesto; what behaviours would you add for *your* team?

Figure 3.8 Agile behaviours underpinning success

Focus on individuals and interactions (over processes and tools)

Customer collaboration (over contract negotiation)

Responding to change (over following a plan)

---

16 http://bluegrassiiba.wildapricot.org/what-is-business-analysis [accessed 30 June 2016].

In the exercise in Section 3.6.4 on developing your team charter, it is not enough to write down only what behaviours we would expect; how would you be able to tell whether people were exhibiting those behaviours? What evidence would you like to see in your team for agile working?

3.4.2 Becoming agile – adapting style to context and environment

Insanity is continuing to do the same thing but expecting to get a different result.

Albert Einstein

One of the presuppositions of NLP, based on the field of cybernetics, is: 'The person with the most flexibility in a system controls the system.' This is not about stopping what we were doing. As another presupposition states, 'All behaviours are useful in some context', otherwise we would not have embedded them in the first place. When we have problems with behaviour, it is usually that we are transferring a strategy that was successful in the past to a context where it is no longer useful. 'Choice is better than no choice'; wouldn't you agree?

Having worked out where your natural preferences are in Section 3.3 on self-awareness, you now have a picture of where you are naturally strong and where you might want to develop flexibility. Alternatively, you could just focus on your strengths and natural preferences.

When we are no longer able to change a situation we are challenged to change ourselves.

Viktor E. Frankl, published psychiatrist and Holocaust survivor

Figure 3.9 illustrates the cycle in which we can start to develop flexibility in behaviours.

Once I have identified a situation in which I am having difficulty, then I identify someone who has achieved success in a similar situation. Ideally, I will look for several people that have solved similar problems in different contexts and in different ways and try to identify common elements to form a new strategy. We can then feed this new strategy into the TOTE model described below, test if it works in a non-threatening environment, and go around the loop until we have sufficient improvement. As we shall see in Section 3.10 on modelling, it is something innate in our nature – NLP just helps to make it more explicit.

3.4.3 The TOTE model – a strategy for personal change

Everyone thinks of changing the world, but no one thinks of changing himself.

Leo Tolstoy

Figure 3.9 Adapting style to context

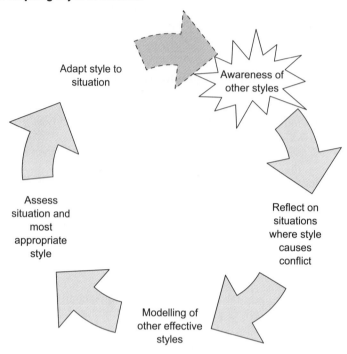

As human beings, we have strategies for doing everything in life, whether it is motivation, learning, relaxation and even finding love. When things do not work, it means that our strategy is not working in that context. For example, most of us would not talk to our boss in the same way we that talk to our kids, as the context and purpose is different. The TOTE model can help you to understand the current strategy you have, and if it is not working in this context, how you can develop a new strategy. The strategy may be one that is successful for you in another context, for example dealing with your spouse, or from someone that you observe as having success in this area. You may recognise that the TOTE model is widely used in testing, for example whether the code in a computer program actually achieves the desired outcome in real life situations. Here we are applying TOTE to your own strategies/programs to see if they are effective in the context you are applying them.

Exercise 3.4 The TOTE model for internal strategies

1. Think of an outcome that you want to achieve and are having problems with. Maybe you do not seem to be able to get on with your sponsor, or maybe you have had a series of miscommunications with one user in particular.
2. Test:
    a. Notice what is happening in the situation. What do you think about the other person? What do they think about you? Are there any peculiarities? Does it remind you of similar situations from your past?

      b.   What would be the desired outcome?

      c.   What are key differences between what happens and what you want to happen?

      d.   What will you notice to be different when things happen the way that you want them to?

3. Operate: The idea here is to generate different ways of doing things.

      a.   Think of another area of your life where you deal with similar situations or where you have achieved similar outcomes.

      b.   What were the key features of the successful behaviour?

      c.   What are the main differences in behaviour? Maybe what you thought about the person, maybe tone of voice, maybe use of language such as motivation style, or even choice of words.

      d.   Identify some aspects of your behaviour and actions in the problem situation that might be changed.

4. Test:

      a.   Ideally in a non-threatening environment or situation, test whether the revised approach has got you nearer to achieving your desired outcome.

      b.   If the approach works to some extent, continue to cycle through the TOTE model until you are happy with the results.

      c.   If the approach does not work then consider looking for external resources, for example modelling people who do achieve success in this area (see next example).

      d.   Future pace. Think about a time in the future that you will have to deal with the same person in the negative situation. Imagine that you have all the new resources from (c); notice how you act differently and, therefore, how the situation will turn out much better.

5. Exit:

      a.   When you are happy with the results then the TOTE model is complete. Were your success criteria met?

I used to clash with the finance department on a regular basis. 'Why did they need all this information from me, and why don't they give me reports in the format that I want them?' The finance department can be a strong ally, but they can also make a bad adversary. Things had to improve.

I realised that I did not appreciate the role of 'bean counters', and was going along to meetings expecting a fight in order to put them right. It had not even occurred to me to explore their map of the world, or understand why they were asking me to fill in forms. Outside this minor conflict, relations with others were good.

I decided that the desired outcome was that both parties had to be listened to (rather than me ending up shouting at them). Both parties smiling would be a good indicator of this, followed by common courtesies and show of appreciation for help.

When I thought about the 'test' part of TOTE, I realised that the present state was vastly different compared to the desired state, that is, neither side was smiling.

I considered how I could reduce the difference between the two states and used the strategy that seemed to be successful for other requests for information, such as with railway enquiries or customer services. On comparison, the two similar situations could not have been approached more differently. My body language, use of words, tone, expectations, and so on were all at opposite ends of the spectrum.

To put this idea into action (operate), I translated the strategy across situations and made a non-urgent enquiry with accounts. (Fortunately, I was able to see a new member of the department, so the relationship was not tainted by previous experiences.) I merely asked for help on how I would go about getting financial approvals, how they could help me, pitfalls to watch out for, and so on. I hope you will not be surprised that the meeting took a completely different tone (test). Having given them personal and professional respect, we had a constructive conversation. Asking for help, instead of telling them what I wanted, removed barriers and built bridges instead.

I could exit as there was no difference between the present state and the desired state.

It was easy to visualise future meetings, where I would go to ask for help, and at worst be redirected (future pacing).

When I was later managing implementations for finance systems, I got to know the world of accounts, processes and financial governance. This gave me an understanding of why they were forced to act as they had. Even later, I ended up as program director with one of the major firms of 'bean counters', so we in fact became friends. (Mind you, I seem to have kept the old strategy for dealing with my own bank.)

3.5 SEEING THE BIGGER PICTURE WHILE MANAGING THE DETAIL

In order to properly understand the big picture, everyone should fear becoming mentally clouded and obsessed with one small section of truth.

Xun Zi

We often hear people talking about 'needing to see the big picture', but what are they actually talking about? Well, some people at work would naturally see a 'helicopter view' of a project, such as purpose, global budget, key stakeholders, rough duration and likelihood of success. Often, they will see this all together in a holistic picture with half a dozen key features. Others would ask to look into the detail of requirements and functional specifications. We need both types of behaviour to deliver a project, though these could be in different team members.

Before you read on, look out of the window for 30 seconds. Now quickly write down the first five things that you remember. Did your words show a clear preference?

Figure 3.10 Finding your preference

Big picture	Detail
• Trees	• Tall tree with golden leaves.
• Wall	• High wall with ivy covering the majority of it.
• Clouds	• Pale blue sky with scattered clouds.
• Buildings	• Georgian double-fronted manor house.
• People	• A family with a young child.

3.5.1 Chunking things up and breaking things down

> Details create the big picture.
>
> Sandy Weill, former chairman of CITI Group and author of *The Real Deal*

It does not matter where we start from in terms of preference for chunk size, as we can arrive at the same place. In NLP, the process of chunking is used extensively to get to the right level of information; for example, chunking up to arrive at a motive in order to establish alternative strategies, or chunking down to arrive at sufficient detail for an action plan. Both have a time and a place.

> Nothing is particularly hard if you divide it into small jobs.
>
> Henry Ford

Figure 3.11 Chunking up and down

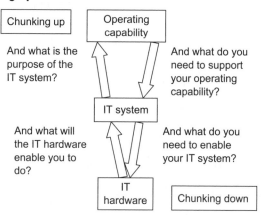

In general, project management tools and techniques cater for the two perspectives, especially phasing of a project and use of work break-down structure. Indeed, on reviewing the UK nuclear industry's £100 billion life-cycle base-line decommissioning program, the whole could be viewed as one entity, important to establish overall budgets and resources for approval, or drilled down through seven layers of work break-down to reveal individual discipline-based work packages in any one of dozens of programs.

3.5.2 Changing meta-programs

We have spoken about the need to develop flexibility, and nowhere is this more apparent than in relation to the meta-program for 'big picture/detail'. Not only are some tasks more suited to one option than the other, but you will need to reflect the bias of your senior stakeholders when reporting to them and also balance this with the preference of your team.

Do not worry, though you probably have a strong preference, it can be changed at will. (Nearly all of us have a strong preference for using our right or left hand, but you can learn to brush your teeth with the other hand with practice, even though you would never be inclined to do so and it does not feel natural until you have made it routine.)

3.5.3 Communicating with big picture and detail

Do your key stakeholders have a preference for 'big picture' or 'detail'? You are likely to have a mixture of both. You would normally expect to get more 'big picture' people higher up the organisation, but this is not always the case, especially where people are promoted within a discipline, for example IT, engineering or finance. Similarly, you would expect to get more 'detail' oriented people doing delivery, but I have been caught out by this when working in creative sectors such as digital media. If you do not communicate with them according to their preferences, then it is going to take a while to develop rapport. Have you ever tried to give a 20-page progress report to your sponsor, or five bullet points to an accountant?

Find out what your client's preference is and communicate with them in their preference, both with written and verbal communication. If you cannot work out your client's preference, then ask them: 'How would you like me to present x?' 'How much detail would you like me to go into?' Remember, if you are communicating with a detail oriented person, make sure that you do a thorough spellcheck or your credibility will be severely questioned. (When getting this book reviewed I picked a mix of types. Some advised that I was missing a section while others would pick up on grammar and spelling – we need both.)

Exercise 3.5 Listening and using appropriate vocabulary

Big picture	Detailed
Summary	Precisely
Overview	Schedule
In a nutshell	First, second, next...
Generally	Plan

3.6 GETTING RESULTS WITH DIFFERENT CULTURES

> You would expect different cultures to develop different sorts of ethics and obviously they have; that doesn't mean that you can't think of overarching ethical principles you would want people to follow in all kinds of places.
>
> Professor Peter Singer, philosopher at Princeton University

Cultural and political awareness were specifically listed in the review of behavioural competencies for BAs in Section 1.4. The wider topic of social awareness is one of the quadrants of the EI framework.

3.6.1 Better together

> Coming together is a beginning; keeping together is progress; working together is success.
>
> Henry Ford

One risk affecting more projects is increased off-shoring, near-shoring and on-shoring, leading to miscommunications from different language and behavioural styles.

Professor Rodney Turner reviewed data on the abilities of different cultures to perform projects,[17] and noted that the Western philosophy of project management did not fit with some cultures. Using some standard parameters for measuring cultural differences, he established that different cultural outlooks were more suited to different phases of the life-cycle. I like this perspective as it reinforces the fact that a diverse group, as long as they have mutual respect and work as a team, creates a stronger entity. He noted that Eastern cultural attitudes were much more suited to initiation and roll-out phases, while Western cultural attitudes were more suited to delivery phases. So, from the table in Figure 3.12, an ideal scenario might be to think like a Latin woman for the initiation stage, turn Anglo Saxon for planning and execution, then Arabic for termination. In other words, you are going to be more successful the more flexible you are.

Figure 3.12 Preferred cultural approach at different stages of the project life-cycle

Trait	Feasibility	Design	Execution	Close-out
Power distance	High	Low	Low	High
Individualism	High	Medium	Low	Low
Masculinity	Medium	Medium	Medium	Medium
Uncertainty avoidance	Low	Medium	Medium	High

17 Rodney Turner, 2008, *The Handbook of Project-based Management: Leading Strategic Change in Organizations*, 3rd edition, McGraw-Hill Education

In her book on the power of the introvert, after pointing out that a cult of the extrovert has ingrained its way into Western societies in recent decades, Susan Cain points out that the role of the quiet, introverted expert is still well respected in Eastern cultures.[18]

We should not pre-judge individuals by their cultural stereotype, but if we treat cultural differences as if they were not there, we will end up disappointed at best. With the growing reliance on multi-country and multi-cultural delivery, I am being asked to facilitate workshops helping teams to work better together, a kind of 'project kick-off +' workshop, though they have usually already attempted to kick off and re-started when difficulties have emerged.

I was called in to one global company, which was Indian owned but with headquarters in London and operations in the Americas. The newly appointed global head of projects had been asked by the new CEO, both from England, to consolidate all project groups and activities across all project types across all countries to create a portfolio management capability. The problem was, people just did not seem to want to do what they were asked and started to become entrenched in whose fault it was. People did not turn up on time for meetings, reports were not submitted, processes were not followed, and so on. This was taken as evidence of unprofessional conduct.

The opportunity was created to get representation from each of the regions in the same room. To me, it seemed evident that the problems arose from a lack of appreciation of the different maps of the world, or even lack of appreciation that there were different maps of the world. Since we were in effect initiating a change program, I took the opportunity to get them to co-create a team charter. The organisation actually had a very good set of corporate values which everyone could buy into. Differences soon surfaced, however, on the behaviours behind those values. The action of one, with good intent, might be taken as a slight by another. Showing respect by remaining with the person you were talking to was disrespect to the person you were late for. Sending report templates to help standardise could be interpreted as undermining trust in ability. Centralisation of process might hamper the way you got things done in another country. Any of this sound familiar yet? As time to get results was short, I facilitated a process of finding accommodations. Having emphasised the source of conflict and the desire to be better together, the result was inevitable. Once everyone started to appreciate that they saw the world differently, the team started to gel.

The effort required to integrate teams can be overlooked when we are asked to migrate diverse organisations onto common platforms and systems. How can you start to resolve differences in your team and find accommodations?

Think about where your preference lies, then think about where that of other parties might be. Better, why not do it together. The simple act of exploring it, working together and appreciating difference will work magic. Better still, put a motivating frame around it such as: 'In order to work even better together, would you like to explore our different behavioural preferences and how we might make a stronger team?' How would that make you feel?

---

18 Susan Cain, 2013, *Quiet: The Power of Introverts in a World That Can't Stop Talking*, Penguin.

3.6.2 When yes might mean no

> The art of leadership is saying no, not saying yes. It is very easy to say yes.
>
> Tony Blair

I was speaking to the head of delivery of an international telecoms company recently who was saying that he was having trouble trusting the on-shoring team because, although they always agreed, sometimes they did not deliver.

> It reminded me of when I was working in the nuclear industry, back in the days when most people did not travel much, and our biggest clients were Japanese utilities. I was being considered as the new head of the Japanese office and was speaking to some of the people who had progressed through that office. One of them, who went on to be head of site, advised me, when in Japan, never to ask a question for which the answer might be 'no'. He related the story of when he was in a restaurant there and ordered a specific fish. After a long time waiting, their guide advised him to order something else. Of course, staff had already made subtle hints, but too subtle for his Western ear. As explained to him after the event, they probably felt that they would have lost face by telling him that they did not have what he wanted. I think the world has moved on since, but loss of face remains a big factor in many cultures. He explained how it became a subtle art, like solving a riddle, as to how to infer a 'no' without getting them to say it (for example, 'would you recommend this fish today or a different one?').

Compare 'Will this be ready by tomorrow?', with 'Given your expertise and experience, when could we guarantee this will be ready?' Which question type is likely to give the most reliable answer?

Do you think there are different shades of 'yes'? Usually, I am sure that when you say 'yes' you fully intend to deliver on your promise. Sometimes, perhaps out of a work context, have you ever said 'yes' while perhaps not being fully committed? How about imagining shades of 'yes' from:

> Yes, absolutely – I will do my best – I will try – if I can make time – I will add it to my list – yes, I hear you – yes, please go away and bother someone else – NO!

Knowing this, how might you tell which yes you are getting?

We run this as an exercise in workshops where you think of how you might say 'yes (definitely), yes (maybe) or yes (not likely)' and your partner has to guess which one you are saying. How successful do you think you can be when you really focus on listening to the other person instead of assuming the answer you want?

3.6.3 Cultures within organisations

> Preservation of one's own culture does not require contempt or disrespect for other cultures.
>
> Cesar Chavez, civil rights activist

Of course, we do not have to cross national boundaries to find different cultures. Cultures vary across sectors, organisations and functional groups. How different do you think the cultures of departments for finance, HR, marketing and IT might be? Do we ever implement projects across these boundaries? Of course we do, but how do we go about encompassing these different cultures in our communications?

The first stage is to recognise that, without crossing international borders, we are entering a different cultural group and should modify our language and behaviour to get quicker and easier engagement.[19] The approach remains constant in becoming inquisitive as to their map of the world and how it differs from ours and then tailoring our message to it. Using the techniques described for developing rapport quickly in Section 3.20, especially looking for common ground, is an essential preface to get off on the right foot.

What makes up our maps of the world? Aside from differences in our meta-programs and our preferred representational systems, our values and beliefs really shape how we react to things. If you trespass on someone's belief system, then they are likely to get emotionally involved. How do you find out about people's maps of the world quickly?

> Prior to the days of Wikipedia, a colleague from my executive MBA worked as a salesman for *Encyclopaedia Britannica*. I asked him his top tips for sales and he confided in me that he used a lot of NLP, not to influence but to understand. He said he gave himself 30 seconds to understand the potential buyer's map of the world before deciding whether to walk away or commit to make the sale. Specifically, if education and their children did not seem important to the prospective buyer, and they had no aspiration for their children to progress to university, then he would decide to quickly move on to his next prospect. Lesser skilled colleagues would waste potentially productive time hanging in to try to close a sale. (He is now a director at a head-hunting firm placing CIOs.)

You do not have months or years to work out your stakeholders' maps of the world as you might in operations, but you do have a lot longer than 30 seconds. How might you go about it? What kind of questions are you going to ask? How about some questions like these:

- What is it you value about the work of your department?
- How do you believe this process/system/project might help you?
- What is it specifically that you are interested in?
- Is there anything we could do to help you to create more value?
- How would you like us to involve you?
- How would you like us to keep you informed?
- Will you help us to spread the word to your colleagues?
- Is there anything else we should know?

---

19 PP lost in translation article from project magazine.

If you were asked these questions by someone who had already established some measure of rapport with you, how would it make you feel? That you were involved? That they were trying to be helpful? Would you be tempted to contribute in some way?

3.6.4 Co-creating a team charter to help bridge the cultural abyss

> The best way to predict the future is to create it.
>
> Peter Drucker, management guru

Co-construction of a team charter is an excellent way to get any initiative off to a great start.[20] I have seen very wordy documented team charters, but I much prefer something created in real time using mind-mapping software or even whiteboard/flip charts.

I focus on getting participation and buy-in. Ask questions which help to reveal differences in world-views to make this apparent to all parties so that they realise we are looking for understanding and accommodation, not a set of house rules. I ask questions such as:

- How do you feel if someone doesn't remember your name?
- How do you feel if someone is late for a meeting with you, or forgets?
- How do you feel when someone doesn't supply you with information when they promised?
- How do you feel when you can't seem to get sign-off?
- How do you feel when your team members turn in shoddy work?
- What do you like most about working on projects and in teams?
- What things annoy you most when working in teams and projects?

Notice, I ask a lot of questions based on 'how do you feel...' as no one can argue with the way you feel.

> I've learned that people will forget what you said, people will forget what you did, but people will never forget how you made them feel.
>
> Maya Angelou, international human rights activist and author

I am looking to construct, in some form or another, information similar to that captured in the table at Figure 3.13. But the content is not important once it is written down; the most important thing is to co-create it in order to get buy-in. Better, if you get a physical copy in draft during the meeting, even if on a flip chart or whiteboard, and each person commits to physically signing up to it. It is your contract and understanding as to how you want to work better together. This approach has been very successful in co-creating

---

20 PP blog on co-creating a team charter.

a joint team from different partnering organisations to help resolve different organisational drivers from parent organisations.

Figure 3.13 A simple team charter

Our brand and identity statement: 'We are...'

Common values   **Behaviours we expect to observe supporting those values**

Value 1   Behaviour x
                                       Behaviour y

Value 2

Value 3

Do you see the value in co-creating a team charter? Do you have a team charter? Do you want one?

3.7 FLEXIBLE APPROACH TO TIME – HOW TO BALANCE BEING ON TIME AND 'IN THE MOMENT'

> How does a project get to be a year behind schedule? One day at a time.
>
> Anne Wilson Schaef, *The New York Times* bestselling author

Have you ever noticed how some people always seem to be behind the clock, constantly rushing, often late, while others seem to cruise through life? Have you noticed that some people get reports in on time while others have to be chased? Some people produce a schedule, while others are reluctant to even rough a plan, let alone work to one? On the other hand, which are the people that you would pick to engage a difficult stakeholder, or speak to the unions about a change program? Maybe some of the same people who do not plan?

The essential skill for time management is to be able to assume a 'through time' position. The irony of many time management courses is that they are written by 'through time' people for 'through time' people. They make little sense to people who are predominantly 'in time', yet they are the ones who really need time management tools. (If operating 'through time', you are mismatching people who are 'in time', out of rapport and so the communication is likely to fail anyway.)

In this section we will look at our natural orientation to time and practise techniques for changing orientation to context.

3.7.1 NLP timelines

Timelines were briefly introduced in Section 2.16. The NLP meta-program for time helps us to determine which groups people naturally fall into (see Figure 3.14). Like all meta-programs, however, note that they are context-based, so you may behave differently in work situations than in leisure situations. If so, all the better, as you have a good basis for flexibility.

Exercise 3.6 Determining your timeline
1. Close your eyes and imagine a line containing your past and your future.
2. Does the line pass through you or not?
3. Is your past behind you or not?

For through time:

- Timeline lies outside your body.
- Often the past is to your left and the future to the right.

In time:
- Timeline passes through your body
- Often the future is in front of you and past behind.

Which type are you?

Figure 3.14 Different timelines

	Through time (Typically American–European model of time)	In time (Traditionally Eastern culture, though adapting to working with the West)
Indicators	• You tend to have dissociated memories. • You are dissociated from the 'now'. • You are able to keep your emotions separate from events. • You are aware of time passing. • You tend to plan ahead. • You are aware of deadlines and are good at keeping them.	• You feel your emotions very strongly. • You are associated in the 'now'. • You tend to have associated memories. • You are not aware of time passing. • You like to keep your options open.

(Continued)

Figure 3.14 (Continued)

	Through time (Typically American–European model of time)	In time (Traditionally Eastern culture, though adapting to working with the West)
	• You are very aware of the value of time. • You are goal orientated. • You are conscious of turning up for appointments on time. • You find living in the now is difficult and avoid it.	• You tend not to plan. • You avoid deadlines or are not good at keeping them. • You are good at multi-tasking. • You are good at living in the moment.
Good for	• achieving goals; • planning; • processes; • delivery; • appointments and meetings.	• building relationships; • dealing with difficult relationships; • enjoying yourself; • being creative.

3.7.2 How to be in time, on time

So, now you know what your normal timeline is. Rather than just give you an excuse for not planning, or not being good at one-on-one situations, the main purpose of NLP is to develop flexibility. Wouldn't it be good to choose which timeline you are operating on depending on the task? Well, you can change your timeline because you created it in the first place and can recreate it if you choose.

You can change the orientation of your timeline so that you can experience a different mindset without changing any of the individual memories and events that your timeline is made up of (see Figure 3.15).

I personally found these exercises very useful, but was taken aback by the widespread sharing of techniques to be 'in time', that is, 'in the moment', more of the time. Maybe it is something about the world we choose to live in, or its impact on our lives outside work.

Figure 3.15 Choosing timelines

Through time	Flexibility to choose	**In time**
Planning Being on time		Soft skills In the moment

Exercise 3.7 Changing your timeline

If you are a goal-oriented person who generally operates through time, but you want to operate in time for a delicate meeting, you can, with practice.

1. Close your eyes and imagine your timeline. For through time, this will generally be in front of you running left to right (or vice versa).
2. Now step on to the timeline.
3. Give yourself a minute to adjust as it can be disorientating, especially as you become more practiced at the switch.
4. How does that feel? You may feel more grounded, more in the moment.
5. Turn your head so that it faces your future. Imagine your future.
6. Now rotate your head so that your timeline is running from your future, through your body, to your past.
7. Take a moment to reorient.
8. Immerse yourself in your planned task and let time slip away. (I like to imagine a clock melting away like a Dali painting while I am doing this.)
9. Now open your eyes.

Conversely, if you are generally an 'in time' person but you have a deadline to meet, you may wish to choose to operate 'through time' for a period.

1. Close your eyes and imagine your timeline. For in time this will generally be running through your body.
2. Now step to the side, off your timeline.
3. Give yourself a minute to adjust as it can be disorientating, especially as you become more practiced at the switch.
4. You may feel a little more objective, a little more able to take an overview.
5. Turn your head to look up and down your timeline, which will now be in front of you. You are now observing time and have control over it.
6. Imagine your task superimposed along this timeline, with key activities laid out in the correct order.
7. Feel your internal clock running like your own metronome.
8. Now open your eyes and let your internal clock guide you through the day. As you go through your day, think about the most appropriate way to be operating with regards to time according to what you are trying to achieve. Practise the technique and the changes will move from subtle to dramatic. Being in time or through time is a choice, not who you are.

3.7.3 Gaining rapport through matching timelines

Have you realised yet how much easier it would be to gain rapport and understanding with other people if you could match their timeline? It is difficult to explain to someone who is 'in time' while being 'through time', and vice versa. Some of the give-aways for which timeline people generally operate in are shown in Figure 3.14. You can find out a lot about how people think about time, together with their critical sub-modalities, by listening to their language, for example:

- It was in the dim and distant past.
- He has a bright future.
- I am looking forward to a holiday.
- Put the affair behind you.
- Time is running out.
- Time is on my side.

Think of one of your key stakeholders. Recall how they behave and what they say. Do you think that they operate in time or through time? How could you check? What might you do before your next meeting?

3.7.4 Use of future pacing and 'as if' reframes to aid problem solving

In several of the exercises in this book you will see the final stage being to 'future pace', that is to imagine yourself in the problem situation in the future and imagine how you would react with the clarity and changes of mindset from the exercise. This is similar to one of the exercises on reframing, where we act 'as if' something has already happened, then test our reaction while looking on it with a different mindset. The advantage of going to a future state is that it dissociates the individual from difficult situations. Just as we can have 20:20 hindsight, it also allows people to move past obstacles that they cannot resolve when the obstacles are in front of them.

> Things work out best for those who make the best of how things work out.
>
> Zig Ziglar

Exercise 3.8 Future pacing

- Imagine a problem/obstacle preventing project completion.
- Now imagine you have successfully finished the project and are at the lessons learned/celebration meeting.
- Looking back:

  - How did you solve it?
  - Who helped you?
  - What was the critical step?
  - What was the one thing that you had to do to move forward?

Conversely, verb tenses can be used for putting a problem into the past, for example: 'That *has been* a problem, *wasn't* it.' Note that the grammar is purposely mixed to confuse the conscious brain so that the instruction to put things in the past can speak directly to the subconscious. A slight change of emphasis also acts as instruction.

3.8 PLANNING FOR SUCCESS – LOOKING BACK FROM THE FUTURE USING PRE-MORTEM

Tomorrow belongs to those who prepare for it today.

Malcolm X

Too many projects fail, but most of these can be avoided by a simply using a pre-mortem, adopting the NLP concept of future pacing.

As a 'Gateway Reviewer' for mega-projects and high risk projects across the UK plc estate, as well as spending a lot of time on intervention and turnaround, I see more than my fair share of project failure. Often I am surprised that the high failure rates which are widely reported are not even higher. The saddest part for me is that the reasons for failure were probably knowable and avoidable from the outset.

We know why projects fail; we know how to prevent their failure; so why do they still fail?

Cobb's Paradox

This means that when projects do fail, sacrificial lambs are easy to find. When your project has failed, you will probably do a post-mortem to find out what went wrong anyway, so why not do it up-front instead and either save your resources by not starting or manage-out the risks that might knock your train off the rails?

How can we implement the lessons learned before we start the project? In the NLP world we often use the technique called 'future pacing' to get our clients to imagine themselves in the future, both to mentally rehearse going through the steps to get there and also to look backwards to help the imagination create insights about what must be done to get them there. Imagining we are in the future beyond the problem helps to set our thinking free and unleash our imagination.

Exercise 3.9 Carrying out a pre-mortem
Set time aside. You can do this exercise quite quickly, but half a day to avoid failure is a good investment. Think of a venue, ideally away from the work environment as you want people to speak freely and be unconstrained (as you read in Part 2, physical locations like the workplace anchor behaviours).

Pick people. Between 6 and 12 is a good number to get enough ideas without losing contributions from the quieter ones in the group. You will want a range of perspectives and thinking styles in the room. Now would be a good time to get your client/end user in the room. Also get your critics and 'black hats'[21] in the room. Maybe you should even consider inviting Cassandra.[22]

If you do not have a good facilitator, then bring one in – the project and people's time are valuable, so do not waste them in order to save a tiny fraction of a per cent of the project value. A good insurance policy is worth the investment.

Tell people why they are here: to help the project to succeed, and success is thinking about as many ways as possible of why the project might fail. Or, rather, to work out, from a future perspective, why the project might fail.

Set the stage – people are most creative when they are having fun, so why not get into the spirit and play-act a little. (How would a 'who dunnit' murder mystery, or even a funeral 'wake', where people reminisce about the dear departed, stimulate the creative process?)

I use 'spatial anchors' to separate out the present and the future in different locations on the floor. In the future spot it is useful to have a flip chart to record ideas, and when we come back to the present we will have another flip chart making action plans for the present.

Initially, I use some Milton language and deliberately confuse timelines to improve chances of side-lining people's conscious minds and assisting creative thinking. Something like, 'Are you curious as to why, in the future, we will look back to when the project was to be implemented; and think about what we could be doing now; and wonder what people will say about why the project failed; and do those things now that will help future success' (no question mark, i.e. no inflection in voice).

Now I play-act a short story to get us from the present to a safe distance in the future. 'We are here today [standing on spatial anchor for the present] to have some fun, by imagining [while walking slowly across to spatial anchor for the future] that we have miraculously been transported to the future, at the company's expense, business class, to look back on our project. And moving forward [while walking], through requirements, specification, design, build, test and roll-out. But the project failed [pause at half way mark]. But five years beyond that, when we have moved on to other successful projects, and maybe met up again like this [now on the future anchor], and look back at today [looking across at present anchor], what are the things, with the benefit of hindsight, that might have been the cause of failure. Shall we see if we can work it out between us?'

Pick someone out to start who is likely to make a good contribution to get things started. We are in brainstorm[23] mode, so do not allow filtering or critique of people's contributions. Use your facilitator's skills to draw out reasons from everyone, especially those who might usually be quiet or reserved. Conclude with, 'So, is our reason for failure in that list, or are we still missing something? And if we were missing something, what might it be?'

---

21 http://www.debonoconsulting.com/black-hat-thinking.asp [accessed 30 June 2016].
22 http://www.britannica.com/topic/Cassandra-Greek-mythology [accessed 30 June 2016].
23 http://www.oxforddictionaries.com/definition/english/brainstorm?q=brainstorming#brainstorm__8 [accessed 30 June 2016].

Now we return to the present. 'So, coming back to today, here in this room, now [while walking to the anchor spot for the present]. Looking at that list, given to us with the benefit of 20:20 hindsight, is that a good list, does it contain that gold nugget that will save our project?' Take confirmation, or recycle back to the future anchor and extract additional learnings.

Next we deal with each of the un-filtered ideas on the flip chart and quickly filter them for likely probability and impact, as we would do in a traditional risk workshop. From the refined list, we can then task pairs or groups to work up initial ideas for mitigation plans for remaining items. If time is short, this can be done by a sub-group after the event.

Bring the session to an end by thanking everyone for their input and creativity and pledge to work up the outputs to improve the risk register.

If you have found the thing that everyone knew but no one wanted to talk about, the elephant in the room, or some other nugget, then you will have saved everyone from a lot of wasted effort and maybe saved your project. Wasn't that much better than waiting a while to present at the project autopsy?

If there was nothing new, then you have done a fantastic job at project assurance, done an excellent job at stakeholder engagement with your client, and carried out a first class team-building event– well done!

The process of 'future pacing' helps us to gain emotional distance to speak freely. If you are new to this game it may sound fanciful, but the results are well researched by Daniel Kahneman.[24] If you are not yet brave enough to try it out, you can start with a tame version from the *Harvard Business Review*[25] based on research at the University of Colorado in the late 1980s.

When working in the automotive industry we carried out an engineering technique with some similarities called Failure Mode Effects Analysis (FMEA), where you predict what symptoms a failed component might display, once built and in operation, and then work backwards to identify candidates for the root cause. From there you go into re-design, and work out tests to identify and eliminate root causes should symptoms manifest in operation.

A fellow author related to me a second hand story about a similar kind of workshop for Richard Branson's Virgin Galactic project. I have to admire a man for whom the epithet, 'The sky is the limit' is not empowering but a limiting belief! For him it was a window to an opportunity for a new line of business. What could go wrong?

Well, his team did not find it difficult to come up with a few potential showstoppers: they did not have a space plane, if they built one it might blow up, they might not get a licence to fly a commercial plane in space, they did not have a space port, no customers, no money ... 'Enough,' he cried, counting the risks and issues and the number of people around the table. 'Right, you [pointing], sort the funding out, you get me a space port, you build me a space plane, you make sure it doesn't blow up, you get it licenced ...

---

24 Daniel Kahneman, 2012, *Thinking, Fast and Slow*, Penguin.
25 G. Klein, 2007, Performing a Project Pre-mortem, *Harvard Business Review* 85(9), 18–19.

Well that was easy.' I saw their program manager present at APM's annual conference in 2011; they had funding, customers, a futuristic spaceport in New Mexico, and a space plane which hadn't blown up when I first wrote this as a blog.[26] (OK, so the project is really behind and the customers have not flown yet, but they still seem happy, because their imagination bought into a story.)

Do you or your sponsor or any of the other senior stakeholders have an uneasy feeling about any of your projects?

I was invited to give a talk to a large community of practice and spoke on the topic of a forthcoming book, *How to Make all Your Projects Succeed*.[27] I had trained many of the people in the room, so was intent on 'walking the talk' and demonstrating some of the NLP tools and techniques on public speaking, presenting yourself and use of stories and metaphors, so I was actually training while talking. For emphasis, I focused on five topics. Afterwards, one of the earlier speakers, who had presented lessons learned on a major project failure, confided to me, 'I spotted four of the five reasons in my feedback report.' I had spotted all five while the project was still alive, so it was little surprise to most people that the project failed.

Would it be useful to give yourself and your sponsor assurance through a technique like this? So that you can honestly say after the event, 'it was not foreseeable'?

There are known knowns. These are the things that we know that we know. There are known unknowns. That is to say, there are things that we know we don't know. But there are also unknown unknowns. There are things that we do not know we do not know.

Donald Rumsfeld, former US Secretary of Defence

3.9 DEVELOPING FLEXIBILITY IN LEADERSHIP STYLE

There is nothing more difficult to take in hand, more perilous to conduct, or more uncertain in its success, than to take the lead in the introduction of a new order of things.

Niccolo Machiavelli

---

26 http://www.peakperformance.gb.com/making-all-our-projects-succeed-using-premortem-and-future-pacing/ [accessed 1 September 2016].
27 Peter Parkes, forthcoming, *How to Make all Your Projects Succeed*, Peak Publishing.

'Leadership and influencing' is one of the three core skills assessed for the 'Expert BA' qualification. Leadership invariably comes up when I ask audiences for the key behavioural competencies. But that label means different things to different people, in different cultures, and indeed morphs over time. Historically, in most cultures leaders were born into position, and in the past our military officers could only gain that rank through birthright rather than ability or experience. Note how such world-views have moved on in the light of overwhelming experience over the last century. Now, it is widely appreciated, and readily measured, that high scores for EI make for better leaders as well as all round better performers.

3.9.1 The rise of emotional intelligence in leadership

I think for leadership positions, emotional intelligence is more important than cognitive intelligence. People with emotional intelligence usually have a lot of cognitive intelligence, but that's not always true the other way around.

John Mackey

Figure 3.16 Schools of leadership

School	Period	Main ideas
Trait	1930s–1940s	Effective leaders show common traits Leaders born not made
Behaviour or style	1940s–1950s	Effective leaders adopt certain styles of behaviours Leadership skills can be developed
Contingency	1960s–1970s	What makes effective leaders depends on the situation
Visionary or charismatic	1980s–1990s	Two styles: 1. Transformational concern for relationships 2. Transactional concern for process
Competency	2000s	Effective leaders exhibit certain competencies, including traits, behaviours, styles Certain profiles of competency better in different situations
Emotional intelligence	2000s	Emotional intelligence has a greater impact on performance than intellect

Professor Rodney Turner observes that there is little work setting leadership in projects within the context of the emotional intelligence school, but there is a significant relationship between project success and inner confidence and self-belief.[28] The latter element is what NLP refers to as the self-reference meta-program (as against the opposite, external reference). Note that self-reference tends to make people more resilient, though less open to feedback.

Turner also observes that, while some say leaders are born not made, and some people are naturally more suited to leadership than others, everyone can improve their leadership skills.

> My hope was that organizations would start including this range of skills in their training programs – in other words, offer an adult education in social and emotional intelligence.
>
> Daniel Goleman

3.9.2 Six styles of leadership

> As we look ahead into the next century, leaders will be those who empower others.
>
> Bill Gates

Turner wrote a comprehensive series on leadership in the project context based on research as to whether different leadership styles influenced project success, and whether different leadership styles were more appropriate to different types of project.[29] There is no right or wrong style, only the wrong context. I think each of these styles has use for some types of project in some situation or other. What is your preferred style?

Figure 3.17 Six styles of leadership

Style	Defining characteristic	Useful when	Harmful when
Directive	Tell employees what to do and expect them to do it.	Organisations are going through a crisis, a period of turmoil or significant change.	The bureaucratic, imagination-stifling nature of the style means that it's inappropriate in situations where staff need to be creative or innovative.

(Continued)

28 L. Lee-Kelley and K. L. Long, 2003, 'Turner's Five Functions of Project-Based Management and Situational Leadership in IT Services Projects', *International Journal of Project Management* 21(8), 583–591.
29 J. R. Turner, 2006, 'Leadership: The Project Context', *Project Manager Today*, November: 29.

Figure 3.17 (Continued)

Style	Defining characteristic	Useful when	Harmful when
Visionary	The objective is providing long-term direction.	Use it when you need to galvanise people and get them to see the bigger picture or motivate them for an unpleasant phase.	Don't use it in a crisis and it would not be effective if the person articulating the vision did not have credibility.
Affiliative	The primary focus is about creating harmony in the team so that they all like one another.	To get a group of creatives or scientists to overcome egos long enough to perform as a group.	Don't use in a crisis at any time when performance issues need to be addressed.
Participative	Likely to hold a lot of meetings and ask people for their ideas and opinions on what should happen next.	Good way of getting fresh ideas from a team of people who know what they are doing.	Terrible in a crisis. Asking for people's input on a decision that you've already made will damage trust and credibility.
Pacesetting	The underlying concern is about getting work delivered to a high standard, but what it looks like in practice is leaders effectively showing people how to do things.	Effective when in charge of a competent, achievement-focused and highly motivated team of people, for example in consulting or professional services.	Poor for long-term results as lack of delegation limits development of the team and creates clones. Burns out the leader.

Source: Compiled from leader articles in *The Sunday Times*, January–March 2008.

Reflecting on the past, do you think you have flexed your style to situations and been as effective as you could be? What style do you think works best in an agile environment? Looking to the future, can you think of a situation where you might want to flex your style?

At times in my career my strategy was so forceful and aggressive that I effectively bludgeoned dissenters and got my own way without taking any prisoners (including the client on some occasions). This might kindly be referred to as an extreme instance of the 'directive' style of leadership. The directive style can be useful in turnaround situations and projects where there is no clear plan and lack of direction. When I moved on to change management projects, however, I quickly realised that this approach was not achieving desired outcomes. I had to learn to do things more elegantly; that is, develop more flexibility in style and approach. If we do not adapt our style to the situation, aside from achieving limited success, we are liable to suffer excess strain and burn-out.

Reflecting back, I can see a progression in my career from a pure directive style, through pacesetting to be more facilitating. I now focus on spending more of my time in a coaching style. Of course, that is my own opinion. In a survey by the CMI Institute, most managers said that they used a coaching style, yet replied that their managers used a directive style. Perhaps CMI members are truly different, but perception obviously comes into it. There is in fact no best style of leadership, as it should be contextual. So, how do you plan to become more agile in your leadership style?

3.9.3 Supervising, managing or leading – what got you here might not get you there

Leaders are people who do the right thing; managers are people who do things right.

Warren Bennis, leadership guru

I was in the headquarters of a professional body when someone asked the question in relation to an application for chartered status, 'Can I put my time as a supervisor down under leadership experience?' 'Yes', came the reply. I disagree; though both have a part to play, leading and supervising are poles apart. If someone is not sure what they are doing and does not know how to do it, then we might have to give them detailed instructions if we are short of time in order to meet a deadline. Ideally, we would have sufficient time to bring them up to speed and coach them to an acceptable standard.

When I started my career, I was informed about 'The Peter Principle',[30] which says that people are promoted to a level at which they become incompetent, and then they do not rise any more. Years later, Marshal Goldsmith, probably the most influential executive coach in the Western hemisphere, penned the bestseller, *What Got You Here Won't Get You There*.[31] Basically, you need to stop doing some of the behaviours that served you in the past in order to adopt those which will serve you in the future.

---

30 The Peter Principle http://www.businessdictionary.com/definition/Peter-principle.html [accessed 20 June 2016].
31 Marshall Goldsmith, 2010, *What Got You Here Won't Get You There*, Profile Books.

This reminds me of a story I was told on my slow path towards enlightenment in martial arts. A novice in a Shaolin Buddhist temple, perhaps Kwai Chang Cain himself, goes to have tea with the wise old monk (a man as bald and eminent as Marshal Goldsmith himself). The novice holds out his cup for tea. The monk delicately pours tea, and continues to pour. Eventually, still holding a serene smile that only an enlightened one can, the monk pours until the cup overflows. The novice, at first reluctant to interrupt the monk, now says, 'Master, there is no room in the cup for more tea!' To which the master replies, 'So student, how will you empty your cup to receive the new knowledge that you seek?'

Exercise 3.10 Progressing from supervising to leading

1. Look at the mix of words below

> checking quality describing tasks listing activities describing a vision disciplining staff coaching managing your state managing stakeholders using stories and metaphors

2. Where do you think these fit along the path from supervising to leading?

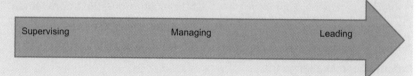

3. On that continuum, where do you see yourself now?
4. Where do you think others see you?
5. Where do you see yourself in the future?
6. Before you take on those new behaviours ahead of you, what behaviours which served you in the past might it be worth doing less of in order to practice more of the behaviours which will serve you in the future?
7. When will you start on your future path and let go of what got you here?

Your attitude determines your altitude.

Zig Ziegler

During training courses, we do a kinaesthetic version of this exercise where we get delegates to write words associated with supervising, managing and leading and place them on a continuum on the floor. We then walk along this timeline to where they think others see them, envisioning letting go of some of the behaviours behind them in order to focus on the behaviours in front of them. The effects have proven to be profound. Why do you think it works?

So, should a BA/change manager be a manager or a leader? I think an effective change manager requires awareness of the context in order to flex between managing and leading depending on the activity being undertaken. Does the table in Figure 3.18 reflect your map of the world?

How can you spend more time on leading change?

Figure 3.18 Change managers need to be both managers and leaders depending on context

---

Leading	Managing
• Create the vision	• Implement the blueprint
• Motivate and inspire	• Plan, budget and organise the team
• Bring stakeholders on board	• Maintain effectiveness
• Build the team	• Manage the impact of change
• Align people and inspire them	• Assess progress
• Create change proactively	• Solve problems
• Keep the values visible	• Seek step-by-step improvement
• Collaborate	• Implement processes
• Keep a helicopter view	• Facilitate workshops
• Continue to challenge the status quo	
• Coach team members	

3.10 MODELLING EXCELLENCE

> Modelling is the pathway to excellence.
>
> Anthony Robbins

Do you know any really good BAs, or ones that do some aspect of the job really well, for example run a workshop? You are in luck, as the primary approach of NLP has been to model effective behaviours. I gave a brief introduction to modelling in Section 2.17, and will now introduce the practical steps of modelling. Please note, however, that effective modelling requires a number of competencies in itself, some of which have been introduced to this point, but it is not usually taught until Master Practitioner level. Of about 50 NLP books on my shelf, half only mention modelling in passing and the rest contain only a cursory outline for modelling of simple strategies. Proper coverage, aside from facilitated practice, needs a book all to itself. The pioneering work for modelling in business was by Robert Dilts,[32] based in large part around modelling of leadership skills at Fiat. My own modelling project, on entrepreneurs in the project management sector, took over a year to complete and achieve my desired outcomes. But BAs are clever people, and we are already familiar with modelling, so we will make a start.

> Nothing in the world is difficult if you break it down in to small enough steps.
>
> Henry Ford

3.10.1 From complex behaviour to modelling of simple strategies

Many areas of excellence that we experience are complex composites of many beliefs, values, behaviours and skills. For example, 'presenting' could be broken down into a number of components, such as: presenting yourself, engaging your audience, use of language, projecting your voice, dealing with questions, use of tools such as PowerPoint, and so on. The more finite the process is, then the better your chance of achieving the same outcome.

Where you are trying to master a larger topic, some success can be achieved by spending a lot of time with people who are experts and subconsciously mimicking what you see and hear. Some of your preference for approach will depend on your own meta-programs; for example, for process, big picture, and so on. For martial arts, this is equivalent to just mimicking the master, which was the common form of instruction when it originated. For BAs, I certainly recommend spending time with your peers and getting involved in best practice groups. Aside from picking up knowledge, some of the behaviours will 'rub off'.

Think of a simple skill that you would like to learn; for example, remembering names. I use this as a warm up for my training as usually, at most, only one person in the group might consider themselves good at remembering names, even though all agree that it is important in building rapport. At the end of the exercise, most people remember all the names in the room.

My first experience of explicit modelling was in the early 1990s. In the days before mobile phones, I was not comfortable using the telephone, but had the fortune to witness a colleague in the PMO who appeared confident and achieved good results. I will use this example for illustration in the process below. Please note that, although the process is shown linearly and can be read through in a minute, it usually requires repeat cycles for you to be able to replicate the skill. Yet more time and practice is required to move it from being consciously competent to a subconscious and internalised skill. The true test of whether you have accurately modelled a skill is whether you can transfer it to a third party. Of course, it can all happen much quicker with appropriate facilitation. Remember that it is your job to discover what it is the person is doing to be successful because they will not have conscious awareness of it.

---

32 Robert Dilts, 1998, *Modelling with NLP*, Meta Publications.

Exercise 3.11 Modelling process for a simple strategy

1. Identify a gap or improvement that you would like to address through modelling.

2. 'Chunk down' the skill until you have something small and concise enough to complete in a reasonable time frame.

3. Identify suitable resources who seem to have this skill. One will do, but more helps in later stages to identify core and non-essential components.

4. Ask permission to model the skill. Most people will be flattered. Usually they do not realise they have this skill, as it is 'natural' to them and they often assume that everyone can do it.

5. Spend time observing people with this skill to get a kind of holistic overview of things they seem to have in common. During this time, you will also be doing some subconscious modelling through the natural process of induction, similar to how you learned most of your skills early in life.

6. Establish rapport. You are well placed to make this easy as you have genuinely praised their skills and you should be listening intently to them. Later, you will also be mimicking both their body language and verbal communication, which naturally leads to rapport.

7. As important as how people do things is why they do them. Values and beliefs underpin success. Where we have recognised a skill gap, we probably have a belief that we are not good at it, which needs to be addressed. The negative language can be easily corrected, for example, 'Now that I have an excellent model I will soon be even better at (communicating by telephone)'. In this instance, my model had a clear belief that information should be shared to avoid confusion and mistakes, so would routinely phone people up just to ask them if they had heard about so-and-so and generally how things were going. People often do not know why they do things, so some gentle questions along the lines of, 'And why is that important?' help them to explore what is buried between their ears.

8. Ask what their desired outcome is, and how they will know when they are achieving it. How will they know when they are not moving towards their desired outcome?

9. What starts the sequence? What are they doing? What are they seeing/hearing/feeling/saying to themselves?

10. Observe people's physiology when you get them to act out the task. In this example I observed that my model always stood up to make important phone calls. He said he liked to imagine walking up to them when he said 'hello'.

11. The most important revelation to me was that he managed to completely ignore the telephone, which had become a negative anchor for me. Instead, he recalled a picture of the person he was going to call, heard their voice and then, in his head, he was effectively having a face to face conversation. Usually, people who have a skill are not aware of how they do it, but these features can be elicited by a combination of focused questions, such as, 'And what are you thinking about now?' and 'Why is that important?'

12. If you have developed sensory acuity, observing the model's eyes when they are mentally replaying the activity will reveal any incongruence in what they say is happening. In this example, the model said that they imagined the person's voice, but their eyes revealed that they were recalling visual memories first, and subsequent questioning revealed that they first accessed the face to help to retrieve the voice, which would be normal for someone with a visual preference.

13. Ask what they will do if they are not achieving their desired outcome. How do they recover the process?

14. Once you are happy that you have elicited a good enough model to make an improvement, try it out. Ideally, get your model to watch you, as seeing a 'mirror' will remind them of any steps or thought processes they have missed out. This learned strategy for the telephone proved a very effective starting point for me, especially in overcoming the barrier of making more calls in the first place and relying less on email.

The real test for a model though is to be able to transfer it to someone else. If you cannot, then there is probably a step missing.

As with any skill that we start to see an improvement on, I was motivated to improve further as I got the hang of it. You can refine the model by testing for bits that can be taken out without affecting the result. Modelling of other 'callers' also revealed that it was not necessary to stand, only to be comfortable, avoid looking down and relax the diaphragm in order to project your voice for clarity.

Is the strategy effective in all situations in which you want to use it? The strategy was not effective when calling strangers, and had to be adapted. I gleaned this from a 'cold caller' in sales, who told me they imagined they were phoning up someone they already knew.

Models can be improved over time as you discover new resources. Matching of pace and energy, matching of language and preferences, and so on, all built on to this skill over subsequent years. I later realised that my mother disliked using the telephone and would avoid answering it, so I was unpicking my unconscious modelling of her.

If you study NLP and modelling further you will see notation for modelling relating to this, particularly to the eye-accessing cues. It is, however, easy to misread these cues unless you have had practical training in sensory acuity and have 'calibrated' for your model; that is, tested how far and fast their eye movements are for a range of questions related to the senses.

In our training courses we include a modelling project to achieve 'NLP Business Practitioner' status. Seeing a group of a dozen people presenting back the skills they have learned from those around them is a humbling experience. You can download the guidance notes for this from the supporting website www.NLP4BA.com.

> If you are going to achieve excellence in big things, you develop the habit in little matters. **Excellence** is not an exception, it is a prevailing **attitude**.
>
> Colin Powell, diplomat and military leader

3.11 BE YOUR OWN COACH

> Everyone needs a coach.
>
> Bill Gates

Coaching skills were specifically mentioned in the review of competencies for effective BAs in Section 1.4. and form one of the three specialist skills assessed for the 'Expert BA' qualification. We can also be a coach to ourselves.

It is expected in sports that you need a coach to achieve your potential, but it is relatively new to business, and usually confined to those in very senior positions. While writing, I am employed as a coach for senior staff across a portfolio of major programs, including their business change managers and lead team in the IT department. But we can all be our own coach with the help of a few techniques and a bit of NLP.

3.11.1 From knowing to being

In Section 1.4 we talked about competencies and becoming competent, and how this was achieved through a combination of knowledge, experience and behaviours. Figure 3.19 is a popular model of this process. I have shown it as a cycle as, hopefully, like top tennis and golf players, we continue on the cycle towards our ultimate goal.

A similar model to this, which I have seen promoted in recent years to assist in sales, suggests a progression from 'just do it', to 'being it'. I think it better represents the journey from understanding, to practising, to feeling fully comfortable in the role (see Figure 3.20).

> We are what we repeatedly do. Excellence then, is not an act, but a habit.
>
> Aristotle

3.11.2 Compassionate coaching and the inner game

> We are shaped by our thoughts; we become what we think.
>
> Buddha

Figure 3.19 Towards unconscious competency

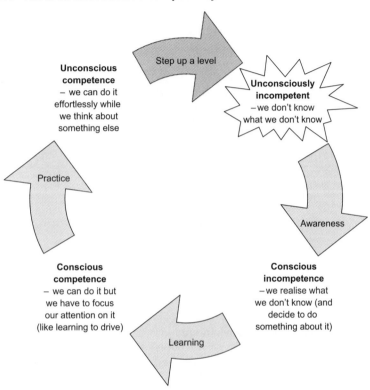

We sometimes make the mistake of thinking that the, sometimes harsh, inner voice is 'me'. It is not, though it is a part of us. We have the most effective learning machine ever developed between our ears, and yet when we try something new we tend to over-rationalise it. Our inner voice did not teach us to crawl or walk, and certainly was not around to teach us to speak, so put it aside. Top athletes have learned 'the inner game' of practice without judgement.[33] This results in the ultimate experience of what has been referred to as 'flow',[34] or 'up time' in NLP speak.

As described in Section 2.6, the subconscious mind is what drives us. If you want to put an internal voice to good use then let it be 'your compassionate coach',[35] and be gentle and encouraging to yourself. Know and repeat your goals. The more solid they are and the more you can visualise them and experience them with all your senses, then the stronger will be the compulsion of your subconscious mind to attain them.

---

33 W. T. Gallwey, 1986, *The Inner Game of Tennis*, Pan.
34 M. Csikszentmihalyi, 2008, *Flow: The Psychology of Optimal Experience*, Rider.
35 A. Essex, 2004, *Compassionate Coaching*, Rider.

Figure 3.20 Being there

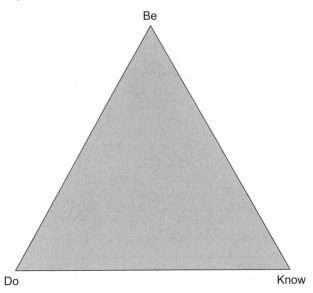

Exercise 3.12 Conquering negative language

Look at the table in Figure 3.21. Do you recognise some of the negative words there? Negativity puts us in an un-resourceful state and holds us back, and that affects both you and the people that you influence. It is easier to start with what we write rather than what we say, so check what you put down on paper/screen and edit out that negativity. Now that it is in your conscious mind, catch yourself if you use a negative word and correct it. It will start to affect your outlook and put you in a more resourceful state. Others will also start to see you as a much more positive and competent person and have more trust in you.

Figure 3.21 Using positive language

Negative language	Positive language
Can't	Working out how to
Difficult	Stretching
Problem	Challenge
Have to	Want to
Failure	Learning
Complaint	Feedback

Next time you catch yourself or one of your team saying something like, 'We can't get the users to sign-off requirements', use a re-phrase like, 'We are getting good feedback from users and exploring ways to articulate their needs.' We are not talking about putting a positive spin on things here – it may sound like just words, but it will frame how you behave and what you do subsequently. Similarly, lessons learned are not about looking at what went wrong and attributing blame, as we see on a TV episode of *The Apprentice*, but a time of reflection on how we will do even better next time.

What are your 'favourite' negative words? What would be a more positive way of expressing them?

Mike Nichols, former chairman of the Association for Project Management until he passed away in 2014, refused to acknowledge any negative language or talk of failure in whatever he said or wrote. Was this a reason why his company was so successful, for example being a family business that leads on mega-projects like Crossrail in London and also operates globally?

Exercise 3.13 Taking control of your inner critic using sub-modalities

Does a voice in your head sometimes hold you back? Do not worry, it is part of the human condition. As you have heard, with NLP everything that we experience is subject to the way our brains code it. Making subtle changes to the language of our code can cure people from severe phobias, and we can use the same technique to quieten our inner force if it misbehaves. Here we will be making use of sub-modalities, as described and illustrated in Section 2.12.

1. Call up that negative inner voice.
2. What does it sound like? Do you recognise that voice? What are the sub-modalities (volume, pitch, near or far)?
3. If you can locate it, for example on your right ear or behind you, then move it to the opposite place.
4. Turn down the volume.
5. Change the pitch.
6. How about giving it a new character? Daffy Duck?
7. Now, let it say some stupid negative thoughts, but in that stupid little voice.
8. Now, that is easier to ignore, isn't it?
9. Imagine the future where you are going to do something where the voice used to hold you back. Now see yourself successfully doing it, with that funny little voice keeping you amused.

That was easy, wasn't it?

3.11.3 The virtual mentor – imaginary friends for grown ups

Before 're-engineering of corporations',[36] there used to be multiple tiers of managers, and people stayed in their jobs for a long time. Nowadays, a couple of years in the same role seems to be a long time, and many people freelance. Hence we have fewer opportunities to 'learn on the job' through informal mentoring.[37] I would strongly advise you to find mentors for all aspects of your life wherever you can. Sometimes you may really wish that you had one there and then. Well, with a bit of imagination you can. I have a collection of virtual mentors that I use in different kinds of environment. I am using Genghis Khan a lot less than I used to, and relying more on Mahatma Gandhi to do things a bit more elegantly. I think of it as a metaphor to put a bit of distance between me and the situation to allow more creativity (rather like 'as if' reframing). For this next exercise, imagine a mentor called 'John' – perhaps someone that you have encountered and admired in your career. I think my father would have chosen John Wayne.

Exercise 3.14 The virtual mentor

1. When you find yourself in a situation where you feel you need more resources, ask 'John' to come and help you.
2. Imagine John next to you and get into his character.
3. Ask him what he thinks about the situation and imagine what he might say.
4. Ask him for some options.
5. Have a think about them – do any sound like they might be promising?
6. Ask for some tips on what to look out for.
7. Note down a plan and the first steps.
8. Thank John and ask him to look over your shoulder until you are comfortable and back on track.
9. Remember, John and his friends are there whenever you need them.

On paper it might look a little strange, but be brave enough to give it a try and judge by results. (That is what John would do.) When we are in a tight spot we could use all the help and advice we can muster, and 'John' is always willing to help.

3.11.4 Action learning sets and communities of practice

Action learning is essentially where you agree a common development aim as a group and agree to work on it individually and share experiences.[38] It also acts as a support group. I have been involved in action learning sets as a senior manager. A related principle is

---

36 M. Hammer, 1996, *Beyond Re-engineering*, Harper Business.
37 P. Matthews, 2013, *Informal Learning at Work: How to Boost Performance in Tough Times*, Three Faces Publishing.
38 M. Pedler, 2008, *Action Learning for Managers*, Gower.

that of communities of practice.[39] A number of large organisations are now setting up communities of practice to share resources and support. I set up an online community on LinkedIn to discuss application of NLP to business analysis and project management, which is now as big as most other special interest groups of the professional bodies.[40] What experiences can you contribute?

3.12 GREAT LEADERS USE STORYTELLING AND METAPHOR TO GET THE MESSAGE OVER

> The universe is made of stories, not of atoms.
>
> Muriel Rukeyser, poet and political activist

In a creative paper on why and how BAs and PMs should work better together, 'The Marriage of Professions; Business Analysis and Project Management can live happily ever after...together',[41] Chuck Milhollan makes the case through the medium of story, including 'The Monster' (legacy system), the heroine (BA) and hero (PM) who go on to live, well, happily ever after.

British sociologist Anthony Giddens (Lord Barron),[42] argued that we derive our sense of self, not from what has happened through our lives, but from our capacity to weave those episodic events into a consistent story. Our story is consistent with, and a constituent of, our personal map of the world.

Use of stories has become ubiquitous across analysis to bridge the gap between what a user wants from a system and the specification for the system. In recent years books have been published on use of storytelling and metaphor as a medium for teaching leadership[43] and lessons in project management.[44] I am currently modelling exponents of storytelling like Steven Carver,[45] who has gone beyond incorporating stories to delivering whole talks within a single story, including post-graduate lectures as Professor at Cranfield Management School.

Legendary orators made extensive use of stories, including religious leaders. Well, the ones who remember anyway, as storytelling aids memory, and masters of memory make extensive use of stories and imagery.[46]

---

39 E. Wenger, 1999 *Communities of Practice: Learning, Meaning, and Identity*, Learning in Doing: Social, Cognitive and Computational Perspectives, Cambridge University Press.

40 LinkedIn group NLP for Project Management https://www.linkedin.com/topic/neuro-linguistic-programming-(nlp) [accessed 20 June 2016].

41 http://www.pmi.org/~/media/PDF/learning/business-analysis/business-analysis-project-management-marriage-professions.ashx [accessed 30 June 2016].

42 http://www.lse.ac.uk/sociology/whoswho/academic/Giddens.aspx [accessed 30 June 2016].

43 For instance, Nick Owen, 2001, *The Magic of Metaphor: 77 stories for Teachers, Trainers and Thinkers*, Crown.

44 T. Taylor and R. Dee, 2012, *Sixteen stories for Projects, Programmes and Enterprises*, Dashdot Enterprises Ltd.

45 http://www.peakperformance.gb.com/leading-with-a-story/ [accessed 30 June 2016].

46 Joshuer Foer, 2011, *Moonwalking with Einstein: The Art and Science of Remembering Everything*, Penguin.

Why do these stories and metaphors work? As the great orators and religious leaders have found, they provide a low resistance **doorway to the unconscious mind**. Marketers and brand managers have also discovered and perfected these techniques. The unconscious mind is the world's greatest pattern recognition system and looks for hidden meaning in all things. Hence I make extensive use of stories.

I recruited a scientist named Dominic Rhodes. Like most general recruitment processes, candidates gave a presentation. I remember being really taken aback by his. Instead of the usual PowerPoint, he showed a set of photographs in sequence of threes; a picture of a site as context, an image of the cause of the problem uncovered through his analysis, and a final slide illustrating the solution to the problem. By way of introduction he also told a story, with graphic use of language, about how he ended up working in a gold mine in South Africa, and extracted a parable about what he learned about life and the work of an analyst. I do not know how much preparation Dominic put in to that presentation, but I have never seen anyone appear more structured, succinct or persuasive. Of course I gave him the job, and a great job he did too. More recently he has been an ambassador for university collaboration and also a science, technology, engineering and maths (STEM) ambassador to schools. He also serves on the Smallpiece Trust, running a series of residential courses to help inspire young people in science and technology subjects. A number of the young people who have been inspired by Dominic's involvement through his outreach work now work alongside him as colleagues. I last saw him in June 2014, 20 years after I recruited him and the day after he found out he had been awarded an MBE for his work with universities and schools.[47] Not a bad story to tell the kids.

How will you inspire your audience? A start would be to use the often quoted but usually forgotten rule of stories – to have a start, a middle and an end. Far too often I have had presentations which seemed, at best, to be a stream of consciousness. Start with a simple message and build out.

3.12.1 Be the STAR of your story

If you can't explain it simply, you don't understand it well enough.

Albert Einstein

One of the most effective ways of conveying information is use of the STAR model below. Recruiters use this technique to establish areas of competency, and I described it as such in Section 1.5 on assessing competency. So, if you want to sound competent, practice the STAR model in Figure 3.22 (the example is from a presentation I gave to a community of practice in Canada).

---

47 http://www.nnl.co.uk/news-media-centre/news-archive/mbe-for-nnl-research-fellow-dr-dominic-rhodes/ [accessed 30 June 2016].

Figure 3.22 Storytelling using the STAR model

Situation or Task	Northampton's city council was struggling to embrace national Modernising Government and eGovernment agendas to a reasonable timescale. The council had 250,000 citizens supported by 250 lines of business.
	I was sent in by a central government agency as interim CIO to facilitate turnaround and develop internal delivery capability.
Action you took	I established cross-party governance, facilitated ICT strategy, pulled together delivery capability and delivered a portfolio of ICT enabled change.
Results you achieved	The council's KPI for eGovernment improved from 36 per cent to 91 per cent within 12 months, resulting in markedly improved customer satisfaction.

How does that sound to you? Does it influence you to think that I am competent? How long did that take, less than a minute? (Sometimes I would ramble when asked these questions at an interview, so it is a great structure for me.) Think of a message that you want to get over and practice writing/telling it in this STAR format.

3.12.2 Use of ambiguity to gain agreement

> Storytelling reveals meaning without committing the error of defining it.
>
> Hannah Arendt, political philosopher

If you want to engage people, and also get them to agree with you, be specific about immaterial things, but use ambiguous terminology where people might associate values and beliefs. This, alongside storytelling and metaphor, is one tool which accomplished politicians, and lawyers versed in the art of rhetoric, use to influence people. We might all agree that 'education is good', but if you go into specifics like 'online training is good', then you run the risk of people disagreeing with you. This is especially true in a group, where they will not agree amongst themselves on specifics and your first task is to get general agreement of direction of travel before considering options.

In the early days of NLP, the founders derived the meta-model for specific questioning by modelling the renowned hypno-therapist Milton Erickson. Erickson used what was described as 'artfully vague language' to persuade mentally ill people to become well again. It can also be used to help mentally tired people to see clearly.

An over the top example of its use might be something like:

> The decision to move forward can only be a good thing. People are behind this. It means we can increase performance and become more competitive while reducing inefficiency. The problems of the past will be behind us as we create new capabilities which give us a competitive edge. Let's do it now.

All great empowering words. Don't you just want one? Would your governing body want one? Have you heard people in your organisation speaking like this? If so, they are probably on the top floors as they know how to sell a story.

By lightly applying the meta-model questions in Section 2.15, we can start to pick it apart.

> The decision (nominalisation) to move forward (how?) can only be a good thing (complex equivalent – this means that, really?). Everyone (generalisation – everyone?) is behind this (what?). It means (complex equivalent) we can increase performance (lack of referential index) and become more competitive (than who?) while reducing inefficiency (inefficient at what?). The problems (which?) of the past (when?) will be behind us (who?) as we (who?) create (how?) new capabilities (which?) which give us (who specifically?) a competitive edge (lack of referential index – against who?). Let's (who?) do it (what?) now (why?).

When the head of performance management from Rolls-Royce went back to work after attending one of my courses a few years ago, her boss, the head of capability, asked if she had been 'programed'. 'No', she replied, 'I think I have been de-programed.'

3.12.3 Using metaphor ... is like painting a picture to help people see what you are talking about

Use of metaphor helps to make change less threatening by associating something new with something they already know and are familiar with. For example, you might warn someone that they risk just repeating what they used to do on the old system with the new system, which does not sound particularly motivating. But if you warn them that they are simply 'digitising the dinosaur', they might imagine that they could face extinction unless they change their ways.

When presenting options, you could advise that you can:

Figure 3.23 Presenting options using metaphor

Factual	Metaphoric
Upgrade current systems	Fix the leaky roof
Increase functionality	Give them a paint job
Implement a new system	Design them a modern new house built for the information age

From the first column, do you think people might be tempted to play safe? In the second column, do you think this approach might tempt people to enter the information age? How can we paint a rosy picture of the future, ideally one so bright that they have to wear shades?

> When you're a carpenter making a beautiful chest of drawers, you're not going to use a piece of plywood on the back, even though it faces the wall and nobody will ever see it. You'll know it's there, so you're going to use a beautiful piece of wood on the back.
>
> Steve Jobs, founder of Apple and Zen Buddhist

3.13 PRESENTING YOURSELF AND MANAGING YOUR PERSONAL BRAND AND REPUTATION

> Presence: 1. The state or fact of being present; 2. The impressive manner or appearance of a person.
>
> *Oxford English Dictionary*

The term 'presenting yourself' implies being 'present' in that moment in time. When we looked at flexibility with timelines, we saw that we should be 'in time'. It also implies having some 'presence', an aspect of charisma which can be thought of as 'self-confidence'. Being 'present' helps to build rapport, and appearing confident helps to build trust. Are you fully in the moment and self-confident when meeting people? If not, you can model people who are.

3.13.1 Modelling the structure of charisma

> Being a leader gives you charisma. If you look and study the leaders who have succeeded, that's where charisma comes from, from the leading.
>
> Seth Godin, author, speaker and blogger on the digital marketplace

Charisma – 'The impressive manner of a person', as the Oxford English Dictionary terms it – can be learned. I remember seeing the CEO of the Confederation of British Industry (CBI) speak at their annual conference and remarking to one of my colleagues that he came over as quite charismatic. 'You should have seen him when we got him', she replied. Model strategies for behaviours that are considered charismatic and use this simple tip: start any presentation you make by beginning in a lower and slower voice than you would naturally use. You only have to do this for a few seconds. After this you will already have made your impression and you can let your voice move to its natural pitch and pace. Because I 'eat my own dog food', as my Canadian colleagues say, I explored 'NLP for public speaking' courses. Aside from addressing beliefs, state management and a few other strategies which I might address in another book, my main tips are these, echoed by courses delivered by RADA.[48]

- **Pitch** – as above in the structure of charisma, drop the pitch of your voice, because a high voice is an indicator of tightening of the vocal chords due to stress. You achieve this by relaxing the diaphragm, which has the secondary benefits of forcing you to breathe deeply and release stress in your body.

- **Pace** – 'say half as much and appear twice as smart'. Speaking fast indicates nervousness, as well as making it difficult to establish rapport. Speaking more slowly also gives your audience a chance to process what you are saying.

- **Pause** – a continuous monologue does not give opportunity to punctuate and emphasise your key messages. A short pause might seem a long time when you are in front of an audience, so allow yourself a count of five. Silence is very effective in communication as well as establishing hierarchy.

Watch and listen to effective speakers and notice their body language, pitch, pace and pause.

3.13.2 Achieving congruence in word and deed

Congruent: in agreement or harmony.

Oxford English Dictionary

One of the NLP presuppositions is, 'The meaning of the communication is the response that you get', that is, you are responsible for ensuring that meaning has been understood as intended. Studies have shown that the words we use account for less than 10 per cent of the message that we deliver.[49] The tone alone counts for far more, while body language accounts for over half of the message as received. Saying, 'I'm not angry' through gritted teeth is not congruent behaviour. Some tips for aligning words, voice and body language are given in Figure 3.24.

It is not that you have to do these things all the time, just when you need to deliver important messages or when you need to convince people of your authority. The more you practise, however, the more natural it will feel and the less you will have to think about it.

3.13.3 Self-confidence and feeling good about yourself

One important key to success is self-confidence. An important key to self-confidence is preparation.

Arthur Ashe, former world number 1 tennis player

---

48 https://www.rada.ac.uk/courses [accessed 30 June 2016].
49 A. Mehrabian and M. Wiener, 1967, 'Decoding of Inconsistent Communications', *Journal of Personality and Social Psychology*, 6(1), 109–114.

Figure 3.24 Congruence in words, voice and body language

Body language	Voice	Words
• Stand/sit straight with shoulders back • Engage your core muscles (if standing, stand feet hip width apart with weight evenly spread between both legs (i.e. no leaning) • Maintain appropriate eye contact (varies between cultures) • Dress appropriate to the situation • Move towards people (but don't get too close and cause discomfort) • Avoid fidgeting and tapping	• Steady • Paced • Fluid • Audible • Avoid 'ums', 'errs', 'you know', etc. – slow or pause instead	• Simple • Never use jargon • Avoid abbreviations • Match key words to recipients vocabulary where practical • No swearing

One of the traits of 'the human condition' is that we lack confidence in some situations. As seen in the belief cycle, the behaviour is self-fulfilling, but no one wants to follow a leader who lacks confidence in themselves. So how do you appear confident even if you don't feel it inside? NLP can help by using change techniques based on the way we code beliefs. Revisit 'Beliefs' and 'Belief change' in Sections 2.7 and 3.2.4.

The way we view or frame a situation also affects the way we feel, which in turn will affect the way we behave. Look at the table in Figure 3.25. Keep yourself in the outcome frame to make the most of your internal resources and look confident.

Figure 3.25 Feelings associated with blame and outcome frames

Blame frame	Outcome frame
Stagnant	Moving forward
Limiting	Choice/opportunities/possibilities feels
Frustrating	Freeing
Negative	Positive
Disempowering	Empowering
Pessimistic	Optimistic

The 'circle of excellence' technique in Section 3.29.2 is often used to 'anchor' confident states.

3.13.4 Developing your personal brand and reputation

> You have to understand your own personal DNA. Don't do things because I do them or Steve Jobs or Mark Cuban tried it. You need to know your personal brand and stay true to it.
>
> Gary Vaynerchuk, serial entrepreneur and bestselling author

Companies and celebrities place great emphasis on developing, exuding and promoting their personal brand. This same concept should be applied to career professionals seeking to differentiate themselves in a competitive global job market. Building your brand boosts your professional credibility, propels your chances for a job interview or promotion, positions you as an aspiring leader and, ultimately, fosters an increase in earning potential.

So, what makes for a good personal brand? A captivating personal brand is:

- A representation of your character and identity.
- Authentic and unique to you.
- Well understood by your target audience.
- Consistently portrayed in person, online and in writing.

If I were to ask you 'What is your unique promise of value', do you have an answer?

After successfully delivering a number of courses to one large organisation, the head of delivery asked us to take his team to 'the next level'. We agreed development requirements, designed and piloted the second level course.

> The best yet; very powerful.
>
> Marco Altieri, portfolio manager

As the delivery director had a degree in marketing, he was keen for us to address 'personal brand' in the content. What is personal brand? Like established corporate brands, it is a shortcut to our identity and capabilities, and whether we consciously take control of our brand or not, we all have one in the minds of our stakeholders. What would you like yours to be?

Like all good brands, our statements and 'elevator pitch' need to be congruent with our behaviours and how we present ourselves. Indeed, with development of social media, there are a number of guides out now on how to develop and maintain your online presence and branding too.[50]

How do you develop your brand? I was surprised at how easily NLP can be applied to this emerging concept. Of course, congruence, establishing rapport and trust, and ethical behaviour are core to NLP from the outset. Understanding yourself and how others see you is the next step, that is, self-awareness. As for corporate brands, this must be linked to your personal values. You may think that they are generic, but we have not yet had two people stating the same values within a group doing nominally the same job

---

50 http://www.businessinsider.in/Social-Media-Series-A-basic-guide-to-managing-your-online-presence-yourself-when-theres-no-budget-to-hire-an-expert/articleshow/52042540.cms [accessed 30 June 2016].

in the same organisation. Then, using some of the communication techniques in this book, refine your words and test them with one of your clients or colleagues until they confirm that your statement is congruent with how they see you. The words you use in your brand statement will become consistent as you start to feel comfortable with them.

Try the exercise below.

Exercise 3.15 Develop your personal brand

- Establish your goal – how do I want people to see me?

- How do you want to position and present yourself to make this a reality? Remember, people will naturally assume that you like what they like until you actively re-position yourself.

- Gather information, for example strengths and weaknesses, feedback, aspirations.

- Since brand has to be congruent with values, do the values elicitation exercise first (Section 3.28.1) so that you have something to guide you. Write down key words.

- Get some feedback on how others see you as part of your general good habits of eliciting feedback at every opportunity. I use the following construction to gather information while priming my stakeholders: 'I believe we have had a successful partnership here in delivering a good result. For my own personal development, would you mind sharing with me one thing which you valued about my contribution, and one thing which I can work on to become even better?' How do you think this phrasing will impact your client? Add some key words to your list.

- Look at the results from your assessment of your meta-programs in Exercise 3.2 in Section 3.3.2. Add some words to your list; for example, detailed, process oriented, completer–finisher, and so on.

- Next, what kind of activities do you want to do more of/less of?

- Now, while looking over your list of words for inspiration, think about how you want to be seen. If you heard people talking about you, what would you *like* to hear? If someone recommended you, what would you like them to say about you?

- Write down your statement and spend 10 minutes reviewing the words to make it punchy and memorable, but remember, it has to be 'you'.

- Test your statement with friendly stakeholders; do you think this is me? Refine your brand through feedback.

- Review – is it working, do people see you as you see yourself?

So, since you have a personal brand and reputation whether you want one or not, what would you like your personal brand to be?

Your smile is your logo, your personality is your business card, and the way you make others feel is your trademark.

Zig Ziglar, marketing guru

3.14 CREATIVITY AND PROBLEM SOLVING – USING WALT DISNEY'S STRATEGY

> It's kind of fun to do the impossible.
>
> Walt Disney

'Creative problem analysis and resolution' is one of the three core skills assessed for the 'Expert BA' qualification. There is a lot written about creativity and problem solving, including by de Bono,[51] the 'inventor' of brainstorming and mind maps. Along with fellow scientists and engineers, I remember going on a week-long graduate training program on creativity as part of my preparation for the world of work. So what does NLP have to add to the mix? Of course, NLP did not invent anything, it just modelled people who were really good at stuff. One person who was really good at being creative was Walt Disney and his 'imagineers'.[52]

> The true sign of intelligence is not knowledge but imagination.
>
> Albert Einstein

3.14.1 Modelling Disney's strategy for creativity

Aside from creation of characters and stories with global and cross-generational appeal, Walt Disney was also responsible for a number of important technical and organisational innovations in the fields of animation and film-making in general. I remember visiting his Experimental Prototype Community of Tomorrow (EPCOT)[53] in Florida 20 years ago and being educated through entertainment as I travelled around on his pioneering magnetic monorail.

It is clear that one of the major elements of Disney's unique genius was his ability to explore something from a number of different perceptual positions. From the analysis of Dilts and DeLozier,[54] it would seem that Disney the 'dreamer' functioned primarily through a strategy of constructed visual images. Disney then made his fantasies 'real' by associating into the feelings of the imaginary characters and acting them out to give them life. The spoiler comes from taking a second look at these creations from the point of view of a critical audience. The strategy can be used in any situation where creativity is required. Balancing the fundamental perceptual positions of the dreamer, the realist and the spoiler (or critic) in the service of a common vision is no doubt a fundamental strategy of all genius and had many common elements to self-analysis by Einstein.

> Creativity involves breaking out of established patterns in order to look at things in a different way.
>
> Edward de Bono

---

51 E. de Bono, 2009, *Lateral Thinking: A Textbook of Creativity*, Penguin.
52 The Imagineers, 2010, *Walt Disney Imagineering*, Disney Editions.
53 http://www.wdwinfo.com/wdwinfo/guides/epcot/ep-overview.htm [accessed 30 June 2016].
54 http://www.nlpu.com/Articles/article7.htm [accessed 29 July 2016].

Exercise 3.16 Disney strategy

1. Mark three positions or chairs in a triangle which are observable from a fourth 'meta-position'.
2. Label them (1) 'Dreamer', (2) 'Realist' and (3) 'Critic'.
3. Anchor the appropriate strategy to each physical location.
4. Think of a time you were able to creatively dream up or fantasise new ideas without any inhibitions. Step into location (1) and re-live that experience.
5. Afterwards, move to a neutral position.
6. Identify a time you were able to think very realistically and devise a specific plan to put an idea effectively into action. Step into position (2) and re-live that experience.
7. Afterwards, move to a neutral position.
8. Think of a time you were able to constructively criticise a plan – that is, to offer positive and constructive criticism as well as to find problems. Step into location (3) and re-live that experience.
9. Afterwards, move to a neutral position.
10. Pick an outcome you want to achieve and step into the dreamer location. Visualise yourself accomplishing this goal as if you were a character in a movie. Allow yourself to think about it in a free and uninhibited manner.
11. Step out into the neutral meta-position.
12. Step into the realist location, associate into the 'dream' and feel yourself in the positions of all of the relevant characters. Then, see the process as if it were a 'storyboard' (a sequence of images).
13. Step out into the neutral meta-position.
14. Step into the critic position and find out if anything is missing or needed. Then, turn the criticisms into questions for the dreamer.
15. Step out into the neutral meta-position.
16. Step back into the dreamer position to creatively come up with solutions, alternatives and additions to address the questions posed by the critic.
17. Continue to cycle until your plan congruently fits each position.

Can you imagine situations where this strategy will prove useful?

3.15 CO-CREATE THE BUSINESS

Of all the things I've done, the most vital is coordinating those who work with me and aiming their efforts at a certain goal.

Walt Disney

I started this book relating my experiences around BPR. Back in those days we were all about 're-engineering the corporation',[55] 'down-sizing' and 'right-sizing'. Internal and external consultants were sent away to do MBAs, learn consultancy skills and BPR. Indeed, I sent my own staff away to become qualified.[56] While working with local government, however, I had a revelation. Local government is made up of more than 200 lines of business, with many thousands of business processes – far too many for a single person to remain expert. But it did not require someone with a huge brain and an MBA to design processes which cut out waste. With a little facilitation, those involved in the end-to-end process, when put in the same room so that they could reproduce and comprehend the 'Frankenstein's monster' which processes often become through repeated evolution and change, were quite capable of optimising their own processes. Perhaps more importantly, they would own the process and any perceived resistance to change would evaporate.

> Tell me and I forget. Teach me and I remember. Involve me and I learn.
>
> Benjamin Franklin

Of course, the concept of self-managing teams is not new. We used to advocate them when total quality management and Peter Drucker's *The Toyota Way*,[57] was fashionable. Here the facilitator only manages the co-creation process, ensuring input from all team members, ideally only contributing questions to lead the team towards the goal. I have found questions like those below useful for drawing out contribution:

- Who is our customer?
- What do they want from us?
- What are we trying to achieve?
- How will we know when we have succeeded?
- What would that enable us to do?
- What do we need to do?
- Does the customer value that?
- What can we stop doing?
- Are we finished, is there anything else we need to do?

Note that I avoid using 'why?' questions, as these can lead to justification and entrenchment rather than facilitate change (see Figure 3.26). You can read more about question types in Section 3.16.

> There is nothing so useless as doing efficiently that which should not be done at all.
>
> Peter Drucker, management guru

---

55 Michael Hammer, 2001, *Reengineering the Corporation: A Manifesto for Business Revolution*, Nicholas Brealey Publishing.
56 Peak Performance is an accredited SPRINT partner.
57 https://blog.deming.org/2013/07/deming-and-lean-the-disparities-and-similarities/ [accessed 30 June 2016].

Figure 3.26 The 3Es – efficacy, effectiveness and (only then) efficiency

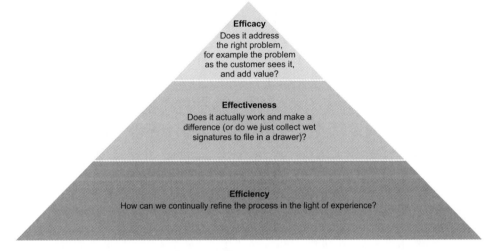

In terms of tools to help you to do that, while yellow stickies work; personally I use mind-mapping software, which enables co-construction in real time (see Figure 3.27). The one I use readily exports to process flowsheet software such as Visio as well as the rest of the Microsoft suite,[58] including MS Project.

> A leader is best when people barely know he exists, when his work is done, his aim fulfilled, they will say: we did it ourselves.
>
> Lao Tzu

So, I urge you, if you want to see effective and efficient processes which work and are happily adopted and supported by those responsible for doing them, then put aside any ego and dedicate yourself to becoming an excellent facilitator and coach in order to support them in finding their own solution. The quicker you can make yourself redundant from the process then the more value you will add. But do not worry, I know from personal experience that there is always a next job for those with that skill set.

3.16 REQUIREMENTS – BETTER ANSWERS THROUGH BETTER QUESTIONS

Understanding requirements is obviously a fundamental part of the role of any BA, but the role is much more than listing stated needs. As BABOK® v2 says, 'The BA is responsible for eliciting the actual needs of the stakeholders, not simply their expressed desires.'

> You can't just ask customers what they want and then try to give that to them. By the time you get it built, they'll want something new.
>
> Steve Jobs, founder of Apple

---

58 http://www.mindgenius.com/ [accessed 30 June 2016].

Figure 3.27 Mind-mapping software is an effective tool for facilitation and co-construction

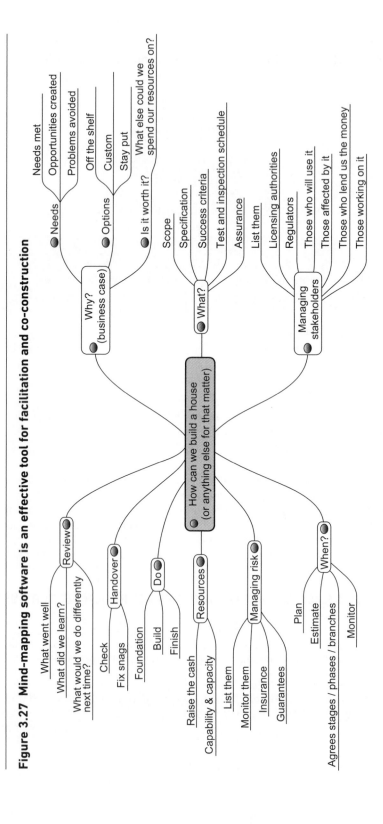

Remember, a key part of our interaction is to build rapport and trust, and we should spend just as much effort thinking about the way we will encourage the customer to feel, as they might not remember what was actually said. Some say that we decide emotionally then rationalise logically after the event. What do you feel?

3.16.1 World-views and perspectives – a different kind of elephant in the room?

> You have to get along with people, but you also have to recognize that the strength of a team is different people with different perspectives
>
> Steve Case, former CEO of AOL

We all have different perspectives, and from different perspectives we form different views and imagine different paths to get there. But, sometimes, we let our ego get in the way and imagine that our map is the only true map or even the only map. As you know, unfortunately some people are prepared to make huge sacrifices to prove their view. But when we appreciate variety we can create a beautiful functioning thing that everyone has part of. Harvest the views and perspectives of your stakeholders to enrich you vision and shun none. If their view is radically different then see it as a challenge to understand why, rather than dismissing it as wrong simply because it does not fit with your view or that of the majority.

The story of the elephant and the blind men[59]

Once an elephant came to a small town. People had heard of elephants, but no one in the town had ever seen one. Thus, a huge crowd gathered around the elephant, and it was an occasion for great fun, especially for the children. Five blind men also lived in that town, and consequently, they also heard about the elephant. They had never come across an elephant before, and were eager to find out about it.

Then, someone suggested that they could go and feel the elephant with their hands. They could then get an idea of what an elephant looked like. The five blind men went to the centre of the town where all the people made room for them to touch the elephant.

Later on, they sat down and began to discuss their experiences. One blind man, who had touched the trunk of the elephant, said that the elephant must be like a thick tree branch. Another who touched the tail said the elephant probably looked like a snake. The third man, who touched the leg, said the shape of the elephant must be like a pillar. The fourth man, who touched the ear, said that the elephant must be like a huge fan; while the fifth, who touched the side, said it must be like a wall.

They sat for hours and argued; each one was sure that his view was correct. Obviously, they were all correct from their own point of view, but no one was quite willing to listen to the others. Finally, they decided to go to the wise man of the village and ask him who was correct. The wise man said, 'Each one of you is correct; and each one of you is wrong. Because each one of you had only touched a part of the elephant's body. Thus you only have a partial view of the animal. If you put your partial views together, you will get an idea of what an elephant looks like.'

---

59 http://www.cs.princeton.edu/~rywang/berkeley/258/parable.html [accessed 30 June 2016].

Figure 3.28 Different perspectives are needed to progress from true to truth

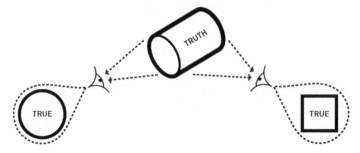

3.16.2 Balancing open and closed questions

While delivering workshops in a large engineering company, I was surprised when I was asked on several occasions what the difference is between open and closed questions. So, for completeness, a refresher on that topic is provided now in Figure 3.29, to draw out how an NLP perspective can be applied to them.

It is easier to ask closed questions rather than open questions because we can readily perform a quantitative analysis of the results. But quantity does not always relate to quality, and in the field of performance management we say, 'Just because something is easy to measure does not mean that we should measure it, and just because something is difficult to measure does not mean we should not try.' Or more succinctly, 'Rubbish in, rubbish out.'

Figure 3.29 Properties of open and closed questions

Closed questions	Open questions
Framed to illicit a short binary answer to provide specific information	Encourages the second party to express their opinion
Projects our map of the world	Elicits their map of their world
Enables us to make decisions quickly	Provides us with the opportunity to listen to indicators of their preferred language patterns, sensory preference, meta-programs, values and preferences
Transactional	Builds rapport
Encourages the second party to use unconscious 'fast thinking'	Encourages the second party to consciously think about what they want using 'slow thinking'

(Continued)

Figure 3.29 (Continued)

Closed questions	Open questions
Isn't this easy?	Why do you think that I end most sections with questions for you to reflect on?
Provides a universally understood answer	Open to interpretation
Easy to capture in questionnaires and spreadsheets and perform numeric analysis	Requires skill to elicit and interpret
Provides quantity	Provides quality
Useful in getting people to do what you want	Useful for finding out what people might actually want
Use after we have established the scope and frame of the topic through use of open questions	Use to build rapport and understand the client's map of the world
Readily automated	Encourages us to interact with our customers

Exercise 3.17 Reducing filtering by asking open rather than closed questions
In the table at Figure 3.30 I offer a reframe of some popular closed questions. Fill in the blanks to practise switching between open and closed.

A sub-set is the use of leading questions, which primes the client with the answer that we want. Note that this is usually done subconsciously rather than deliberately and is a key area of discipline for those conducting opinion polls. As Daniel Kahneman showed through research, it is fairly easy to get people to reverse their answer depending on how you frame and phrase the question.

Figure 3.30 Examples of open and closed questions

Closed question	Open questions
Would you like tea or coffee?	What would you like to drink?
Do you prefer SAP or Oracle?	Is there a customer relationship management (CRM) system which you prefer (leading to, 'What is it that you particularly like about that system?')?

(Continued)

Figure 3.30 (Continued)

Closed question	Open questions
Do you want a blue screen or a green screen?	Do you have a preference for screen colour?
Would you like weekly or monthly progress reports?	How would you like me to keep you informed?
Will you sign-off these requirements?	Is there anything else I need to do for you to be comfortable enough to agree that we have adequately captured your requirements?
How long have your worked here?	What do you like most about your role?
	What application of NLP do you think would be most useful to you?
Do you think soft skills are important to a BA?	
	How could you explore a client's map of the world?
Do you think open or closed questions are most useful?	
	How could you become a more effective BA?

3.16.3 World-views, meta-programs and sample size

> Given a choice between their worldview and the facts, it's always interesting how many people toss the facts.
>
> Rebecca Solnit, author and political commentator

In Section 2.5 we introduced the concepts of world-views and filters, and the role of behavioural meta-programs in determining preferences. If you were to characterise your sample user population, which you are gathering requirements from, what proportion are:

- detail oriented rather than big picture?
- reflecting on the past rather than focusing on the future?
- process oriented rather than outcome focused?
- looking for variances rather than seeing commonality?

When I conduct well-formed outcomes exercises for personal change during group coaching sessions, I endeavour to demonstrate some of the basic errors we are programd to make because of our own maps of the world and filters. In one exercise someone wanted 'to be fit'. I elicited their requirements, asking a member of the group to capture them, while at the same time remembering them as accurately as I could myself. When I asked for the requirements to be read back, they bore little resemblance to what the client had actually wanted, let alone said; they were what the BA would have wanted in his shoes. When I said, 'That's strange, I thought I heard him say that he wanted x, y and z', repeating the exact language of the client, he smiled and nodded. First, his requirements had been respected and accurately captured. Second, I had made the effort to actually listen to him, rather than thinking that I knew what he needed better than he did.

Have you ever asked for something and been surprised when it didn't turn out the way you expected? Has someone asked you for something and been disappointed with what they ended up with? What are your preferences? How might these be biasing your proposed solution? How will you compensate? In the future, how are you going to change your behaviours to accurately capture people's stated requirements?

3.16.4 Ask how not why

Successful people ask better questions, and as a result, they get better answers.
Tony Robbins

When I worked for one of the large consultancy firms, we were drilled with the '5Ys' technique. I felt like I was interrogating people in client organisations by asking a succession of five 'why' questions before we moved on. An example might have run along the lines of the example given in Figure 3.31.

Figure 3.31 The '5 whys' men

---

5 whys	Possible responses
1. Why isn't the product available?	The project got behind
2. Why did the project get behind?	Because the contractor didn't deliver
3. Why didn't the contractor deliver?	Because he didn't have enough resource
4. Why didn't he have enough resource?	They are on higher priority work
5. Why are they on higher priority work?	Because that was behind schedule

---

Being on the receiving end of this interrogation, how do you think you might feel? (There I go again, slipping into use of framing and priming to lead you to say what I expect you to.) In my experience, it led to people becoming defensive, even when given assurances such as, 'Hello, we are from Y consultancy preparing a report for internal audit on your project and are here to help you.'

> Far better an approximate answer to the right question, which is often vague, than the exact answer to the wrong question, which can always be made precise.
> John Tukey, professor at Princeton and leading statistician

In contrast, explore the types of responses you might give to 'how' questions in Exercise 3.18.

Exercise 3.18 Ask how, not why
How do you feel when asked this type of 'how' question? Personally, I feel like I am being engaged and asked for help rather than being offered up as a sacrificial lamb on the altar of doomed projects. It helps to move us from a 'blame frame' to an 'outcome frame' (see Section 3.23.1); from being stuck in the problem to thinking laterally and coming up with options. Add your responses to the 'how?' questions in Figure 3.32.

Figure 3.32 Ask how, not why

Examples of how questions	Your possible responses?
How could this product be made available sooner?	If we could have more resources, or maybe defer some of the features to the next release
How can we recover time on this project?	
How can we help the contractor to deliver on time?	
How can we get enough resource?	
How can we prioritise our work?	

Peter always had the right questions to ask.
Frank King, technical assurance lead, HMRC

3.17 REQUIREMENTS – THE AGILE ROAD TO 'MOSCOW'

> The fast-paced digital age has accelerated the need for companies to become agile.
> Nolan Bushnell, founder of Atari

Adolf Hitler, like Napoleon before him, after stunning 'quick wins', finally bit off more than he could chew when he tried to go for a 'big bang' and implement his Russian campaign in one phase. Synchronicity, then, that agile methods make extensive use of with the term 'MoSCoW' to capture the principle of prioritising requirements in terms of (my interpretations):

- **Musts** – we must have these requirements as a minimum to function effectively.
- **Shoulds** – these requirements have obvious value, so we should do them if we have sufficient resources, but the system functions without them.
- **Woulds** – these would add value, and would be worth developing if we have time before the deadline.
- **Coulds** – I could do them if I have time, somewhere down the line. (But probably will just put them on this 'car park' instead, and maybe fold them into a future release.)

In traditional agile 'sprints', delivery is 'time-boxed', that is, after establishing a reasonable duration to check progress, say a week to a month, the team works down from the highest priority requirements until they run out of time. Delivery of functionality over time establishes the team's 'velocity' for planning future sprints. A series of further sprints are scheduled, each going through their own development and test cycles, until the agreed release date.

Think about release of your next smartphone; the provider will not be pinned down on functionality until close to the release date, usually set by the marketing team, because they are not sure how much they will fit in, but it must have the Musts. Other software functionality from the desired requirements list can be added after you have purchased the phone. Customer feedback and research and development (R&D) then pave the way for a re-visitation of customer requirements, including those anti-gravity and teleportation features for the release of iPhone 99.

But it is not my job here to teach you the benefits and formalities of agile, which should be self-evident. Aside from the exercises below, which will help you to separate needs from wants and overcome some of the barriers to getting buy-in to an agile approach, I want to draw out a more general application of agile thinking.

As we have said from the start, agile is about approach and mindset. When I look at any task, including writing this book, I visualise it in terms of a standard consultant's 2×2 matrix, as illustrated in Figure 3.33.

I want to exclude anything that I can from the top left box of Musts and establish the minimum that I can get away with while still fulfilling the customer needs.

For those familiar with bidding for contracts, a successful approach is to submit the minimum specification compliant with the request for tender, sometimes even knowing that it would not be fit for purpose. After all, if you do not win the work then you are not

Figure 3.33 Boxing in MoSCoW

What is the *minimum* I **must** do to achieve the desired outcome in the shortest time with the least resource?	What work **would** I do if I still have resource and *time* before the final deadline?
What questions do I need to ask to get to the core of the opportunity or problem?	
What additional work is there which has *clear value* to the client which I **should** do if I have resource?	What work **could** I do if I had available resource and inclination, bearing in mind the *opportunity cost* of staying on this task?

going to be able to add any value to the client anyway. A more expensive 'value proposition' can then be added alongside the compliant bid. Alternatively, a value proposition might be submitted after securing the contract.

This approach gives me a number of immediate benefits:

1. I am de-risked in that I have a working solution in as short a time as practical.
2. I only need to ring-fence my resources for a short period but more importantly,
3. It focuses my attention on questioning what the customer really needs.

3.17.1 'Old wine in new bottles' – haven't we tasted this before?

Of course, much like NLP, a lot of this can be thought of as 'old wine in new bottles'. Things that make sense and are practical will re-surface time and again in the colours of the new fashion (or 'flavour of the month', 'à la mode', 'smells familiar', or 'reboot/upgrade/v2.0', depending on your sensory preference).

Value management[60] has been around for a long time in engineering circles, though not so visible in recent years. I remember the textbook exercise of assigning value to the functionality of a bus stop, and in combination with assessed cost/effort, working out how to 'get the most bang for our buck' (see Figure 3.34). Of course, it is the client's perception of value which we have to get an understanding of; we need to get into their world. That raised curb at the bus stop might be of little value to me, but my brother is in a wheelchair, and I might not need that timetable on display while I have my phone app, but what about my grandfather who does not have a car or smartphone? How will you find out how your client values things differently to you, as they surely will?

Note the parallels with Section 3.18.10 on **benefits management** in the delivery of change programs where value is added incrementally with each tranche. Added advantages are that our cash and business exposure is greatly reduced. It is politically much more acceptable to walk away from the project at any time without having to face the psychological burden of sunk cost as in a traditional 'waterfall' approach from requirements to test.

---

60 https://ivm.org.uk/what-is-value-management [accessed 1 July 2016].

Figure 3.34 Value and cost

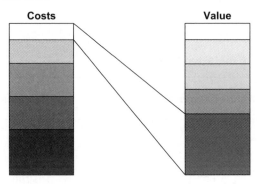

And let us not forget the **Pareto Principle**,[61] usually referred to as the 80/20 rule, which states that you can usually get 80 per cent of the value of an activity from only 20 per cent of the effort. This was taken a stage further by The Lazy Project Manager,[62] who asked 'Can't we just get 80% of the 80% with 20% of the 20%?' Yes, in principle, you can get two-thirds of the value (64 per cent) from less than 5 per cent of the effort.

3.17.2 Needs from wants using the meta-model

> You get what you need in life, not what you want.
> Anthony Robbins, master wizard and advisor to past and
> future presidents of the USA

Having travelled on that long road to MoSCoW several times, it is a challenge to help users on the journey to understand what good enough might look, sound, feel and function like. Forget perfection; the best is the enemy of the good. Good enough is, well, good enough.

A fundamental of NLP is the meta-model (see Section 2.15), which helps us to develop precise language by minimising distortions, generalisations, deletions and equivalences. As I said in the introduction of Part 2, and you saw from the history of development of NLP in Section 2.2, little in NLP is new, being a synthesis and modelling of strategies which have been found to work. The meta-model is one of those few developments which was developed at the core of NLP, being reverse engineered from Erickson artfully vague hypnotic language.[63] It is perhaps the most effective structure for exploring other people's maps of the world and clarifying what the words and phrases they use actually mean to them, rather than what they mean to us. Meta-model questions will help you to uncover all the types of distortions that fall out of our mouths all of the time (all of the time leads to distortion). Hence, our words provide a print-out of our internal map of the world to those who invest enough time to listen and understand them.

---

61 https://betterexplained.com/articles/understanding-the-pareto-principle-the-8020-rule/ [accessed 1 July 2016].
62 http://www.thelazyprojectmanager.com/peter-taylor [accessed 1 July 2016].
63 John Grinder and Richard Bandler, 1975, *The Structure of Magic I: A Book About Language and Therapy*, Science and Behaviour Books.

The table in Figure 3.35 shows the 12 types of meta-model violations with typical responses which could be asked to explore the elements that are obvious and redundant in the client's map of the world.

Figure 3.35 Using the meta-model in negotiation

Type	Example	Response
Comparative deletion	'This is the best deal that you will get'	Compared to what?
Simple deletion	'I'm disappointed'	Disappointed about what?
Unspecified verbs	'You explain things badly'	How specifically do I explain things badly?
Cause and effect	'What you say makes me angry'	How specifically does what I say cause you to be angry?
Complex equivalence	'You didn't deliver on time, you are a failure'	How does an unavoidable change to the plan make me a failure?
Mind reading	'You think that I don't know what I am doing'	How do you know what I think?

I recommend that you play with the meta-model questions with friendly colleagues and move on to listening for the patterns before trying them out in real work situations, as they can come over as abrasive if used without finesse.

3.17.3 Getting requirements signed off

> Unless commitment is made, there are only promises and hopes ... but no plans.
> Peter Drucker

Finally, when we believe we have adequately captured requirements, we sometimes still have a problem getting the client to sign-off on them. Why might that be? Let us consider for a moment life in the client's shoes. To take second position, if you will. What do they have to lose by signing off requirements, and how might they think that their position is better if they don't?

Reasons may include:

• They do not want to be held accountable (and we might not want to either).

• They do not want to be charged for any changes down the line (and we do not either).

- They do not want to be seen to be the cause of delays further down the line (and neither do we).

- They do not understand the requirements document (and we probably have a limited understanding of their business, otherwise we might not need to behave so contractually about requirements).

- They don't understand the language in the document – for example, 'use cases'.

- The language preference in the document is that of the analyst, translated from their sensory-based language (or lack of it in the case of a high proportion of BAs being naturally AD).

- They are not actually sure what they want (as am I, when I am looking for something that I am not familiar with, such as when I recently bought my first telescope and ended up with a great specification which I found difficult to use; it remains in the garage to this day).

In one organisation, users' reluctance to give up wants in order to get their needs sooner appeared to have been due to the fact that, in the past, they never got their next release. As we have discussed elsewhere, trust underpins everything, and it takes a long time and lot of effort to build. It can, however, easily be lost. How long does it take to recover a lost reputation?

Why do you think users sometimes resist signing off? How might you overcome those barriers in advance by thinking about it now?

Should we even be trying to get a 'sign-off' of these technical specifications by the end user? What I am looking for is ownership rather than accountability or blame. I want the client to help me if we hit problems, rather than us wasting time working out from the requirements whose fault it might have been.

To test whether I have captured what will satisfy them, and expressed it in their language, I usually use the phrase, while holding out my hand, 'If I had this in my hand, would you take it now?' This is a phrase we often use in behavioural change and personal coaching. If the person does not make a movement towards the hand you offered, then they are still not sure and you need to cycle around phrases such as, 'Imagine what might we need to add or change for you to really want it' or 'Now it has that feature, how much do you want it?' Always look for the body language rather than the words. Now you have commitment rather than a reluctant signature.

If you still feel that you need a formal sign-off, I use the phrase, 'Now, in order to give you what you need, I need to get this closed-out with an email so that we can move forward and deliver it to you by your required date.' Remember though, their map of the world and language patterns are different from yours, so keep your eyes and ears open for the subtlety of what they are saying, not what you think they mean.

3.18 DELIVERING TRANSFORMATIONAL CHANGE

Business analysis is the practice of enabling change in an enterprise.

IIBA *BoK* v3

145

The BCS survey discussed in part 1.2.3 lists 'business transformation' and 'organisational change' as two of the top three current management issues. Perhaps it is fitting, then, that the whole of the BA skill set in the SFIA framework is aligned to the 'business change' category.

Year after year, more change initiatives fail than succeed, particularly in not realising the promised benefits from the resources invested. As a member of the UK government's accredited 'Gateway' reviewers for high risk projects, I see more than my fair share of them. But failure is avoidable. As quoted previously, what is now widely known as 'Cobb's Paradox'[64] points out:

> We know why projects fail; we know how to prevent their failure; so why do they still fail?

So, enough of failure; in NLP we model what works rather than what does not, so let us focus on making all of our projects succeed.

3.18.1 Do you want incremental improvement or transformational change?

Start with the end in mind.

NLP presupposition

Often when I am called in to review or support programs of change I find that they are still using linear project management methods with the emphasis on incremental milestones from the current situation. However, to achieve true transformation we must start with the end in mind, as walking forward in a direction with which we are familiar is unlikely to take us to new places. The table in Figure 3.36 shows the difference in application and emphasis for the two approaches.

Figure 3.36 Do you want incremental change or transformation?

Incremental change	Transformational change
Suitable for stable business environments	Required when business environment changes
Focus on efficiency	Focus on efficacy – doing the right things, and effectiveness – achieving results
Need to understand processes	Need to understand customers
Competitive advantage is cost or time	Competitive advantage is in creating new services and value

(Continued)

---

64 Cobb's Paradox.

Figure 3.36 (Continued)

Incremental change	Transformational change
Efficiencies of a few per cent can be realised	Transformation should target at least 30 per cent improvement to outweigh barriers
Only refinements to processes are required	Changes to mindset and to behaviours are required
Forward looking	Imagine a point in the future where you are successful and look backwards to understand how to achieve that
Operators best placed to identify efficiencies	Operators can be blinkered by 'as is' situation so best facilitated by external change team
Improvements can be captured and measured easily	Benefits require formal methods to realise and track

In the following sections I will focus on transformational change, but incremental change should still be carried out after transformation to realise further improvements in performance and operational excellence.

3.18.2 Be customer centric

> We think that our job is to take responsibility for the complete user experience. And if it's not up to par, it's our fault, plain and simple.
>
> Steve Jobs

After central government modernisation and technology-enabled transformation initiatives, which basically migrated processes from being paper-based to being web-enabled, another transformation was initiated which still has a long way to run. Of course the driver was to reduce the number of civil servants by migrating customers to the lowest cost channel, that is, self-service via the web. While high-volume services in central and local government mimicked operating models and processes in the financial services sector, the words around valuing 'the customer' rang hollow in both, especially after a couple of instances of wasting hours hanging on the telephone waiting for 'customer services'. In the private sector, such a commodity market differentiated on cost rather than service destroys brand loyalty and customers migrate to the lowest cost provider. Margins are lost and quality is on a downward spiral of cost cutting.

Bizarrely, in spite of the old adage in retail that 'the customer is always right', it can appear from down in the operational engine room that customers are a pain. Life would be a lot easier if we did not have them, or at least if they would stop bothering us and stick to the process as we designed it. In financial services and utilities these are usually

147

designed to maximise cross-selling rather than delight us, the customer. These attitudes and behaviours prompted fellow NLP practitioner, Shelle Rose Charvet, to write her excellent follow-up book *The Customer is Bothering Me*.[65]

> My first experience of this type of transformation was in local government with the introduction of customer-focused services into so-called Adult Services, that is, social service support to adults in need. The operating model changed from professional staff determining what was best for the client to the customer deciding what they wanted from a service menu. Horror! What does the customer know; they will mess up! Of course, much higher levels of satisfaction were reported. It came as a surprise to many in social services with less vision that the main part of the program was in behavioural change on the delivery side, not the enabling IT and systems.

So, strangely, real customer-focused service is revolutionary. Instead of us, as the professionals/experts, telling people what is best for them, we should give them the choice. To get around our own biases, we have to develop the ability to ask questions without imposing our own filters. You can practice structures for eliciting what the customer might actually want in Section 3.16 on 'better answers through better questions'.

> Another area of local government services which many of us have come into contact with is town planning, which gives permission on changes to our houses. We used a similar approach to develop a revolutionary customer-centric virtual reality model to guide developers and citizens into perspectives bespoke to them. The approach was successful in winning the 'Customer Excellence' joint award from the Society of Local Authority Chief Executives (SoLACE) and Society of IT Managers (Socitm). It has gone on to become an exemplar for similar services.[66]

One expert in selling and buying, and associate NLP practitioner, Michael Beale, summed up current thinking around creating a sustainable business as:[67]

1. Maximise the proportion of 'good sales' from bad, that is, focus on products and services that the customer is happy to pay for rather than charging them for things that they do not want or use your market position to bully or penalise them. (Think of examples such as phone roaming charges, lock-in periods for gym membership, obfuscating tariffs from utilities, and so on, as great ways to tarnish your brand.)

2. In your requests for customer feedback you only really have to ask one question: 'Would you recommend us to friends and colleagues?'

   And I will add a final follow-up question.

3. What is one thing that I could do more or less of to improve the value and quality of our services to you?

---

65 Shelle Rose Charvet, 2010, *The Customer is Bothering Me*, Kendal Hunt Publishing.
66 http://www.investilford.co.uk/newsandevents/news/10-10-15/Ilford_Blueprint_Wins_Top_Award_for_IT_Excellence.aspx [accessed 1 July 2016].
67 Seth Godin's blog @ http://sethgodin.typepad.com/ [accessed 1 September 2016].

Would you happily and unreservedly recommend your service providers to friends and colleagues?

How do you think that your customers might respond to those questions? You can practise using the exercise on second positioning your customer in Section 3.17.3 to help you find out.

3.18.3 For transformational change think programs not projects

> The greatest danger for most of us is not that our aim is too high and we miss it, but that it is too low and we reach it.
>
> Albert Einstein

Figure 3.37 Behaviours of effective program and project managers

Effective behaviours for a project manager	Effective behaviours for a program manager
Focused on delivery of assets to time and cost	Focused on operational outcomes and realisation of benefits
Drives out risk and uncertainty ('Away from' risk)	Comfortable with risk and uncertainty in order to maximise opportunity ('Towards' opportunity)
Manages internal stakeholders and suppliers	Navigates through external stakeholders
Supervisory or directive leadership style	Coaching style of leadership
Suited to detail	Likely to be 'big picture'
Resilient and may be dissociated from feelings	High degree of empathy to tune into feelings of stakeholders
Comfortable telling	A natural listener
Driven by schedule	Directed by business case
Might be introverted	Might be extroverted
Task focused	People focused
Asks 'why' questions	Asks 'how' questions
Explains project view	Elicits other people's perspectives and world-view

To be honest, for many years I was a sceptic of the adoption of program terminology and had many discussions on the topic with my colleagues in the best practice group for program management.[68] I was not alone in reluctance to adopt the developing world-view around programs. The APM only restructured its body of knowledge to address the different perspectives of programs and projects (and also portfolios) in its sixth edition in 2012 under the chairmanship of the late Mike Nichols of the Nichols Group,[69] with whom I was honoured to sit on the steering group.[70] US-based PMI has also supplemented its 'Project Management Professional' qualification with a similar one for program management.[71] Today, roles and terminology have been clarified and codified to the point where they are coherent and practical.[72] To cement my conversion, I now deliver master classes in program management for my former employer BNFL, now Sellafield Ltd, and re-purpose some of that slide-ware in this section.

So, what promoted my change of mind? Basically, I saw that, in general, projects were still focused on delivery of assets rather than realisation of benefits, and even today, benefits as stated in the business case are not achieved in the majority of IT projects. Whether I agree with it or not, the PM role remains largely technical and supervisory rather than one of leadership, consigning the BA to a role of requirements gathering and testing. Program management, however, promotes the BA to undertake change management and benefits realisation, often with the title 'business change manager'.

One of the exercises we conduct in workshops is to imagine the behaviours of ideal program managers and PMs to help crystallise the differences in roles. Some of the responses are captured in the table in Figure 3.37. Most of the behavioural aspects can be readily matched to the NLP meta-programs.

Irrespective of what it is currently called, do you think that you are working on a project or a program? More importantly, is the approach suitable for realisation of the benefits articulated in the business case?

3.18.4 The role of the executive in sponsoring change

> Leadership is the capacity to translate vision into reality.
> Warren Bennis, widely regarded as a pioneer of
> the contemporary field of leadership studies

When I first became involved with the APM best practice group for governance in 2004,[73] I realised from the UK National Audit Office's list of reasons for project failure – gleaned from several thousand independent gateway reviews[74] – that failure was usually outside

68 https://www.apm.org.uk/group/apm-program-management-specific-interest-group [accessed 1 July 2016].
69 APM, 2012, *Body of Knowledge* 6th edition, APM https://www.apm.org.uk/BOK6 [accessed 1 July 2016].
70 https://www.youtube.com/watch?v=fWwKJYNcvH8#t=197 [accessed 1 July 2016].
71 http://www.pmi.org/certification/program-management-professional-pgmp.aspx [accessed 1 July 2016].
72 http://www.apmg-international.com/msp.aspx [accessed 1 July 2016].
73 https://www.apm.org.uk/group/apm-governance-specific-interest-group [accessed 1 July 2016].
74 https://www.nao.org.uk/wp-content/uploads/2013/12/10320-001-Over-optimism-in-government-projects.pdf [accessed 1 July 2016].

the direct control of either the BA or the PM. Those causes of failure, however, should be under the influence of the sponsor, otherwise you have the wrong sponsor appointed. A standard model for program governance showing the leading role of the sponsor, sometimes referred to as the senior responsible owner (SRO), is shown in Figure 3.38.

Figure 3.38 How the sponsor supports delivery

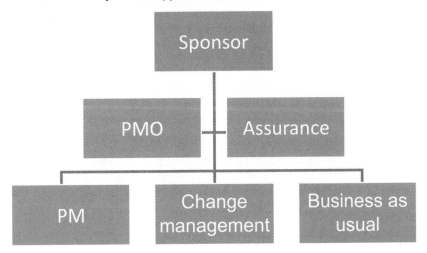

In 2005, when we published the first guidance on project governance,[75] even the word 'governance' had not yet made an appearance in APM's *BoK*, PMI's *BoK* or any of the OGC (now Axelos) publications such as PRINCE2 (the IIBA had not yet been founded). The role of sponsor was even less well defined, and so our guidance on the role of the sponsor in delivering change,[76] published by the APM, was readily adopted by the OGC, now the Cabinet Office, and distributed to senior sponsors. Recognising the gap that had been filled in this age of governance and oversight, a launch event was hosted at the Institute of Directors' London headquarters[77] and introduced by the then chairman of the IoD, Sir Neville Bain.

Personally, I did my best to avoid sponsors right through the 1990s as I did not understand their role any more than they did. But now I say to you, 'sweat' your sponsor; that is, give them tasks and make them work to support delivery. Not only should they be considered as part of the team, think of them as team president. They should be working behind the scenes to make your life easier. Under formal methods, they are actually the ones who 'own' the business case, that is, present it for funding approval, and who 'own' the benefits, as benefits are usually only realised after the resources have moved on to the next project. Of course, they will probably get you to write it for them.

---

75 *Directing Change: A Guide to Governance of Project Management*, 2004, Association for Project Management.
76 http://knowledge.apm.org.uk/bok/sponsorship-0 [accessed 1 July 2016].
77 https://www.apm.org.uk/news/governance-change-institute-directors [accessed 1 September 2016].

To me, sponsorship is all about leadership, which is the ability to get people to want to follow you, and they should practice the language of leadership. While you should use very concrete, specific and detailed language to elicit requirements, a leader needs to paint a picture in people's minds of where they want to take them. For this we use what NLP refers to as 'artfully vague language'.[78]

> Have you ever wondered why Dilbert has an uncommon first name, no last name, a nameless boss, and he works for a nameless company, making nameless products, while living in a nameless city? That's hypnosis. By omitting those details, I allow the reader to better feel some version of 'that's me!'.
>
> Scott Adams, author of *Dilbert*

Artfully vague language is the approach of choice for politicians and those seeking to build a following and achieve consensus. Basically, you make generic 'motherhood and apple pie' statements that everyone thinks they understand, interprets in their own map of the world, and few have reason to disagree with. Any devil is in the detail. In training I use videos of great orators and politicians to illustrate common language patterns established millennia ago by Aristotle as part of the art of rhetoric,[79] and more recently mastered by US President Obama. It is the polar opposite of the meta-model introduced in Section 2.15 to uncover specific meaning. Basically, use:

- Global and inclusive terms – We (everyone, really?).
- Nominalisations (verbs used as nouns) – took 'the decision' (which?).
- Words and phrases with generic or global meaning (though not common meaning) – to achieve improvements (value, customer satisfaction?).
- Lack of specificity – and things (which?) will be better (how?).
- Lack of referential index –in the future (when?).

It is also the language of hypnotists,[80] and allows people to tune out and feel that they are part of something global. You can deal with specifics with individuals, according to their maps of the world, further down the line, but it removes many roadblocks if people feel that they want to be part of the change, even if they have suspended disbelief for the time being.

> When you criticise Donald Trump for his vague policies during his election campaign, you should know that it is intentional. The empty spaces are provided for you to fill in with whatever you think a good idea. For a skilled wizard (trained by Anthony Robbins), the less he says, the more you like it. The wizard lets your brain fill in all the blanks with your personal favourite flavor of awesomeness.
>
> Scott Adams, Ericksonian-trained fellow wizard and author of *Dilbert*

---

78 J. Grinder, 1975, *Patterns of the Hypnotic Techniques of Milton H. Erickson*, Meta Publications.
79 You talking to me? Rhetoric from Aristotle to Obama.
80 My voice will go with you: The teaching tales of Milton H Erickson.

3.18.5 Imagining end state and creating the future together

> Change is the law of life. And those who look only to the past or present are certain to miss the future.
>
> John F. Kennedy

As you would expect, use of the NLP technique of future pacing can be applied directly to development and description of the future state resulting from transformation. We have used this technique successfully for not only new systems, but also organisational strategy and very large support frameworks. Use Exercise 3.19 to create a robust 'end state' which is agreed to by your stakeholders.

Exercise 3.19 Creating the future together

Choose a cross-section of stakeholders with different perspectives, motivational biases and behavioural preferences. Take them to neutral territory where distractions of the day job, functional hierarchy and un-resourceful anchors to the workplace are reduced.

Frame what we are going to do: have some fun creating the blueprint for what **we are going to deliver**.

Some facilitators start with the current problem state. Given your new understanding of how the mind is primed with what has been suggested beforehand, I prefer not to taint thinking with what is not working now. Instead, I always start with getting people to imagine and buy-in to the future state.

I use physical and temporal spacing and anchors, so when I talk about going from *now* (emphasising and pointing down to the floor at the left of the room, or furthest away from the window), I talk about moving forward to a point in **the future**.

Next I make the future as real as practical. 'Now in the future', when we are celebrating success together, what might people be saying? What might we see? How will we feel? How will we *know* that we have been successful. (No question mark, i.e. no upward inflection of voice here as this is a suggestion to help the group associate with success.)

Now we start to capture how they will know that a successful outcome has been achieved. Ensure that everyone is talking in the present tense about the future: *we* need to create a compelling vision for the future, a future that we will (not would) be proud of being a part of, a future so bright that we have to wear shades.

While facilitating APM's 2020 strategy for 'A world in which all projects succeed', we had them transported to the future and writing catchy tabloid-style newspaper headlines on the topic, because gaming releases the playful and creative part of us.

This co-creation process not only gives us multiple perspectives so that we are less likely to miss significant aspects, but it also gives us immediate and almost unconditional buy-in to the future state; a positive anchor, if you will. I no longer attempt to guide people to the solution I used to think it was my job to be the expert in, but rather submit myself to the wisdom of crowds.[81]

Next, *travelling back* while moving across the floor to the spatial anchor for the past, we create an uncomfortable anchor for the current state. Here we use the language of pain through problem statements. Now those running 'away from' meta-programs come into their own. Pour on the pain until the present state seems like it cannot go on, even though it probably has for many years and people have got used to it. (In sales training this is known as the SPIN technique.) If we do not have a 'burning deck' for change then we need to fan the embers until at least our feet are uncomfortable.

The rest is the usual process and mechanics to develop an 'as is' and 'to be' description. (When we write it up, it is useful to match off the problem statements to future state and vice versa as a gap analysis.)

- Is there sufficient buy-in to your end state?
- Is it innovative?
- Is it robust?

3.18.6 People take action when standing on a burning deck

When you can't make them see the light, make them feel the heat.

Ronald Reagan

Basic management theory from the time of Henry Ford says that some people are more motivated by fear and others by greed; the proverbial 'carrot or stick'. NLP says that people have a behavioural bias 'away from' problems or 'towards' opportunity, and we captured this meta-program in your self-assessment in Exercise 3.2. But why take a chance guessing what motivates someone when you can 'buy one, get one free'? Accomplished NLP practitioners, like accomplished politicians, attempt to cover both ends of binary pairs for meta-programs using inclusive statements. As well as removing the need to make assumptions about the target audience, it also reduces inadvertent projection of our own biases. The technique can be used to add shade to the usual black and white presentation of 'as is' and 'to be'.

It is often said that transformation, especially of large organisations, rarely exists in the absence of a so-called 'burning deck'. You might recognise other kinaesthetic based metaphors around 'doing' when encouraging people to take action, like 'holding their feet to the fire'. Pick up on them to encourage feelings of discomfort with the current state.

We often hear of politicians putting a 'spin' on things, and even employing a 'spin doctor'. The sales technique of SPIN selling[82] was actually taught to me during my NLP practitioner course by NLP trainer Paul Matthews, now managing director (MD) of People Alchemy and former European head of sales for a large software vendor.[83] The steps are shown in Figure 3.39:

---

81 https://www.youtube.com/watch?v=iOucwX7Z1HU [accessed 1 July 2016].
82 N. Rackham, 1995, *SPIN®-Selling*, Gower.
83 https://www.alchemyformanagers.co.uk/index.php?target=login [accessed 1 July 2016].

Figure 3.39 The steps in SPIN selling

Situation questions	Deal with the facts about the buyer's existing situation.
Problem questions	Focus the buyer on the problem while clarifying it.
Implication questions	Help buyer recognise effects and seriousness of problem.
Need Payoff questions	Directly connect the problem with your value proposition.

Notice that this method of selling is not about talking someone into action, but in asking questions that allow them to talk themselves into it. The approach is parallel to that used successfully in coaching interventions. How can this technique help you to create the impression of a platform which, if not actually burning yet, might be about to burst into flames?

3.18.7 Getting stakeholders on board

> Communication is a skill that you can learn. It's like riding a bicycle or typing. If you're willing to work at it, you can rapidly improve the quality of every part of your life.
>
> Brian Tracy, author and authority on personal effectiveness

'Communicating ideas and getting buy-in' was a specific skill gap in the BCS survey reviewed in Section 1.2.3. The success of your project is often more about perception than reality, so best to start to influence perception in key stakeholders from the outset. Your initial stakeholder map should be a living document which evolves as your map expands through each new contact. Personally, I use a mind map to capture the evolving picture. When you get down to mapping all of your stakeholders, I expect there to be too many to meet up with on a one-on-one basis. The table in Figure 3.40 is an established tool to help prioritise who to talk to, basically anyone who can accelerate your project or derail it. For the rest of those affected by your project, roadshows and online information usually suffice.

Figure 3.40 Stakeholder power versus interest grid

Interest in your project→		Focus your efforts here
	Amount of power that individuals and groups can yield →	

While facilitating a stakeholder management plan for a large organisation in the nuclear sector, I discovered that being led by their corporate communications team, where the focus was on the public perception of their operations, 'the public' and 'the trade unions' were assumed to be their priority stakeholders. In fact, no resource had gone in to planning, let alone engaging, stakeholders within the company who had an interest and leverage in helping the program to be successful, or identifying those who might slow it down.

Who can help you overcome barriers? Who can stop your project? Who has the most influence? What is their map of the world and how might your project benefit them? How are you going to engage them?

Be sure to maintain a stakeholder engagement plan to monitor and record stakeholder activities and the evolving stakeholder landscape as a mechanism to share progress. Fields for a stakeholder engagement plan might include:

- Category (from power versus influence grid).

- Stakeholder position.

- Name.

- Who in the team owns the relationship?

- How will engagement be managed, that is, through existing committee structure, Friday morning coffee, over golf?

- What events are scheduled?

- What engagement has occurred to date?

- What do you think their current position, needs and wants are?

Personally, I also grade the relationship from green – strong supporter – through to red – active blocker. No colour means I have not found out yet, while amber means they are still making up their minds. Over time, how does your stakeholder landscape change? How could you make further improvements?

Once you have constructed your initial stakeholder grid then you may want to think about an analysis of your stakeholder social network. As you already know, network relationships are all the buzz with social media. Who are the key 'connectors' influencing perception of your outcome?

I presented on development of internal capability at the IPMA's global congress in London in 2000. Of course, the 'Millennial Projects' were high on the agenda; essentially a set of vanity projects funded to help celebrate the turn of the year 2000. Two iconic projects in London were held up for comparison; the London Eye and the Millennium Dome, now the O2 Arena. Public perception invariably refers to the Millennium Dome as a failure, yet it was one of few projects to be completed on time for New Year 's Eve celebrations, let alone within cost and to scope. The London Eye, however, sponsored by the British Airways marketing team, is seen as a success, and it remains a great ride. But it over-ran, despite being 'shrunk'. Whereas the Eye team actively engaged the mass media, as after all it was a marketing exercise, the Dome discouraged disruption by the press in order to meet committed deadlines. The Dome also suffered from an overly ambitious business case, but that was in place before the project team were assigned.

Figure 3.41 Example of a network diagram

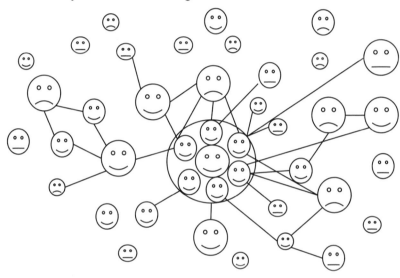

Which projects that you were involved in do you think have been presented as successful, and which were considered failures? Do you think that opinion, if not the result, could have been influenced by more robust stakeholder engagement?

> You can't win an argument; both sides lose over time as resentment builds up and relationships suffer.
>
> Dale Carnegie in *How to Win Friends and Influence People*

Personally, I do not attempt to directly influence those whom I consider to have already made up their minds. I do, however, employ advocacy; that is, influencing people who have influence on those people. Who do you know, or who could you get to know, who could help you to influence, or at least neutralise, any remaining potential blockers? Remember that you do not need to do this directly, and your sponsor may be better placed to manage the politics. Being responsible for change, however, you are responsible for deploying appropriate tools to manage the stakeholder process. (This often leads to confusion over the term 'stakeholder management', with many preferring 'stakeholder engagement'; 'stakeholder management' is management of processes, which encompass stakeholder engagement, but engagement needs to be prefaced with analysis and summarised through tracking for broader stakeholder management.)

Tools and techniques for one-on-one engagement are illustrated in Section 3.20.

3.18.8 Managing expectations

> A genuine leader is not a searcher for consensus but a moulder of consensus.
> Martin Luther King Jr

Do you like unpleasant surprises? Neither will your sponsor or other stakeholders. It becomes rather boring to see highlight reports in the sequence: green-green-green-red! Red from nowhere on a highlight report is also red on the face of your sponsor when they have to explain to their customer that they did not have proper oversight in place. Expect a debilitating program of external assurance as a consequence. Trust takes a long time to develop but a moment to lose forever. The golden rule is:

No Surprises!

Do you think that the public consider the iconic Sydney Opera House a success, despite it being an order of magnitude over budget and a decade late? How does Richard Branson hold on to the deposits of paying customers for his Virgin Galactic flights into space, despite a history of delays and even the demonstrator blowing up? In a world where perception is the only reality, it is down to active stakeholder engagement and managing customer expectations.

Of course, marketing, sales or the account manager might have already set expectations too high in order to close the sale and secure their bonus. I know many in the business analysis function try to get involved as early as practical to inject a dose of realism; keep at it, as a sale that does not make money is not even good for the client or the salesman in the long run.

Senior management are conversant with the phrase:

Under-promise and over-deliver

but often we get the opposite. Professor Bent Flyberg at Oxford Said Business School's centre for complex projects makes a living describing people's natural 'optimism bias', resulting in delivery that runs late and over-cost.[84] Compounding the fact that most organisations systemically under-estimate resources, however, humans are loss averse.[85] Psychologists such as Daniel Kannerman demonstrated that we are happier getting less but more than we were promised, rather than getting more but less than we were promised. Assume that you have an 'intelligent client' and do not oversell, or you will come to regret it.

> Keep it real.
> Ali G

Most of us involved with corporate buying are familiar with 'the hype cycle' (see Figure 3.42),[86] and I find it makes a useful tool to keep things light and recalibrate expectations

---

84 B. Flyvbjerg, 2003, *Megaprojects and Risk: An Anatomy of Ambition*, Cambridge University Press.
85 D. Kahneman, P. Slovic and A. Tversky, 1982, *Judgment under Uncertainty: Heuristics and Biases*, Cambridge University Press.
86 http://www.gartner.com/technology/research/methodologies/hype-cycle.jsp [accessed 1 July 2016].

at project initiation with the client. Keep the illustration visible to remind us all that current difficulties are only a phase in what will be a successful journey.

Figure 3.42 The Gartner Hype Cycle

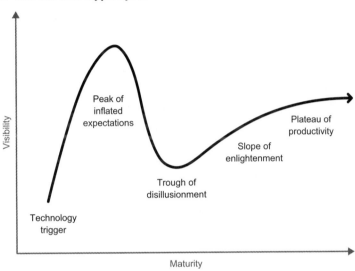

If you were in a position of oversight for a major change initiative, what would you like to know, and how would you like that information communicated to you?

3.18.9 Overcoming resistance to change

> If you really want something, you will find a way. If you do not, you will find an excuse.
>
> Jim Rohn, entrepreneur, bestselling author and motivational speaker

As Machiavelli pointed out,[87] transformation upsets the status quo and so will inevitably be resisted by established stakeholders. Whether conscious and deliberate or not, this is human nature. Hence, transformation programs will often default to incremental change, which is not disruptive and hence not threatening. Unfortunately, it does not result in transformation of performance either. But we can still 'cherry-pick the low hanging fruit', as getting some early successes under our belt will help enormously in managing dissenters. But what does it mean, and how do you do it?

Personally, I use the grid in Figure 3.43 and organise a workshop of stakeholders to help to populate the squares with examples of services / features / benefits. Different perceptions of value and resistance quickly emerge, which helps to inform the client of the difficult choices you have to make, but hopefully you will gain at least some consensus.

---

87 Machiavelli, The Prince, chapter 6: 'it ought to be remembered that there is nothing more difficult to take in hand, more perilous to conduct, or more uncertain in its success, than to lead in the introduction of new things.'

Figure 3.43 Value versus resistance

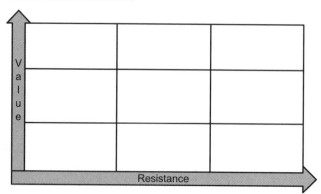

It also creates some buy-in to the early implementation plan, and you could go further to encourage them to become evangelists for the project.

During master classes on change management, after first establishing an overwhelming vision for what we are trying to achieve, I tease with the phrase, 'It all seems so easy, doesn't it. So what is stopping us?' After a long pause, I get the delegates to list on a flip chart everything that they think is preventing them from moving forward quickly enough. Of course, it is all specific to each change initiative, each industry, each organisation … No, generally it is not. Barriers to change are fundamentally part of human nature and fairly generic, as are methods of dealing with them. But first we must assess their magnitude, and decide whether we have enough push from the problem, pull from the opportunity and management support and resource to overcome them.

Some people, especially analysts, like to make tables of barriers and levers, score them and weight them and decide on the likely outcome. Personally, I like to visualise them in a force-field diagram as shown in Figure 3.44.

Figure 3.44 Lewin force-field diagram illustrating barriers and levers for change

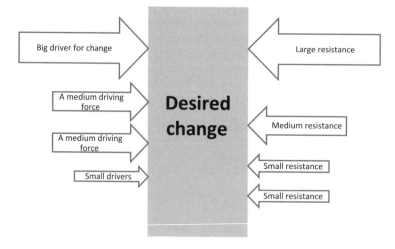

What do you think barriers to your outcomes are?

Of course, sometimes there appears to be just one awkward individual who takes malevolent delight in ruining your day. But I am of the belief that no one comes to work to mess up. Perhaps I am misguided, but usually I find that the individual just has a different map of the world. My own reframe is to see this as an opportunity to practise my skills of eliciting this strange creature's world-view, and then finding their levers for change. But if we do not have time or energy for that, then try the simple but effective Exercise 3.20.

Exercise 3.20 Do you want to celebrate success together, or blame each other for failure?
When you recognise that something needs to change in a conversation, affect a 'pattern interrupt'; that is, abruptly change your body language, position and tone. This signals something has changed and renders the subject prone to suggestion.

Now, hold out your left hand and say, 'If this left hand holds out the risk of arguing about blame for failure, (move your right hand very slightly upward and forward as you speak) 'and my right hand holds out the opportunity of basking in success together, which hand do you *choose* now' (no question mark, this is an embedded command to choose now using subtle command tonality).

Having forced that choice on the other person, you can now consolidate progress with an inclusive, but non-specific, statement along the lines of, 'So, how are we going to start working better together from now on?' And wait as long as it takes for them to fill the silence. And they will.

I have never had a client who hesitated, let alone choose the wrong hand.

Resistance in a client is a sign of lack of rapport.

NLP presupposition

3.18.10 Focus on delivery of benefits

As you might expect, the SFIA framework includes 'the quantification of potential business benefits' as part of the BA role, and benefits realisation mapping was added to the second edition of BCS's book *Business Analysis*. A formalised benefits management process helps to work backwards to focus on activities which are essential to delivery of outcomes and realisation of business benefits.

Some people struggle with constructing benefits maps, confusing activities, capabilities, outcomes and benefits, but they are quite easy to construct by asking questions of the right format. In Section 3.16 we discussed getting better answers through better questions. Figure 3.45 illustrates how the sometimes confused terms outputs, outcomes and benefits are related:

Figure 3.45 Benefits in the context of a healthcare program

	Project outputs/ capability	Outcome	Benefit
What	Enables a new outcome in part of the operational organisation	Is the desired operational result	Is the measurement of (a part of) an outcome
Answers the question	What new or different things will we need to realise beneficial change?	What is the desired operational state using these new things?	Why is this operational state required?
Example	A new hospital building	A fully operational hospital servicing regional demand	Wait time for hip operations reduced from 10 weeks to 3 weeks (on average)

Now, starting with the example of the benefits being measured in Figure 3.45, do you necessarily have to create that asset, that is, build a new hospital? In fact, these targets were largely met by alternative activities. What alternative ways can you think of for reducing wait times in this example?

I have seen benefits-mapping exercises to back-fit this approach to large programs which reveal tens of millions of pounds of unnecessary scope, and at the same time illustrate that the scope was missing which would have been necessary to realise the benefits from the assets being created. The impact of the latter would, of course, have led to significant delays when discovered later, affecting not only time and cost, but also functionality, risk and stakeholder confidence.

Can you relate all your activities to operational outcomes, and how you will base-line and measure the benefits?

3.18.11 'Let's not blow everything up in a big bang' – agile thinking and use of tranches

Nothing is particularly hard if you divide it into small steps.

Henry Ford

If we imagine ourselves on a boat, it would be straightforward to plot a course from the front to the back, bow to stern. Unless the boat was very big, or we could not see the other end because of large obstacles, or it was very foggy, especially if we were in rough seas. In these cases, we would be advised to plot our course to the next point where we could stop and rest, then revisit our course with better visibility. Though we might appear to be zig-zagging to someone on solid ground, we would in fact be maintaining forward direction by the most practical route. And so it is with programs of change where we have an overall direction but cannot see clearly quite how to get to our destination at the time we set off.

That is why we use tranches in programs, to provide resting places where we can harvest benefits of progress from creating new capabilities while re-assessing future direction in a changing environment. In this respect, a program approach is similar to an agile approach. With an agile approach, strictly speaking, we should be able to envision the whole development before we decide to break it down into time-based 'sprints'. With a program approach, tranches are based on achieving capabilities rather than a duration or phase of working. Thus, a program approach embodies the traditional change management cycle illustrated in Figure 3.46.

Figure 3.46 Unfreezing and freezing meta-states

Because tranches are based on delivery of distinct capabilities, they give us natural 'walk-away' decision points where we can harvest the benefits of investment to date, rather than committing ourselves to an all or nothing investment cycle. For large investments, it is easy to fall in to the 'sunk cost fallacy', which might otherwise keep the team working long after hope of achieving the business case has, in reality, already been lost.

Calling things by their proper names – tranches, stages, phases or sprints
In NLP we aim to be very precise with our language. As we demonstrate in workshop exercises, the same common words are understood to mean quite different things in different people's heads, despite being in the same function of the same organisation with similar cultural and educational backgrounds. So, let us be clear with terminology regarding work break-down, as words are often used interchangeably, causing needless confusion.

A programmatised approach to business change is similar in many respects to agile methodology, especially in the agile mindset, for example:

- Focus on early realisation of benefits.
- De-risk implementation by avoiding a 'big bang'.
- Focus on stakeholders.
- Adaptable approach to changes in environment.
- Plan from a helicopter view around building blocks.
- Adopt a facilitative style and involve the team and stakeholders in co-construction.
- Engage business users directly inside the delivery team.

The main difference should be that, by using agile in developing system architecture, we should have a good picture of what it is we are building before we set off, but choose to deliver in 'sprints' in order to realise benefits incrementally. This brings forward the benefits curve and reduces the peaks of the risk profile. While agile **sprints** should deliver progressive functionality, the main driver for their length is duration, which should not be more than a few weeks, whereas **tranches** in change management, based on delivery of new capabilities rather than time, are more likely to be months and years.

Stages are sub-divisions of the life-cycle and a very convenient point to reconsider the merits of the business case and reformulate team membership for change in focus. Stage and gate originated in new product development[88] and is extensively used in pharmaceutical development, where most projects are expected to be terminated early. The method is also extensively used where development periods are long, including the automotive and aerospace industries. So, use of stages and gates is a portfolio process for opportunity and risk management rather than one supporting benefits realisation. The stage and gate process is used by many central government departments to review status before allocating the next round of funding in very large, high risk projects. While stages and gates are extensively used in projects, only a 'Gate Zero' is used in programs as an assurance mechanism to ensure that organisation, processes and documentation is in place to support successful delivery.

Many people used the terms tranches and phases interchangeably, but **phases** are only convenient points in planning, such as handover from one contractor to another, or financial periods. An example would be in construction where first phase electrical fit-out would put wiring in, followed by plastering, that is, a handover to another resource skill set, followed by second phase electrical fit-out. None of which necessarily indicates any realisable benefit to the customer.

When you are using tranches correctly, you will always have the option of closing out the project and mobilising your resources to other initiatives, as benefits of work to the last tranche should have already been realised.

3.18.12 Selecting options for implementation

> The best is the enemy of the good.
>
> Voltaire

Consider Figure 3.47. A 'perfect' solution, but with a lot of resistance, or which is difficult to embed, does not result in any more benefit than a simple solution, such as a spreadsheet which is widely adopted. A simpler solution also minimises disruption by the program. Hence, I council you from experience: look for options which are likely to result in sufficient benefits with lower risk and disruption. Having constructed your benefits map, look at it again from right to left. If what you want to achieve is on the right, do you really need all the stuff on the left to achieve it?

> Start with the end in mind.
>
> NLP presupposition

---

88 http://www.stage-gate.com/ [accessed 1 September 2016].

Consider Figure 3.45, showing the relationship between building a new hospital and the measured benefits which we are expecting to result. If we start on the right with the goal of reducing waiting time for hip operations, do we really need to build a new hospital, which will take years to complete, irrespective of the cost? In master classes on this topic, delegates have no problem coming up with a long list of alternative ways to achieve the benefits more quickly and cheaply. (Many of these were in fact used by the health service when it considered the same approach.) Unfortunately, sometimes 'the tail wags the dog', and we become the slave of a system implementation.

Figure 3.47 Options – the best is the enemy of the good when it comes to implementation

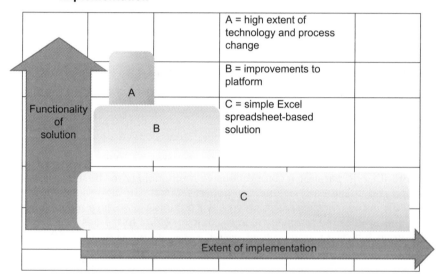

I was responsible for a program of technology-enabled transformation in a local authority and was called in by the executive team to explain the benefits of putting in the new enterprise resource planning (ERP) system. I was, however, working under an outsourced service provider, and explained that our business case in offering it was to secure a 12-year service contract. I was not able to discern what their business case was as they already had a good system. It turned out that they were asking this question because they were due a visit from the now defunct Audit Commission. To support my client, I gave them some examples of things which might have been benefits in a business case – had one been written – including financial governance, process efficiency and cost saving, to enable mobile working and to migrate away from out of date and costly line of business systems, hardware and so on.

They sent me away, and called me back a couple of days later to tell me that they decided that the business case was financial governance, and I should say so if asked. A good call given that a big over-spend had revealed itself as a surprise at the previous year end. 'Oh dear', I replied. When asked why, I explained that the new system was just a modern equivalent of the perfectly good system they had before, and it would not stop the same problem from occurring. They needed personal accountability in job descriptions, financial controls in place, process re-engineering and a lot of training, including of suppliers. They responded, 'We assumed that you might have been doing that already?' ('Assumed' makes an 'ass' of 'u' and 'me'.) No, came my reply, I am just putting the asset in; you are supposed to be managing business change. We were running a project without the umbrella of a program on the client side. As above, a right to left perspective is a great sense check, and we might have chosen not to put that new system in. Since we now had it, we used it to harvest other benefits too. The balancing activities were back-fitted in time and benefits realised, and the partnership went on to win major PPP of the year.

Hopefully, your sponsor understands the boundaries of work-scope and relevant responsibilities, but is it worth checking that what you are delivering makes sense on their map of the world?

3.18.13 Methods, tools and behavioural competencies

A fool with a tool is still a fool.

Grady Booch

The UK government's transformation agenda popularised structured delivery methods such as PRINCE2. In parallel, a comprehensive methodology for business process re-engineering and change management in public services, SPRINT, was developed by a lead authority in collaboration with a university's organisational development function.[89] The resulting SPRINT methodology is in my opinion equal to the best out there and is actively supported by a community of practice and annual conference. (I should say here that I am biased, as Peak Performance is a SPRINT accredited organisation.) As described in Section 1.3 on qualifications, since then, IIBA was formed (in Canada), qualifications by BCS have become more popular and PMI piloted a BA qualification in 2014.

Why was it felt, so late in the day, that these capabilities needed to be developed? Because it was realised that progress on the five-year funded program was not where it should have been.

I was engaged to turn around one such transformation program in local government which was lagging four years on a five-year schedule. I realised that the focus had been on the bulk of a thick report on failings complied by the Audit Commission, which had been 'projectised' by one of the leading management consultancies. I thought the route to success was contained in the opening paragraph of that thick report: 'This organisation has no credible capability in delivery or change management.' This is what I addressed, creating delivery and change management capabilities, including a business analysis function. After that, delivery was relatively plain sailing, and massive improvements in audited key performance indicators were achieved within the final 12 months and reported in the national press.

---

89 http://www.managingbydesign.net/SPRINT/ [accessed 1 July 2016].

Funding enabled a lot of people in local and central government to be trained in the PRINCE2 method. Unfortunately, conferring the title of 'PRINCE2 Practitioner' was mistaken as a qualification in project management itself, whereas, as the lead author and accompanying manual says, it is (only), a method to support project management. When Andy Murray of Outperform, now part of global consultancy RSM, was commissioned to update PRINCE2, he reported that the overwhelming feedback was that behavioural competencies need to be added. They do indeed need to be added to create capability, but do not belong in the method document itself. Rather they should be developed through a professional cadre or academy using similar group coaching methods to those we deploy within large corporates.

> Peter shows a path to maturity that starts with self-awareness and progresses through self-regulation, social-awareness to social-regulation. It is the latter that most people will find will transform their performance as it includes the ability to influence groups.
> Andy Murray, Partner of RSM and lead author of PRINCE2

Maturing your change management capability – mindset and toolset

> Organisational maturity is directly correlated with organisational success. Higher maturity yields higher performance.
> PWC state of PM annual survey

Organisations are maturing from heroic endeavours of change and program management to codifying methods and processes that improve chances of success. Indeed, PWC's survey for the PMI 'State of the profession' highlighted a stark difference between high performing organisations, with a better than 80 per cent success rate, and low performing organisations, with a large correlation to maturity.[90] Hence the opportunity arises to assess the likelihood of success of programs and projects across an organisation by assessing maturity.

Maturity models were reviewed in a guide by the APM,[91] and include the CMMI model and PMI's OPM model. More recently, the IPMA have introduced the Delta model, which is perhaps the best in addressing the maturity of behaviours likely to lead to success.[92] As an accredited maturity assessor, I still consider assessment of behavioural maturity to be lagging significantly.

Another approach to assessing maturity of delivery is the Portfolio, Program and Project Management Maturity Model (P3M3).[93] As a trained and accredited assessor, I find in particular that the program management dimension provides reasonable assurance for change management, covering blueprint, benefits, processes, stakeholder management and roles. Some organisations, including the State of Queensland in Australia,[94] have mandated use of maturity assessment using P3M3 for their departments, and many large organisations in the UK have not only assessed maturity but also have improvement programs in place.

---

90 PwC PPM Global Survey, 2014, *Insights and Trends into Current Project, Programme and Portfolio Management*, https://www.apm.org.uk/news/pwc-ppm-global-survey-insights-and-trends-current-project-programme-and-portfolio-management [accessed 1 September 2016].
91 *Models to Improve the Management of Projects*, 2007, by Association for Project Management (Author).
92 http://www.ipma.world/certification/certify-organisations/delta-benefits-and-references/ [accessed 1 September 2016].
93 Portfolio, Programme and Project Management Maturity Model (P3M3) https://www.axelos.com/best-practice-solutions/p3m3 [accessed 1 September 2016].
94 Consistent feedback when we released early drafts of PRINCE2 was the need to describe those vital behavioural competences (or soft skills) required for successful project delivery. At last there is now a book that describes those skills.' Andy Murray, Lead Author of PRINCE2 (2009).

Successful delivery is a combination of mindset and toolset; toolset is somewhat overdone and we need to focus more on mindset. This book will help you.

Steve Wake, chairman of the APM

3.19 MINIMISING ORGANISATIONAL DISTRESS DURING TRANSFORMATION

It is time that we admitted there is more to life than money, and it's time we focused not just on GDP (Gross Domestic Product), but on GWB – General Well-Being.

David Cameron, former UK prime minister

We will deal with managing stress and building resilience in ourselves, alongside broader aspects of the emotional intelligence quadrant of managing ourselves, in Section 3.29. Here we look at ways of minimising stress in an organisation during transformation. Addressing organisational needs forms part of the fourth quadrant of the emotional intelligence framework under social influence. I find this particularly important, not just for ethical reasons, but because an organisation under excessive stress is likely to freeze and resort to passive aggressive behaviour rather than make life easy for us as managers of change.

Stress seriously affects people's health and wellbeing and it is the number one cause of lost working time through sickness in the UK, with one in four working adults suffering from a stress-related health problem in their lifetime. Organisational restructuring is perhaps the biggest source of stress in the workplace. Hence, as agents of change, we should optimise our approach to reduce the effect we have on the health of others.

3.19.1 Causes of stress in the organisation

Remember that stress doesn't come from what's going on in your life. It comes from your thoughts about what's going on in your life.

Andrew J. Bernstein

I run an ongoing stress survey,[95] and results to date are:

- **Causes** – 55 per cent reported being hopelessly under-resourced.
- **Symptoms** – only 30 per cent did not feel overwhelmed, and 46 per cent were very anxious about work.
- **Business impact** – only 30 per cent would stay if they had another job offer.
- **Wellbeing** – only 27 per cent had confidence in their leadership.
- **Support** – only 30 per cent had any training in managing stress or building resilience.

Do you think stress helps an organisation to move from good to great?[96]

---

95 http://www.surveymonkey.net/stressman2 [accessed 4 July 2016].
96 J. C. Collins, 2001, *Good to Great: Why Some Companies Make the Leap...and Others Don't*, Random.

I supplemented a review of literature with input from more than 20 workshops around England speaking about the causes and impact of stress. Common causes of stress given at the workshops are shown in Figure 3.48. Consider how could you modify your approach and behaviours to reduce your impact against each of these.

Figure 3.48 Causes of stress in the organisation

Cause	Mitigation
Uncertainty	
Change	
Lack of trust	
Lack of control	
Lack of leadership	
Being micro-managed	
Unrealistic targets and deadlines	
Lack of recognition	
Lack of support and coaching	
Not enough rest	
Inter-personal conflict	
Uncertainty	

3.19.2 How the organisation performs better without stress

As in shown Figure 3.49, when under stress we exhibit classic responses of 'freeze, flight or fight'.

In Figure 3.50, consider how each of these might manifest itself in your organisation.

Stressed people under-perform and make poor decisions at best. Conversely, in the absence of stress, individuals are more likely to collaborate, motivate and create. Which team culture would you prefer if you were in charge? What can you do about it?

3.19.3 Minimising the impact of stress from change management initiatives

Having been responsible for bid and transformation through large PPPs, I have seen change management done badly, and witnessed the effects on the workforce in general as well as on the wellbeing and careers of individuals. In PPPs we have an extreme, but mergers and acquisitions are similar. Put yourself in their shoes: your employer

Figure 3.49 Stress pyramid

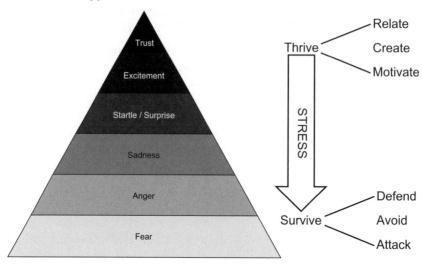

Figure 3.50 Manifestations of stress in your organisation

Stress response	Manifestations in your organisation
Flight	
Fight	
Freeze	

is changing from a 'cosy local government job for life' to working for a profit-centred private sector company with aggressive performance management. You may be re-located. Your job description will change. Your boss will change. The systems and processes you use will change. Efficiency targets mean there are likely to be fewer of you. Your outputs will be measured and your performance will be managed. Your output and performance is expected to go up markedly immediately after transition! In their shoes, how do you feel?

I saw one of these transitions drag out for three years waiting for supporting technology platforms and new facilities to come online. Performance declined rather than increased due to the long-term impact of stress, which in turn led to more pressure. When it came to my turn to manage a similar portfolio of technology and facilities through transition, with the benefit of hindsight I realised that performance would be better if we did things quicker and tried our best to keep stakeholders involved through the process. This was underpinned by:

- Setting up joint governance involving leadership from all stakeholder groups with communications top of the agenda.

- Getting agreement at the governance level that the implementation would be as clean and swift as practical, shortening analysis of the stagnant 'as is' stage and adopting 'vanilla' implementations of key systems such as enterprise resource management and customer relationship management systems with minimal customisation and configuration.

- Only adopting common off the shelf technology (COTS) where we had reference transformations. Avoiding 'bleeding edge' technology, no matter how good the sales pitch.

- Working hand in glove with corporate communications to tell people what was going to happen, what was happening and celebrate what we had achieved. Planning media campaigns to work across all channels, appealing to different representational systems and meta-programs, especially away from problems and towards solutions.

- Having a dedicated ring-fenced budget to manage the change and supporting training. Note that this is normally excluded from capital expenditure (CapEx) proposals.

- Employing a dedicated change management professional to augment the program in addition to the business analysis and BPR resource.

- Having a dedicated HR change management professional to promptly deal with queries regarding working conditions. You might already have an HR business partner who would love to be involved and bring additional resources to bear.

- Avoiding 'big bang' change-overs by piloting all roll-out of systems through lead groups with close support.

- Involving local subject matter experts in the specification and design, especially 'black hats' to look for what might go wrong.

- Majoring on active stakeholder management with ongoing engagement of all groups including workforce representatives.

- Training up a group of 'change champions' within the workforce to act as local ambassadors and points of contact.

- Holding regular 'town hall' meetings where anyone had a voice to ask any questions.

- Celebrating success at every opportunity.

Award for 'Major PPP of the year' was in no small part due to the way we managed the transition. Having made life-long friends with some of those affected was the real measure of success. What approach will you use to minimise road-kill on the road to change?

3.20 FAST RAPPORT BUILDING WITH STAKEHOLDERS

Rapport is meeting someone on their map of the world.

NLP presupposition

Stakeholder relationship management is one of the three core skills assessed for Expert BA. You will be aware that there is a whole host of people who have an interest in your project, including perhaps many outside your own organisation. Some may be initially for it, but you can be sure that for any change initiative there will be an array of people who would prefer things to remain as they are and so will be resistant to you and your project. Some have the influence to stop you achieving your objectives if they are not engaged and managed. Sponsors have accountability for stakeholder management,[97] but you might find yourself carrying out much of the engagement. Things probably go all right with most of them most of the time, but if what you are doing is not working, then you need to understand their map of the world and speak directly to it.

> Resistance is a sign of lack of rapport with your client.
>
> NLP presupposition

Successful people create rapport, and rapport creates trust. Many people think that you either have the ability or you have not. All NLP courses, however, have this as one of the first skills that they teach, as rapport is one of the pillars of NLP. In fact, it is safe to say that without the ability to establish rapport, none of the other techniques of NLP will work. Relationship management was specifically listed under behavioural competencies for BAs reviewed in Section 1.4. The NLP fundamentals of rapport were introduced in Section 2.14, and here we apply the principles to stakeholder engagement.

3.20.1 Prerequisites for rapport

The word rapport stems from the old French verb *rapporter*, which means literally to carry something back, referring to what one person sends out the other reflects back. Today we might say, 'bouncing (ideas) off each other'. The other person might be brought to realise that they share similar values, beliefs, knowledge or behaviours.

Adopting an attitude of curiosity and taking an interest in people in general helps to develop the behaviours to achieve rapport quickly and easily. Often we can be so task focused that we forget about people, especially when we are in virtual teams spread around the country, or even globally, and end up at the extreme of sending cold emails to strangers. Many of us like to people-watch and observe others when we are in public places, but seem to lose this ability when we are under time pressure at work. NLP believes that everything that is going on in the inside is expressed on the outside by language and behaviour, so everything that you may need to know is there to see and hear if you take the time and make the effort to observe. In terms of the meta-programs, this is one of the occasions when you should attempt to be 'in time': fully aware of the moment and in tune with your senses.

> Behind every behaviour is a positive intent.
>
> NLP presupposition

To be able to understand anyone we have to suspend judgement. Even if someone does something that we do not agree with, we should not judge the person. Until we can see

---

97 APM Governance SIG, 2009, *Sponsoring Change: A Guide to the Governance Aspects of Project Sponsorship*, APM Publishing.

things from their perspective and understand why they do things, we are unlikely to be able to anticipate their choices and affect their behaviour. (At the extreme, you can see people in traditional martial arts or cage fighting contests bowing and showing respect to their opponents before and after beating each other up. They are also experts in sensory acuity and rapport, as it is in the interests of their noses to be able to anticipate every move and behaviour of their opponent.) It is an instinctive skill that we all have within us, but which we sometimes just do not get around to practising much after childhood.

3.20.2 Match and mirror, not mimic

Matching and mirroring were described in Section 2.14. When done properly it is a very persuasive technique, and this is not lost on salesmen. Rather than try to establish rapport, however, they often just use physical matching and mirroring techniques to mimic it. If motive and action are not aligned, this comes over as incongruent. It can lead to 'buyer's remorse', where people regret the decision once they are away from the influence. So let us go back to ethics, integrity and desired outcome. If you are trying to establish understanding and trust with someone in order to reach a mutually beneficial agreement, then all of this will work.

Probably the NLP technique most badly performed is mirroring, and that is at least partly due to people reading a book, like this one, and thinking that they are competent to go out and bend the world to their will. If you are able to observe two people who are in love this will be obvious through their body language. Personally, I try to avoid matching and mirroring and instead look for my client to start to naturally match me, indicating that rapport has been established. Once they match me, I can then take on a lead role to take the conversation in the desired direction.

> I was at a meeting at one of the largest IT consultancies and the head of capability knew that I had NLP training. He spent the first 10 minutes adopting unnatural body positions, affecting facial characteristics, displaying negative body language, avoiding eye contact and so on. I guess that he wanted to have some sport watching me attempt to mimic him. Fortunately, I only matched breathing and language, which bought us into line anyway, and he soon dropped the charade and realised that NLP was not so superficial. Later, he endorsed the book.

So, my advice to you, particularly when starting out, is to be aware of body language, but let it fall into line naturally rather than attempting to mimic it. If you match your breathing only, you will find that you soon align in terms of energy, pace and pitch, which are a prerequisite for rapport anyway. If you also match language, then you will quickly notice an improvement in communications that lays the foundation for understanding and trust.

Of course, as we conduct a lot of our meetings over the phone, breathing and language remain good underpinning. For email correspondence, use of similar language, particularly recognising preferred modalities and reflecting any evident meta-programs, improves the chances of common understanding. Ideally though, always build rapport face to face first before allowing yourself to lapse into email and instant messaging. As you may have noticed, you do not build rapport on social networks this way, even though you might find common interest and values.

3.20.3 Hierarchy of rapport

There is a well-established hierarchy of neurological levels for NLP, as discussed in Section 2.7 and illustrated in Figure 2.9. Connection at higher levels leads to deeper rapport.[98]

Rapport established through matching and mirroring, as described in Section 3.20.2, is tackling the challenge from the bottom of the pyramid. It is much more effective to start from the top to look for points of connection. Figure 3.51 captures how I looked for rapport in a large PPP where relations between organisations were initially very contractual and antagonistic.

Figure 3.51 Connecting neurological levels in the project context

Neurological level	Considerations for connection in the project context
Purpose	Joint venture projects and collaborations have been shown to be more likely to succeed if a clear superordinate goal has been established. If two parties are bought into a common purpose then it is more likely that they will work together constructively, even setting aside old rivalries.
	If the stakeholder can align to the purpose that you promote then it will be much easier to work together. You may have to 'chunk up' to identify this common purpose.
Identity	Who we are is very important to the human condition. From a project perspective this supports the need for a clear project identity and branding. When you speak to stakeholders be clear what hat you are wearing; that is, present yourself as 'the project' rather than as an individual. (Where you have an established personal brand or reputation, you may consider switching this around and connecting the project to the brand, just as some successful investment funds promote themselves through the fund manager where they have a strong track record.)
Beliefs and values	It used to be common to see corporate 'value statements' and this has spread to some projects, but avoid the cliché and the superficial. The values are what people do, not what is written down. If the project says that creativity is valued then don't stifle it with process and command and control.

(Continued)

---

98 Robert Dilts, 1990, *Changing Belief Systems with NLP*, Meta Publications.

Figure 3.51 (Continued)

Neurological level	Considerations for connection in the project context
	For projects such as PPPs I found early on that it is essential to bridge the gap in perception of different values between the public sector and the private sector. It is important to stress that all parties are trying to bring about a successful outcome.
Capabilities	People from similar professions or vocations have a natural affinity whenever the link can be established. Aside from the common linkage of the project, many people today have had a range of roles in their career and you may find commonality in history and experience.
Behaviours	It is easier to build rapport across similar behaviours. Where you identify that you normally have different behaviours then look at your preferred options for key meta-programs and consider those of the second party. (There is an exercise below.)
Environment	This can be taken to be working on the same project, in the same location or under the same organisational structure. Whatever it is, emphasise it. 'We are all in the same boat.'

For all of these aspects, where you are looking for commonality, it is obviously easier if you are working from a matching rather than a mismatching perspective.

When leading transformation on my first major PPP, we were paving the way in terms of governance arrangements. The public sector partner would usually insist on chairing project boards, but the expense of the projects was borne by the private sector partner. The potential for massive overruns in scope, cost and time had the potential to make the £250 million contract loss-making.

At the first formal program board, as we did introductions, most of the 20–30 people in the room advised that they were 'representing' such-and-such department. I introduced myself as being accountable for successful delivery of improvements for citizens. This struck a chord with the chairman, who had joined the council from the private sector and was also very focused on delivery of benefits rather than assets. He nodded to me in recognition – we had established common purpose.

After the meeting he contacted me to arrange a more informal discussion. I put my cards on the table, telling him what my internal constraints were with regard to budget and expectations, and he told me what he needed and what his political masters wanted. We traded the stuff in the middle and set about to deliver as much as we could together with the resources that we had. The next thing we did was to communicate a competition and prize for a name for the program. Alongside joint working, we had started to establish a common identity.

Although the program was defined contractually in terms of deliverables, we agreed that we were actually trying to improve outcomes. The most prominent of these were those around customer service, as measured by the national auditing body. The program took on a slightly different direction, with less focus on the IT and more on changing behaviours, improving operating models and providing supporting training.

Private sector capabilities in delivery were acknowledged, and we in turn recognised the public sector knowledge and contact with its own customers. We seconded some of their people into the team and offered training to any who wanted it, creating a whole that was more than the sum of the parts.

During my time there we always behaved as a common team with a common purpose. Differences, potentially backed up by a contract and severe financial penalties, were reconciled in a way that meant that delivery was maintained and neither party was taken advantage of. All of this was underpinned by constant dialogue to get to learn more about each other, in terms of personalities as well as capabilities.

The partnership won major PPP of the year, not for having a brand new IT infrastructure, but for measurable improvements in customer-focused services (which were enabled by the infrastructure). All of this was only possible, not by the latest technology, but from the earliest skill – the ability to connect.

3.20.4 Finding the connection

The business of business is relationships; the business of life is human connection.
Robin Sharma, former lawyer and bestselling leadership author

You may be familiar with the concept of six degrees of separation, which says that we are connected to everyone in the world by no more than six friends or contacts. Since this concept was first postulated in the nineteenth century, my own view is that this route may be even shorter today. Certainly, using professional networking sites such as LinkedIn, I can find my route to some of the most famous people around the world in three connections or under. So, next time you meet a 'stranger' you might like to practise by playing the game of discovering your connection. I like to set myself the target of finding three points of connection as quickly as I can. Now I fall into the habit of doing it automatically every time I meet a new stakeholder. I use this technique as an ice breaker in public talks and have had people finding more than 20 connections with apparent strangers in less than three minutes.

Exercise 3.21 Finding the connection

If you use a stakeholder management grid then consider the dimension of 'connection' for each of your key stakeholders, or at least those where things may not be running as smoothly as you would like. This could be any aspect, for example: having studied at the same university, studied the same topic, worked for the same company, common friend, born in the same town or even sharing the same hobby or football team. You probably do not have enough information for many of your stakeholders to construct this at the moment, but it should give you the prerequisite inquisitiveness to start to find out, which will build rapport in itself. From what you know of them, you might think that you do not want to know more, but they are likely to behave differently in different environments, from the office to the family BBQ, just as you might do. Maybe there is an aspect which you will come to like. How will you start to find out?

Now we have an excellent starting point, but how do we start to understand their map of the world? Of course, we could ask them, and should. This is particularly important when we are dealing with customers and end users. Simple questions like 'How do you see things?', and 'What is important to you in terms of outcome?' can be most enlightening. They can be even more so with the help of NLP to understand the underlying structure of what they are saying, as this will reveal their behaviours, that is, meta-programs, and also their primary representational systems. Knowledge of preferred representational system will help to reflect appropriate language, for example with a bias to visual or auditory words. Very subtle modifications to questioning can also reveal some of their values and beliefs in relation to the topic and context.

3.20.5 Rapport through matching of meta-programs

Having similar ways of looking at the world and similar behaviours will help to establish rapport. But which meta-programs help to establish rapport in the first place? Have a look at Exercise 3.22.

Exercise 3.22 Meta-programs for rapport

For the following meta-programs, choose the option that you think is most appropriate for achieving rapport. For example, if you think that it is easier for outgoing, extrovert people to develop rapport with others then mark this option in the box. On the other hand, you may think that extroverted people only have shallow relationships, and being introverted helps to develop sufficient depth.

Best for building rapport?

Self/Introvert	Other/Extrovert
Need to be alone to recharge their batteries.	Relax in the company of others.
Few relationships with deep connections.	Have a lot of surface relationships.
Interested in a few topics but to great detail.	Know about a lot of things, but not in detail.

(Continued)

Best for building rapport?

Match Notice points of similarity.	**Mismatch** Notice differences.
Associated Feelings and relationships are important.	**Dissociated** Detached from feelings. Work with information. Task oriented.
In time Live in the moment. Creative but poor with deadlines.	**Through time** Good at keeping track of time and managing deadlines.
Proactive Initiates action.	**Reactive** Analyses first then follows the lead from others.
Person Centred on feelings.	**Thing** Centred on tasks.

Do you remember what your orientation was with these meta-programs? Which ones would you like to develop flexibility with to help with this?

3.20.6 The language of rapport

As covered in Section 2.10, we all have a preference for a particular representational system based on the senses. Figure 3.52 shows some examples of words and phrases that you might hear to indicate a person's preferred system, and which you might like to reflect back to them in your conversations.

Note that these are not casually used, but consistently, that is, unless someone is deliberately attempting to vary vocabulary, then they will tend to use the same type of words. (Good authors will attempt to use descriptive words from all representational systems in order to connect with a wider audience, but this takes discipline and practice.)

For example, if someone has a visual preference and uses words like 'Let me see the evidence', you will not be doing yourself any favours by responding with phrases like 'Wait until you hear the results'. Similarly, if people use language appropriate to a particular option for a meta-program, you will struggle to connect if you use language from the opposite option. If they ask for 'the big picture', and you take them through all the detail, will you establish rapport?

By listening to the type of words they use and flexing our language, we 'tune in' to their wavelength much quicker. The signal to noise level increases dramatically and we can get our message received and understood.

The person with the most flexibility controls the system.

NLP presupposition adopted from cybernetics

Figure 3.52 The language of rapport

Visual	Auditory	Kinaesthetic
Appear	Clear as a bell	Those affected
Bird's eye view	Sounds right	Crash
Clear-cut	Let's discuss it	Foundation
Focus	Harmonise	Get a grip on
Illustrate	In a manner of speaking	Impact
In the light of day	Outspoken	Lukewarm
With hindsight	Out of tune	Muddled
Graphic	Hear the results	Nail
Illusion	Hidden message	Pressure

Figure 3.53 The language of meta-programs

You are likely to hear them say:

Proactive
Let's do it!
Go for it!
JDI

Reactive
Analyse, consider, think about
The important thing is to...
Set up a study group

Towards
Outcomes, objectives, results
Achieve, deliver
Milestones, deliverables

Away from
Overcome, solve
Prevent, avoid
Issues, risks

Internal reference
We recommend
We are/will

External reference
What's your opinion?
Has anyone else used this
approach?
Benchmark

Match
Common, same,
I remember a situation like this

Mismatch
Doesn't fit
Different

(Continued)

Figure 3.53 (Continued)

You are likely to hear them say:

General
Overview, executive summary, flavour

Specific
Precisely, exactly, specification, data, specifics

Options
Choice, options, possibilities, alternatives, variety, capability

Procedures
Proven, tried and tested, logical, robust, process, method
Firstly..., then

In time
Let's do that now
I'm sorry that I'm late, I just lost track of time

Through time
Let's schedule that in
I will see you at 1pm
(Where is everyone?)

Sameness
Same, similar
Like this
Replacement
Reminds me of
Usually, normally
That's not the way *we* do it

Difference
New ways of working, radical, transformation, change
Make a difference
Project

Independent
Accountable
Control
I will/have...
When do you need it?

Cooperative
Let's, we, the team
We will start right away
Team-building
Collaborate

Person
People's names and their relationships
Who shall I ask/needs to know?
Talk about

Thing
Where is the procedure for ...?
What software are you using?
Do

Figure 3.54 Rapport bridges the communication divide

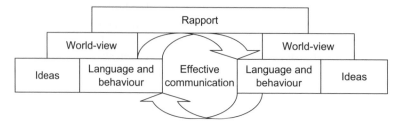

3.21 COMMUNICATING THE MESSAGE AND CHOOSING YOUR MEDIUM

> The single biggest problem in communication is the illusion that it has taken place.
> George Bernard Shaw, author and co-founder of the London School of Economics

When I can get hold of them, I usually incorporate the host organisation's objectives at the start of each workshop to illustrate how the specific training is supporting them. It amuses me to hear, time after time, that people do not recall seeing them before. On one occasion, a delegate came up to me afterwards and said, 'Those senior managers in that room who said they had never seen those objectives definitely have, because I was in the room with them.' But they do not remember them; they did not connect with them. Have you ever been in a meeting and made a suggestion, which was ignored, only to have someone else say something similar later, and everyone pick up on it? Do not worry, it is not personal; our subconscious makes decisions and filters most information so that it does not overwhelm our conscious thought processes. So, how can you increase the chances that your messages are heard, understood and remembered?

3.21.1 What is your preferred style of learning?

> I am always doing that which I cannot do, in order that I may learn how to do it.
> Pablo Picasso

As BAs are involved in the process of educating users, learning and development was specifically mentioned in the review of competencies for effective BAs in Section 1.4. The text on this topic in IIBA's *BoK* makes specific reference to catering to different sensual representation systems, or the 'VAKOG' model as we term it in NLP – visual, auditory, kinaesthetic, olfactory (smell) and gustatory (taste).

The education system in the UK used to be geared to separating out those who learned from books and those who learned by doing. Education establishments are now better at taking into account that people have different learning styles, as credited to Honey and Mumford,[99] and they try to address all of these styles in the one environment. Indeed, I was asked to be opening speaker on this topic at the annual conference for the parents of 'gifted' children.[100] This learning preference has been termed a meta-program. As a comparison, I have shown these styles in Figure 3.55 alongside the main representational systems as introduced in Section 2.10.

Unless they have been trained and have developed flexibility, a trainer, for example, is likely to deliver in their own preferred learning style and preferred representational system, as well as being biased to their own meta-programs. As a consequence, this can result in failure to connect with large parts of the audience.

> We now accept the fact that learning is a lifelong process of keeping abreast of change. And the most pressing task is to teach people how to learn.
> Peter Drucker, change management guru

---

99 P. Honey and M. Mumford, 1982, *Manual of Learning Styles*, Peter Honey Publications.
100 Keynote address 'Learn to fail or fail to learn' for the Potential Plus UK in Leamington Spa, UK, 26 October 2013, http://www.potentialplusuk.org/ [accessed 1 September 2016].

Figure 3.55 Learning styles and preferred representational systems

---

Preferred learning style	Main representational system
Activists Like to be involved in activities Like to seek out new experiences Active supporters of change	**Kinaesthetic** Like doing physical things Use the language of doing
Reflectors Like to collect all the facts and look at things from all angles Risk averse	**Auditory** Like to hear and tell stories Listen to the sound of word Use words related to hearing
Theorists Logical and dispassionate Perfection not pragmatism	**Audio-digital** Led by a constant internal dialogue The language of logic
Pragmatists Full of ideas but little patience Happy to go with the first practical idea rather than search for the best	**Visual** Like to see things Like words relating to seeing things

---

As you might expect from such an important area of our lives, reflective practitioners have written a lot about learning.[101] Thankfully, a lot of it was drummed in to me by someone who holds a master's degree in adult education. The work of Kolb,[102] often referred to as the Kolb learning cycle, is specifically cited in IIBA's competencies. I agree that a BA's ability to switch backwards between abstract concepts and concrete examples is perhaps the key skill in taking an audience on a journey.

Kolb's model outlines two related approaches towards grasping experience: concrete experience and abstract conceptualisation, as well as two related approaches towards transforming experience: reflective observation and active experimentation. In NLP, we refer to these aspects as two pairs of the 60 or so meta-programs. According to Kolb's model, the ideal learning process engages all four of these modes in response to situational demands; they form a learning cycle from experience to observation to conceptualisation to experimentation and back to experience. In order for learning to be effective, all four of these approaches must be incorporated. As individuals attempt to use all four approaches, however, they may tend to develop strengths in one experience-grasping approach and one experience-transforming approach, leading them to prefer one of the following four learning styles:

---

101 https://en.wikipedia.org/wiki/Learning_styles [accessed 4 July 2016].
102 David A. Kolb, 2015, *Experiential Learning: Experience as the Source of Learning and Development*, 2nd edn, Pearson Education.

- **Accommodator** – concrete experience + active experiment: strong in 'hands-on' practical doing (for example, physical therapists).

- **Converger** – abstract conceptualisation + active experiment: strong in practical 'hands-on' application of theories (for example, engineers).

- **Diverger** – concrete experience + reflective observation: strong in imaginative ability and discussion (for example, social workers).

- **Assimilator** – abstract conceptualisation + reflective observation: strong in inductive reasoning and creation of theories (for example, philosophers).

Figure 3.56 Kolbe learning cycle

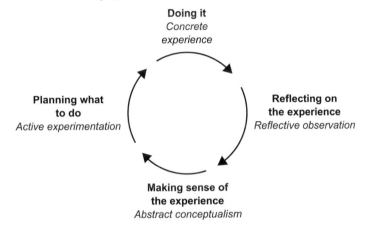

Where do you fit in? When you are learning or self-coaching be sure to bear in mind your own bias for learning style. As a coach to others, you should try to discover the learning styles and primary representational systems of the team members that you are developing.

3.21.2 Getting your message across with the help of the 4MAT model

I'm a great believer that any tool that enhances communication has profound effects in terms of how people can learn from each other, and how they can achieve the kind of freedoms that they're interested in.

Bill Gates

As you have learned, in NLP we do not actually invent anything, we just model it from people who excel. One of the models taught in NLP, and most widely applied across training, is that derived by Bernice McCarthy, a North American schoolteacher. In short, she says that different learners, and ourselves as trainers, have a bias in our focus on each of the four quadrants shown in Figure 3.57, but that we should use structure to establish that we have covered each of them adequately.

Figure 3.57 The 4MAT model for teaching

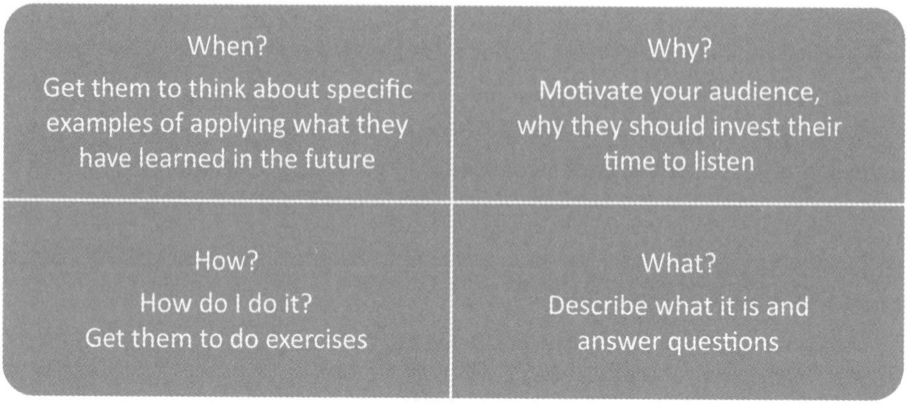

When?	Why?
Get them to think about specific examples of applying what they have learned in the future	Motivate your audience, why they should invest their time to listen
How?	What?
How do I do it? Get them to do exercises	Describe what it is and answer questions

Certified NLP trainers are assessed against more than 30 criteria. The top four from that list are:

1. Choosing and managing your own emotional state.
2. Building rapport quickly with the group and tracking individuals as well as the group.
3. Framing, setting and delivering the desired learning outcome.
4. Using and demonstrating use of the 4MAT model, including quadrants which are not the trainer's own preference.

The 4MAT training model helps to overcome our own bias to get the message over to a wide audience. Before learning the structure, I used to spend too large a proportion of my time on the 'why' and then the 'what', scrimping on demonstrations showing how to do stuff, and often forgetting to future pace the audience to think about specific occasions when they will use what they have learned. I also realised that the trainings which I reacted badly to and learned little from were those that launched into the 'how' without first establishing 'why' it might be useful to me. For those with a different preference, you will still notice this bias towards 'why'. Now to 'future pace': what is your bias, and how will you compensate?

In the first part of trainings I usually cover learning style and get people to do the exercises above to start delegates thinking about how they prefer to receive information. It is no surprise that I usually have all combinations in the room at any given time. This frames my discussion at the start of training as to why I switch between:

- framing;
- why the topic is important;
- why it works;

- theory and background;
- embedding key messages in metaphors, storytelling, and quotations;
- priming;
- abstract concepts;
- concrete examples;
- getting people to reflect (why?);
- showing some video content;
- getting them up doing exercises; and
- back to reflecting on when they will use the techniques in the future.

(Why I switch between preferred meta-programs in my language patterns comes later.)

Then I ask them why I go to this trouble. Why? We trainers still occasionally get feedback effectively saying that we should tailor the training to only their preference. (More theory, more practical, more stories, less stories, shorter, longer.) As I practise and refine my technique, particularly in framing the training, this is becoming rare, but I do not expect it to go away. Why? More importantly, what are you going to do about it in your trainings?

3.21.3 Beyond Kirkpatrick – embedding learning

In a world that is constantly changing, there is no one subject or set of subjects that will serve you for the foreseeable future, let alone for the rest of your life. The most important skill to acquire now is learning how to learn.

John Naisbitt, bestselling author of *Mega-trends*

Figure 3.58 The Kirkpatrick model for evaluating training effectiveness

Level 4 - Results	**What organizational benefits resulted from the training?**
Level 3 - Behaviour	**To what extent did participants change their behaviour back in the workplace as a result of the training?**
Level 2 - Learning	**To what extent did participants improve knowledge and skills and change attitudes as a result of the training?**
Level 1 - Reaction	**How did participants react to the program?**

In the learning and development sector, the Kirkpatrick model is widely known for assessing effectiveness of training and coaching interventions.[103]

Although the Kirkpatrick model is widely known, it is rarely used for formal scoring, as classroom training cannot usually be expected to progress above the learning of knowledge at level 2/4 in the model. I do use it for evaluation of my own workshops, as we use a group coaching format and specific NLP tools to achieve behavioural change. But even the best interventions do not lead to lasting results unless they are part of a longer approach to learning and development. As evaluated by Kirkpatrick's own son, effectiveness is determined as much by setting expectations and pre-work, and follow-up actions, as by the interventions themselves.[104] Figure 3.59 illustrates the approach we use with change management professionals.

Figure 3.59 Beyond Kirkpatrick – effectiveness of training interventions is determined as much by pre-work and follow-up in the workplace as in the classroom itself

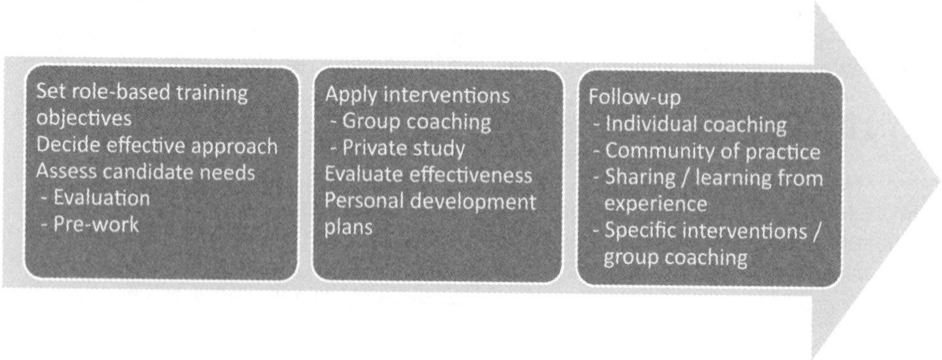

Set role-based training objectives
Decide effective approach
Assess candidate needs
- Evaluation
- Pre-work

Apply interventions
- Group coaching
- Private study
Evaluate effectiveness
Personal development plans

Follow-up
- Individual coaching
- Community of practice
- Sharing / learning from experience
- Specific interventions / group coaching

How can you apply this approach to help to make your messages heard and stick?

3.21.4 Tailoring reports to your audience

To effectively communicate, we must realize that we are all different in the way we perceive the world and use this understanding as a guide to our communication with others.

Tony Robbins, NLP guru

In terms of your stakeholders, knowledge of how they view the world can assist in how you behave and relay information. This can be interpreted from language and actions. In terms of reporting, key meta-programs to consider are their preferences for:

---

103 Donald L. Kirkpatrick and James D. Kirkpatrick, 2006, *Evaluating Training Programs: The Four Levels*, Berrett-Koehler.
104 Doug Kirkpatrick, 2011, *Beyond Empowerment: The Age of the Self-Managed Organization*, Morning Star Self-Management Institute.

- General or specific – it could be assumed that the higher up the organisation an individual is then the more of a 'helicopter view' they may take, but this may not be the case.

- Options versus procedure – hopefully higher management are focused on considering the 'what', that is, options rather than the 'how' of process, but in some professional backgrounds there is an organisational filter that pre-selects people with a disposition to procedure and method. Note that there has been a growing trend in project management since 2000 for procedure-based methods like PRINCE2, which accentuates this filtering.

- Convincer pattern – what is their evidence base? This is developed further below.

There are four basic ways that some people are convinced, as shown in the column on the left of Figure 3.60. You may think that you have convinced someone by telling them about it, whereas their preference could be to read a document. Once we have the preferred channel then we have to satisfy a frequency criterion. Some people will believe what they read/you tell them on face value, while others may take a lot of persuasion through repetition or over a period of time. At the extreme, some will always remain

---

Figure 3.60 Dimensions and options for the convincer meta-program

What convinces someone?	**How often does something have to be demonstrated for another person to be convinced?**
They have to see something to believe it.	Automatic – they take things at face value.
They have to hear someone else say that they can do it, for example a reference.	They need two or three occasions before they make up their minds.
They have to read about it, for example a report or a CV.	They make up their minds over a period of time – no point repeating yourself or trying to rush them.
They have to experience doing something before believing it.	Consistently – they only consider you as good as your last performance (and almost expect to be let down).

---

sceptical. Some people are sceptical for a living. As a former head of the compliance and enforcement division of UK Customs explained to me, they have their own 'ABC' – assume nothing, believe no one, check everything. A rather interesting map of the world, but not unique, and a very sharp tool in the right role.

Perhaps this sheds some light on why we occasionally struggle to convince some people. The safest option, especially when working with groups of people, and now being used in the educational system, is to provide all of these options where practical. For a project this might involve you:

1. Sending out a high level report.
2. Providing all the details in an appendix or through hyperlinks.
3. Getting an advocate or early adopter to talk about it.
4. Giving them a tour/demo.
5. Letting them try it.
6. Maintaining the communications channels rather than just doing it once.

Of course, this sits on top of the other aspects of effective communication which we have already dealt with, such as using both big picture and also detail, and with language appealing to different representational systems. And, of course, you have to keep doing it. This is one of the reasons that we bring in communications professionals to help us with change management programs. Otherwise we might just communicate according to our own meta-programs and in the language of our own representational system and lose the rest of the audience.

3.22 LISTENING SKILLS – HEARING WHAT IS NOT BEING SAID

> The most important thing in communication is to hear what isn't being said.
> Peter Drucker, management guru

Listening skills, for good reason, were included in those behavioural competencies for BAs reviewed in Section 1.4.

An observer from Mars may reasonably conclude that conversation is simply taking it in turns to talk. Sometimes, we even talk at the same time. The most important part of conversation, however, is usually listening, not talking. Listening is more than hearing. Under stress, people's hearing improves, but listening diminishes.

We learned to communicate as animals long before we had language. Some studies have shown that the actual words used in conversation can account for less than 10 per cent of construed meaning, with meaning being picked up from tonality and body language.[105] Hence, the first part of an NLP practitioner course is usually spent on exercises to develop sensory acuity. Being able to pick up and decode what is being communicated outside obvious words will give you an edge in everything from negotiation to leadership. The key starting point, whether we are listening or speaking, is to be 'present' / 'in time' rather than thinking where we need to be next or focusing on our own agenda/ what we want to say. On that foundation, we can really start to listen.

---

105 A. Mehrabian and M. Wiener, 1967, 'Decoding of Inconsistent Communications', *Journal of Personality and Social Psychology*, 6(1), 109–114.

3.22.1 Words, distortions and meaning

The meaning of the communication is the reaction to it.

NLP presupposition

In Section 2.15 I introduced the meta-model, which describes the way the language we use distorts meaning, and ways of challenging it using the 12 patterns of the meta-model. Which of those patterns regularly fall out of your mouth? Have a look at Exercise 3.23.

Exercise 3.23 Clarifying meaning using the meta-model

1. Refer to Figure 2.18 (in Section 2.15) to remind yourself of the 12 patterns of the meta-model.
2. Think of someone to whom you do not relate well, or someone whose behaviours you do not quite understand.
3. Listen to the language they use and note examples against the 12 patterns of the meta-model.
4. What are the common patterns of distortion that they use?
5. What do the common patterns being used tell you about their view of the world?
6. Given that this view is their reality, are there any changes you could make to your language in order to meet them on their map of the world?
7. If you were to challenge their map of the world, what would be the key clarification to use?
8. If they were listening to you, what do you think they would hear?

3.22.2 What makes them tick – meta-programs and preferences

A man's character may be learned from the adjectives which he habitually uses in conversation.

Mark Twain

To get a good connection, it helps to match meta-programs through language. Listen to a stakeholder's language to work out:

- Are they towards goals or away from problems?
- Big picture or detail?
- Options or procedure?

Reflect these meta-programs through complementary words.

Similarly, listen for their preferred representational system. Are they biased towards visual or auditory? What words do they use? Reflect them, and change them according to the person you are speaking to in a group.

Sometimes individuals complain to me that so-and-so does not listen to them. They cite examples where they have said something, and apparently been ignored, only to hear someone else say it and be applauded. Did that ever happen to you? Sometimes in close personal relationships we may swear that we mentioned so-and-so. It may be more than a failure of someone's memory. I clarify, 'doesn't listen to you or doesn't hear you?' Remember, we filter out more than 99 per cent of everything received through our senses to cope with the volume of information. How do we filter it? We filter out information not consistent with our map of the world, our sensory preferences, our behavioural meta-programs, our values and beliefs. If you want to improve your chances of being heard, then tune in to their wavelength.

3.22.3 Modelling of good listeners – some basic dos and don'ts

Practise listening to people whenever the opportunity arises. I learned this from my father, who seemed to make friends with everyone he came into contact with, from the checkout girl to the chairman. Here are some common things to bear in mind:

- Be present (that is, 'in time').
- Give them your attention – this will also help you to move into a situation of rapport.
- Suspend your personal view on the issue while listening and just try to understand theirs.
- Listen from a position of respect for the person.
- Listen without judgement – do not impose your own 'map of the world', values or beliefs.
- Focus on what you have in common rather than differences. (This one is especially important for people like myself who are naturally at the 'miss-matcher' end of that meta-program.)
- Know when someone's style is just thinking out loud.
- Playback and summarise, but do not paraphrase – use their language.

And a few things to avoid:

- Do not 'help' others to say what (we think) they want.
- Do not 'mind read' people's intentions from their actions – keep everything evidence based, or ask them.
- Do not jump in and problem solve –it can be quite insulting.
- Do not tell people that you know how they feel. (We might think we know how *we* might feel, but we are all different.)

Who do you know that you would call a good listener? What is it specifically about them that inclines you to think of them as a good listener? Can you model them, or someone else, to find out what is going on in their head to make them come across as a good listener?

3.23 REFRAMING DIFFICULT SITUATIONS AND DELIVERING BAD NEWS WELL

> The meaning of any experience in life depends on the context that we put around it.
> Anthony Robbins, wizard of wizards[106]

Frames were introduced in Section 2.9. There is no such thing as reality, only the meaning that you give to it, which is dependent upon your past experiences, attitudes, values, beliefs and so on. When the frame changes then the meaning changes with it. How you think about a situation determines your behaviour, which, in turn, affects your outcome. You can use reframing to help yourself in difficult situations and you can also use it to help take the emotion out of situations for other people by offering an alternative perspective.

3.23.1 Breaking bad news

> There is nothing either good or bad, but thinking makes it so.
> William Shakespeare

Although we may adopt the mottos 'no surprises', and 'under-promise, over-deliver, given the range of stakeholders that we have to manage, it is inevitable that there will be things that do not go to plan. It is very tempting to get into a 'witch hunt', but this 'blame frame' is not constructive, especially when we still need to solve the issue and go on to deliver the project. We should adopt an 'outcome frame', which will help us to resolve the problem.

Look at the two lists in Figure 3.61. Think about a recent issue you have had at work and tick either the left or right-hand column depending on which reflects how you were thinking about the issue. If you did both kinds of thinking, which did you spend the majority of your time in?

Think about how the left-hand column leads you to feel and how the right-hand column makes you feel. Next time you find yourself in a problem situation, which frame do you think stands the best chance of getting you out of it? How might you change your language patterns to maximise your chance of a speedy outcome?

---

106 Anthony Robbins, 1987, *Unlimited Power*, Harper Collins.

Figure 3.61 Blame frame versus outcome frame

Blame frame	Outcome frame
What's wrong?	What do we need?
Why do you have this problem?	How shall we resolve this challenge?
How late is it?	How will we know when we have achieved it?
What is holding you back?	What resources would help us to move this forward?
Who's fault is it?	Who has experienced similar challenges?
How could this happen!	What can we learn from this?
What does this problem stop you from doing?	What resources do you have that could help you to move forward?
Why haven't you solved it yet?	What are you going to begin doing now to get what you want?
This is going to reflect badly on us.	When we look back on this, what actions will stand out in helping us to have solved the challenge?

3.23.2 Reframing of context to change meaning and reduce impact

> Entrepreneurs are simply those who understand that there is little difference between obstacles and the opportunity and are able to turn both to their advantage.
> Niccolo Machiavelli

Jokes are an excellent example of context reframe, where the twist at the end 'reframes' the original meaning and makes the thing funny. Here is one of mine:

> How many change managers does it take to change a light bulb? It depends on what you want to change it into.

Politicians are also excellent role models for reframing. During the 1984 presidential campaign in the USA there was considerable concern about Ronald Reagan's age. Speaking during the presidential debate with Walter Mondale, Reagan said, 'I will not make age an issue of this campaign. I am not going to exploit, for political purposes, my opponent's youth and inexperience.' Similarly, when rank outsider Donald Trump, trained by Anthony Robbins, ran for president of the USA, he was widely considered under-qualified for the job because he had never been a politician. After a clever reframe, the chatter was about how it would be good to have someone who knew how to run a commercial enterprise at the helm for a change.

Whenever battle lines start to get drawn, there is always opportunity to reframe where the skirmish will take place and who the protagonists are.

> While leading a change management project in local government, I was warned to avoid a couple of 'troublemakers' who were asking awkward questions during a briefing by their director. When I put on my best innocent face and asked why, I was told that they were cynics. I offered a reframe: I said that I often found that cynics were people with passion about a situation that were brave enough to voice an opinion that was not popular, and some had experience of previous failures that might be able to help avoid making the same mistakes again. If you can win over the cynics, I said, they can become your biggest zealots in a change program.
>
> While not being convinced of this transformation from sinners to saints, the reframe gave me the scope to get a meeting with several 'troublemakers' to hear their concerns. I took the opportunity to ask for help and advice. Feeling listened to disarms much hostility, and asking for help more so. Cynics, for this campaign at least, quietened down, which helped my credibility with the director. One cynic, a prominent union official, joined the change team and helped to forge better working relations with the range of union representatives in the organisation. Inevitably, some changes involved detriment to individuals, including redundancy, but these were resolved through fair process in constructive dialogue, rather than adversarially through lengthy tribunal process.

Figure 3.62 Examples of context reframing

Frame (Problem?)	Context reframe (When/how would this behaviour be useful?)
Too stubborn	Resilient Can be relied upon to get the job done
Can't work late tonight	Honest Prioritises Values work/life balance
Won't delegate	Sees things through Takes care of the details Takes ownership

3.23.3 The 'as if' frame

> Choice is better than no choice.
>
> NLP presupposition

The 'as if' frame is particularly good for resolving conflicts. It allows you to come up with ideas which you might not have already thought of, giving you the flexibility to think outside the box, which will provide more of a chance of gaining a positive outcome. To help resolve problems, try one or more of the 'as if' frames on yourself or with another party. (You can think of it as a grown up version of 'let's pretend'.)

Figure 3.63 Use of 'as if' frames to overcome barriers

As if frame	Steps
Future switch Useful for stepping back from the issue and giving some perspective to enable creative thinking.	1. Imagine yourself some time in the future when this project is finished. 2. Look back to now. 3. Ask yourself how you solved this issue.
Person switch Useful for de-personalising the issue and looking for resources that you might need. (Also a good technique for 'self coaching'.)	1. Imagine that you are someone else whom you respect (famous or a personal colleague, friend or family member). 2. Ask what you would do about the issue if you were that person.
Information switch Good for identifying missing resources.	1. Imagine that you have all the information you need in order to solve the issue. 2. What information do you need to know now to get you to where you want to be? 3. Where might you find it?

3.23.4 Framing the problem

What is referred to as the agreement frame is where we look at scoping the issue in terms of the areas of agreement that sit around it. For example, we agree that we want to finish the project within cost, we cannot use any more time and we do not have any more resources. Now we can explore our common problem with considerations such as 'Which are the parts of scope that can be deferred to another phase?' Discipline yourself to overtly agree on what you agree on, rather than focusing on sometimes relatively trivial areas of disagreement.

If you want to win the game, then choose the frame. Are there any situations troubling you now? Is there another way of seeing things?

3.24 BRIDGING THE DIVIDE – NEGOTIATION, PERSUASION AND MANAGING DIFFICULT PEOPLE

> For me, relationship is very important. I can lose money, but I cannot lose a relationship. The test is, at the end of a conversation or a negotiation, both must smile.
>
> Sunil Mittal, multi-billionaire businessman

Negotiation is at the core of being able to move forward in a timely manner, and negotiation skills were specifically listed under behavioural competencies for BAs reviewed in Section 1.4. The PMI qualification in BA specifically includes 'Negotiation Tools', and 'Negotiation and Conflict Management' is one of the three specialist skills assessed for the 'Expert BA' qualification.

There is a huge body of knowledge on negotiation and arbitration,[107] but here we will be focusing on what NLP can bring to bear, though this covers most of the fundamentals along the way. As NLP recognises that people each have their own views and filters on the world, it also has a range of techniques for discovering them and finding accommodations.

People see things quite differently as they have different maps of the world and apply different filters. They have different values and beliefs, and no matter what you believe, this is their reality, so there's no point arguing with their perception, especially since it has got equal chance of being seen as 'right' to an observer as your perception. The trick is to try to understand their map of the world, values and beliefs and speak to them.

3.24.1 Are you winning the battle but losing the war?

Never argue with an idiot. Bystanders have a problem working out who is who.
My boss's advice on my being promoted into
his job at his retirement

As Dale Carnegie said, 'You can't win an argument'; both sides lose over time as resentment builds up and relationships suffer. You do not have to negotiate or resolve conflicts. You always have other options. You can go into denial and avoid the issue, give in, compromise or even attempt to push out your chest and dominate. All of these options have their own problems, however, even if we can minimise resultant stress. Compromise should be a last resort as it can leave ongoing resentment. Compromise has also been described as the solution where everyone loses the least. As everyone says, you need to look for 'win–win', but this cannot be gained by force or capitulation.

While following up an on-site training with one-on-one coaching, one senior analyst, struggling to get business sign-off to requirements of a large project, was of the opinion that his protagonist liked to see others fail. I wrote down on one card 'celebrate success together' with a cartoon smiley face. On the other card I wrote 'argue who is to blame for failure', with sad faces and a big 'F' on our score card. I said, offer him the choice and see which card his hands move towards. (Note the subtle choice of 'good' and 'bad' words, and effective 'priming' – celebrate / success / together versus argue / blame / failure).

Especially when we are dealing across cultures, we must also remember that issues such as 'face' can be very important. You are rarely forgiven for causing someone

---

107 The Chartered Institute of Arbitrators http://@ www.ciarb.org. [accessed 4 July 2016].

unnecessary embarrassment by publicly airing mistakes or poor judgement. Better to resolve your differences and problems between you behind closed doors and air your cooperation and success publicly.

> To win one hundred victories in one hundred battles is not the height of skill. To subdue the enemy without fighting is true skill.
>
> Sun Tzu, from the *Art of War*

3.24.2 Dealing with anger and other emotions

> You cannot shake hands with a clenched fist.
>
> Indira Ghandi, former Indian Prime Minister

Conflict has two basic types: substantive and emotional. Mostly we are dealing with residual emotional conflict long after the original cause of the conflict has ceased to be significant. We need to deal with strong emotions before attempting to problem solve using logical tools.

In NLP, one underlying principle is to separate out the behaviour from the person and not to take issue with the individual (though it is human nature to do so). It is also very easy for the other party to become the anchor for the issue. Hence, try not to be in the direct line of sight of people experiencing negative emotions. Instead, try to anchor the issue to an inanimate object such as a whiteboard or a piece of paper on the desk and refer to 'how we are going to resolve *this* issue', while pointing to the neutral object.

Should you remain calm in the face of anger and hostility, maybe adopting the demeanour of a Buddhist monk? If you have ever been annoyed enough to have a rant at the 'customer services' of perhaps a utility company, how did it make you feel to be met with a calm and level tone? In NLP terms, they are mismatching you in terms of energy, pace and probably language, and apparently on values and beliefs. If someone is angry with you, then avoid being angry back, but respect their emotion and attempt to match their energy and pace, which will give you much more chance of getting them to tune in to what you are saying. Initially, of course, just let them get it out of their system while checking understanding. What annoys me most is when I feel that my concerns are not being listened to. Once you have listened to them, and they have signalled that they feel that they have been heard, agree to go away and investigate their concerns and make an appointment to come back to discuss 'the issue'. When they come back you may not be able to give them what they need, but most of the emotion should have been dissipated from the situation and you will have a better chance of finding a logical accommodation.

3.24.3 Using the meta-mirror and meta-positions to explore difficult situations

> Everything that irritates us about others can lead us to an understanding of ourselves.
>
> Carl Jung

The meta-mirror technique, developed by Robert Dilts,[108] is based on the assertion that in our subconscious minds we see in others that which we do not like in ourselves. (Perhaps this is why we hear the accusation of hypocrite so often.) Hence, as per one of the presuppositions in NLP, we have all the resources within ourselves to deal with the situation. Personally, I did not relate to this concept during training until I had facilitated a session to deal with a recurring confrontation and figuratively found myself looking back in the mirror. (NLP has a number of techniques for resolving parts of ourselves that are in conflict.)

When one of the founders of NLP, John Grinder, modelled people who were good at negotiations, he found that their core skill was being able to experience situations from several perspectives. It is said that Mahatma Gandhi would sit in the chairs set aside for delegates before important meetings and try to see the world from their perspective, rotating around the seats time and again until he had a good mental model of the overall human system that would play out in the room. Look at Figure 3.64 and try the same in Exercise 3.24.

Figure 3.64 Perceptual positions

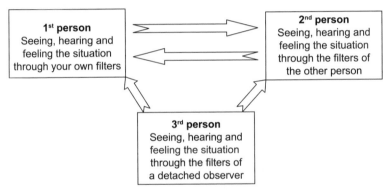

This exercise highlights what is really going on in a situation and helps you to feel differently about the person and situation. It is sometimes referred to as perceptual positions, and was the technique that sold me on NLP 20 years ago when it helped me to resolve repeated conflict with an old boss. I find it best to spatially anchor the positions with chairs set at the appropriate points.

Exercise 3.24 Exploring conflict through meta-positions

1. Think of a situation where you are struggling to build a good relationship or find mutual understanding.

---

108 Robert Dilts, 1990, *Changing Belief Systems with NLP*, Meta Publications.

2. Sit in 1st position and imagine that you are looking across at the other person with whom you are having difficulty (in the 2nd position).

   a. What are you thinking/experiencing/feeling when you see X?

   b. What would you like to say to X?

   c. Say it.

3. Break state by standing up from 1st position and shaking it off.

4. Sit in 2nd position and imagine that you are looking back across to yourself as you were in 1st position.

   a. What are you thinking/experiencing/feeling when you see Y?

   b. How did what they say make you feel?

   c. What would you like to say to Y? Make sure you respond in the first person: 'I ....'.

5. Break state by standing up from 2nd position and shaking it off.

6. Sit in 3rd position so that you have a detached and impartial overview. Looking at yourself in 1st position, how do you now see the person there and the situation? What is really going on?

   a. What would you like to say to yourself?

   b. What would you like to say to X?

   c. Having listened to both sides, what insights do you have that would help to move the situation forward?

7. Break state by standing up from 3rd position and shaking it off.

8. Go back and revisit 2nd position. Ask, 'How is this different now?', 'What's changed?'.

9. Finish by going back to 1st position. Ask, 'How is this different now?', 'What's changed?', 'What's happened for you since the beginning?'

I believe this technique to be life-changing and I measure my own maturity by how often and easily I can jump into second position and lose emotion. Are there any situations where insight from the other person's perspective might help to resolve conflict?

In the house of ignorance there is no mirror in which to view your soul.

Kahlil Gibran

3.24.4 Flexing meta-programs to increase likelihood of agreement

We have seen that NLP describes some people with a meta-program for 'big picture' and others for 'detail'. Neither is right or wrong, but they are more useful in different contexts. In the context of gaining agreement, a 'big picture' approach is much more likely to lead to agreement than a detailed approach. I always coach people not to include anything in a report or proposal that is not necessary, even as an appendix, as it will increase the possibility of someone finding disagreement in some level of detail.

While working in R&D, I was asked to arbitrate in a dispute over which team took control over which laboratory. In short, one project team that had failed to plan properly wished to claim priority and ownership of a laboratory that had been refurbished by a better planned but lower priority project team. Since these were nuclear facilities, the lead time to get a laboratory decommissioned and refurbished to purpose was long, as well as costly, so the stakes were high. Senior people had been brought in to argue their corner. It looked like one of those funny shaped arguments with two sides and no end. It was originally framed as a classic win–lose in game theory; but, if you want to win the game, you have to control the frame.

As insults were already flying, the first thing to do was to try to take the emotion out of the situation. The technique of putting representative bullet points on a flip chart and saying, 'This is the problem that we are trying to solve', while pointing at the board had the effect of starting to move everyone towards solving a common problem. (As these were R&D staff, problem solving was one of their motivating meta-programs.) As everyone was from a research background, however, the predominant meta-program was detail. They were all familiar with work break-down structure, so we were able to chunk up to a common problem of shortage of facilities. With the problem-solving brains of a dozen people with PhDs now engaged in generating options, we were very quickly able to generate a flip chart full of them. About half the room would have been options oriented, with the rest being mainly process oriented. Those process-oriented people were then able to take the lead in putting the options through 'the machine', listing criteria, ranking and rating, and coming up with recommendations.

The preferred solution was one of the options created in the process, which was to do a three-way move, bringing in another lab that required no decommissioning and relatively modest refurbishment. Those with a detailed/specific orientation then happily went away and planned all the component work to make it operational.

Rather than simmering resentment and personal vendettas for years, by chunking up to a bigger picture we were able to align a very creative joint team to imagine options and provide a process for accommodation. Although everyone had to give a little, everyone could see that it was best for the organisation and the process had been fair. As a group we all claimed credit for helping to sort out the department's facilities problems, further cementing us together to make things deliverable.

Which do you think is easiest to gain agreement from: when you are operating from 'sameness' or 'difference'? How could you change that?

3.24.5 Chunking to agreement

Successful joint ventures are said to depend on establishing a superordinate goal that allows both organisations to address a common purpose. In soft systems methodology (SSM) this would be called finding an 'accommodation'.[109]

---

109 P. Checkland and J. Poulter, 2006, *Learning for Action: A Short Definitive Account of Soft Systems Methodology*, Wiley & Sons.

We may disagree on whether we need an IT system, let alone which system, but could chunk up to agree that we need 'a system' (see Figure 3.65). Defining the system and process could then lead to a separate question of 'which is the best option for achieving our agreed requirement?' I have been caught up in arguments over which finance systems to procure, when chunking up would have revealed that the superordinate goal was to improve financial governance, which would actually have been better addressed through clear accountability and training on the existing system, and for a lot less money and disruption.

Figure 3.65 Chunking to common purpose

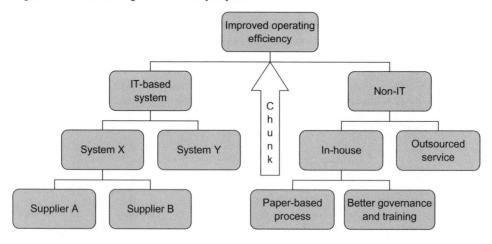

As we have already discussed, people operate on different levels of detail. To move detailed people up the tree, ask the question, 'what would that give you / enable you to do?'. To move big picture people into more specific requirements, ask 'what do you think you might need to enable you to do that?'

3.24.6 Modelling excellent negotiators and end-to-end process

> So much of life is a negotiation – so even if you're not in business, you have opportunities to practice all around you.
>
> Kevin O'Leary, entrepreneur and panellist on
> the Canadian version of *Dragons' Den*

If you are not experienced in negotiation, or not yet confident in it, then you should consider modelling someone who is. Which person is good at resolving conflict or negotiation that you could try to model? What do you think their meta-programs might be? What is going on in their head is more important than the words coming out of their mouths, as they are driven by the former. How can you find out what is going on in their head? (Modelling is covered in Section 3.10.)

As you have read in this section, NLP has a lot to contribute towards finding agreement and resolving conflict. Just to recap on fitting some of these into an overall process:

1. To minimise risk of conflict, have project management processes and tools in place and sorted up-front, especially those around stakeholder management.

2. Be clear of your desired outcome and how you will know when you have achieved it.

3. Be clear on your walk-away position. If you do not have a walk-away position, and are prepared to do so, then you are in a very weak position and relying on bluff or the generosity of the other party. What are your 'deal breakers'? Get them out up-front as it is of no benefit dancing around these.

4. Practise using meta-positions to establish motivation of other parties. Are they motivated by 'towards' opportunity or 'away from' issues? Do you need to 'dangle the carrot' or 'wave the stick'? If you are dealing with a group of people, choose language which appeals to both preferences.

5. Set the frame for what you are doing. What is this discussion about in a longer term context?

6. Anchor resourceful states (such as confidence, enthusiasm, commitment and curiosity) in order to manage your own psychological and emotional state before going into negotiation/persuasion/conflict resolution.

7. Use the techniques that you have started to learn to gain rapport, as without rapport there is likely to be little trust.

8. Separate out your needs from your wants, and be specific in your language.

9. Outline the overview first and then go into the detail afterwards so that you appeal to people with 'big picture' and 'detailed' preferences in order to help them to understand you.

10. Talk less and listen more. Ideally, work in pairs so that someone is always observant, including taking in body language of others in the room.

11. Get good at listening and reading other people's non-verbal communication. Start to recognise when someone really believes what they are saying or whether they are testing your position or being dishonest with themselves.

12. Be prepared to loop through cycles of test, operate and test again before your final exit. Be flexible in your approach rather than trying to force things through by brute force.

13. Use your questioning skills to uncover any deletions, distortions and generalisations, as this will help to ensure that you are both on the same page and that there are no misunderstandings.

14. Reframe situations if there are any obstacles or objections so that the person can look at the situation from a different point of view.

15. Chunk up to a point of agreement before dropping back down to deal with areas of difference one at a time, easiest first.

16. Use metaphors to get your point across on an unconscious level if you meet conscious resistance.

17. Be conscious of your outcome throughout. Summarise after each breakthrough using their language.

18. When you have what you need, be prepared to give a little back as an investment in the relationship.
19. Finish with a conclusion.
20. Celebrate success in resolving conflicts together.
21. Follow up with a thank you email.

Remember, at the end of any negotiation, both parties should leave with a smile on their face rather than play to win the battle and risk losing the war.

3.25 HOW TO BE ASSERTIVE WHILE AVOIDING CONFLICT

> Anyone can become angry – that is easy. But to be angry with the right person, to the right degree, at the right time, for the right purpose, and in the right way – that is not easy.
>
> Aristotle, *The Nicomachean Ethics*

Conflict management is specifically included in the competencies assessed for PMI's Professional in business analysis and also for the 'Expert BA' qualification. Conflict undermines team dynamics, reduces individual performance and causes unnecessary stress. Management of conflict was specifically listed in the review of behavioural competencies for BAs reviewed in Section 1.3.2.

There is a large body of work on assertiveness that I will not reproduce here,[110] but the basic process and skills can be easily covered with an NLP approach. The linguistic part of NLP means that we know how to use precise language, avoid deluding ourselves that we can 'mind read' other people's intent and avoid meta-model distortions such as gross exaggeration. Using these techniques, we can build confidence so that we tackle situations early and head-on by practising assertive behaviours.

3.25.1 Finding the sweet spot between submissive and aggressive behaviour

Submissive behaviour is at first appealing because it seems to avoid conflict. Being submissive, however, usually builds up with bad consequences. Similarly, being aggressive will blow up in your face one day. People who are overtly aggressive can become submissive and compliant after a certain amount of stress. Assert early before you get angry, as anger starts to pass command from the higher brain functions to the primitive brain functions, causing our abilities with language to diminish.

> In my early career, I would become quite aggressive when challenged, though I often felt bad about it afterwards, especially as 'good will' vanished and some tasks became onerous in terms of monitoring and control. After one clash with a newly appointed director, we rightly had our heads banged together by the MD. I licked my

---

110 T. Gillen, 1998, *Assertiveness*, Chartered Institute of Personnel Development.

wounds and bit my tongue in future meetings, which allowed my antagonist to reign free. My resentment built up until I felt like I would explode when we sat in the same meetings. I did not explode, but I was eventually stretchered off-site in an ambulance with a stress-related illness. As I lay on my back in a hospital bed I had time to reflect. Although I was not NLP trained at the time, I found the resources and model that I needed within me. From my martial arts training we had the motto 'the samurai remains outside the battle'. This refers to attaining a state of total unemotional awareness, that is, without anger or fear. From then on I took pride in never losing my temper at work while never backing down from any situation either. I reframed the situation from being some personal conflict to being just a job that I was being paid to do. That approach of letting go helped me to do a much more professional job.

I like the continuum model of assertiveness shown in Figure 3.66.

Figure 3.66 The submissive, assertive, aggressive continuum

| Submissive | Assertive | Aggressive |

- Submissive behaviour is about ensuring everyone else's thoughts/feelings/rights and so on are taken into consideration: 'Don't worry about me.'

- Aggressive behaviour is about ensuring your own thoughts/feelings/rights and so on are taken into consideration: 'Forget everyone else.'

- Assertive behaviour is about ensuring your own and the other person's thoughts, feelings and rights are taken into consideration – part of what NLP considers as the 'ecology' of the situation.

Do you think people consider you as generally submissive or assertive?

3.25.2 Beliefs which can hold us back

We all carry around certain beliefs about appropriate behaviour that limit our repertoire. In some cultures, organisational as well as national assertiveness is frowned upon, especially where rigid hierarchies are in force. Let us tackle a number of general beliefs that many of us carry around with us:

- Despite appearances, none of us likes confrontation. By the time we feel we have no other option, however, we are usually so angry that we overreact and end up regretting it and having to sweep up the damage.

- We do not like to hurt other people's feelings, and we go to great lengths to avoid the possibility of upsetting people.
- We make the assumption that we will not get what we want by asking for it directly. Instead we often assume that we have to be Machiavellian and use subterfuge. In fact, you will get more respect stating expectations clearly up-front.

In terms of beliefs around asserting yourself, these are some that came up in a work-shop with a major consultancy:

- I think I know, but I am not sure.
- It is not my place to say/do that.
- It is above my pay-grade.
- I am not really part of their team.
- I cannot challenge clients.
- I cannot challenge more senior members of staff.
- Someone else will already have thought of this and I will sound ignorant.

If you are carrying around beliefs like these, then it is unlikely that you will assert your-self. Therefore, you can either change these beliefs or you can act 'as if' you are asser-tive by following the models below.

3.25.3 Three-step assertiveness model

Some assertiveness models do not take into account the thoughts and feelings of the other person and border on aggressive behaviour.[111] An NLP model, taking into account the thoughts and feelings of all parties, would be as shown in Figure 3.67.

Think about making a friend, not an enemy, as the only true way to defeat an enemy is to make them your friend. This model needs lots of practice, so try it in everyday life before you try it out on your boss.

3.25.4 Modelling the dos and don'ts of assertive behaviour

Finally, aside from using the models above, in Figure 3.68 I summarise some points to consider in becoming more assertive. Who do you know that you would describe as assertive? What do you think their process might be? Would it hurt to ask them?

Is there a situation where you feel that your boundaries or values have been trans-gressed, that is, where you feel emotion after the event? How can you use the models above to deal with that potential future conflict now and defuse the situation? How much better will you feel when the issue is out in the open and then out of the way? Will you sleep better?

---

111 R. Bolton, 1979, *People Skills*, Touchstone.

Figure 3.67 Three-step assertiveness model

Steps	Personal life example	Work example
Step 1: State behaviour that you have a problem with, ideally expressing some understanding of why they might be doing this. This is about their map of the world.	I know it is Saturday night and you have probably worked hard and want to let off a little steam.	I know you are a top guy and have a lot of calls on your time.
Step 2: State the effect on you. Use the phrase 'this makes me feel...', as no one can argue with how you feel.	But your music keeps my family awake all night and it makes me feel that you do not care about your neighbours.	But when you skip my workshops I feel that you are not committed to the success of this project.
Step 3: Ask for them to consider an alternative behaviour. You might be specific, but I am finding that I do not even have to include this step if I make a good enough job of steps 1 and 2.	Would you mind keeping the noise down after midnight? I will be sure to let you know when we plan to be away so that you can organise your next party.	Will you be able to attend my workshops in the future, or at least send a representative? By the way, I always provide the donuts and coffee, and we always keep the meetings short.

Figure 3.68 Dos and don'ts in assertive behaviour

Do	Do not
• Assert yourself on the real issue, not the symptoms. For example, rather than pick someone up on being late for meetings, if you actually feel someone is not respecting your authority then deal with that. You must, of course, give factual evidence of the behaviour (being late) that causes you to feel that they don't respect you rather than assuming it was their intent.	• Do not let small issues build up into big ones. • Do not try to force your values onto someone else, for example 'It is *wrong* to...' • Do not assume that someone is 'bad' because they do something that doesn't match your values. If you treat the other person with respect you are much likelier to get a positive result with the minimum of defensive behaviour. • Do not assume other people's motives as you are probably not a mind reader and hence are likely to be wrong.

(Continued)

Figure 3.68 (Continued)

Do	Do not
• Separate the behaviour from the person. • Write down what you intend to say and check it. Like most things in projects, it's more difficult to recover from a bad start than to do a bit of preparation. • Pick your place and time. Although you may like an audience, if you cause the other person to lose face then they will not forgive you. Ever. • Use assertive body language, i.e. 　▪ face them square on, but avoid looking aggressive; 　▪ maintain eye contact, but don't try to stare them down; 　▪ breathe from your diaphragm to enable you to speak with a clear voice in mid-tone. • Pick your battles wisely.	• Do not 'wait for the right time'. Arrange it and do it. • Do not use code or 'think' that people got the message – be explicit. • Do not exaggerate (e.g. 'every time'). • Do not use sarcasm, blame or put down – you may feel smart but they will react badly. • Do not hang around afterwards or ask them to go for a drink. Move on. • Do not feel responsible for the other person's reactions. Their reaction is their choice. • Remove aggression from your tone – easier done by tackling things before there is too much pent up emotion.

3.26 ENABLING HIGH PERFORMANCE TEAMS

> Innovation has nothing to do with how many R&D dollars you have. When Apple came up with the Mac, IBM was spending at least 100 times more on R&D. It's not about money. It's about the people you have, how you're led, and how much you get it.
>
> Steve Jobs

Change is delivered through teams rather than by individuals and we need to continuously refine our team-building skills. Teamworking was specifically listed under behavioural competencies for BAs reviewed in Section 1.4. I will not write extensively on leading high performance teams here, as that is a follow-on book in its own right. I do, however, want to bring out a few aspects that have achieved great results in practical workshops and coaching.

3.26.1 Use group coaching to address the common dysfunctions of a team

> You've got a goal; I've got a goal. Now all we need is a football team.
>
> Groucho Marks

It is often said that you cannot teach new behaviours in a classroom. That is not to say that new behaviours cannot be adopted through new experiences in a group environment. Ketts de Vries from INSEAD business school has effectively demonstrated that high performing teams are best facilitated through group coaching rather than one-on-one coaching.[112] Why do you think that might be?

During our in-house workshops, we progress from a standard format where we share information with a group and get them doing exercises, through a facilitation approach where we get the delegates doing most of the work, through to a group coaching approach where we really start to achieve results.

We do not start with group coaching as it does not work until people are comfortable sharing ambitions, strengths and weaknesses with their peers. Bearing in mind that the peer group they are sitting with might be competing for promotion, it is natural to be cautious. While gradually getting people to work together and reveal more about themselves, and seeing the progress that they have made as individuals and a group, trust gradually builds. When you feel that the group has developed sufficiently, and tested it by asking whether to move on to a group coaching, you can start to address, or rather get them to address, the common dysfunctions that limit team performance.

When I ask people who have worked in high performance teams what it feels like, they say things like: energising, exciting, empowering, trusting, provides personal growth, commitment, fulfilling, ambitious, creative and, of course, fun. Most managers want to work with teams like that as they are at the same time very productive.

Hopefully, you are working as part of a high performance team now. Unfortunately, most of us do not most of the time. Why is that? If you picked the most expensive players and told them to turn up for a game the next day without any team-building, how do you think they would perform?

Do you want a group of superstars or a high performance team?

I saw the, then third division, football team MK Dons beat Manchester United 7–0, when United fielded seven players fresh from the 2014 World Cup months before. MK's under-21 striker even managed to put three past them. How did that happen? New season, new manager, and individuals did not play as a team while the opposition found the gaps between them. At the end of that season the Dons finally moved up to the next division after years of trying. Do you think that startling win in the first game of the season might have affected their beliefs?

---

112 Manfred F.R. Ketts de Vries, 2005, 'Leadership Group Coaching in Action: The Zen of Creating High Performance Teams', *Academy of Management Executive*, 19(1).

Exercise 3.25 Addressing common team dysfunctions

The table in Figure 3.69 illustrates the common dysfunctions that limit team perfor-mance.[113] Do you recognise any of them in the teams with which you are working now or in the past?

Against each dysfunction, think of ways that you could improve the situation.

The best way to approach this with a team is to get them to work in smaller groups to come up with their own ideas of how they can improve their own team.

Be sure to get people to write down what *they* can do rather than what they want someone else to do. That way things might happen, especially if they make a com-mitment to do it in front of the rest of the team. Peer pressure is a very powerful force in society.

Alternatively, you can start with a clean sheet of paper and get them to brainstorm anything that would enable them to move to the next level.

Figure 3.69 Addressing common team dysfunctions

Common team dysfunction	What can <u>you</u> do about it?
Absence of trust – unwilling to be vulnerable within the group	
Fear of conflict – seeking artificial harmony over constructive passionate debate	
Lack of commitment – feigning buy-in for group decisions creates ambiguity throughout the organisation	
Avoidance of accountability – ducking the responsibility to call peers on counter-productive behaviour that sets low standards	
Inattention to results – focusing on personal success, status and ego before team success	

How can you follow up on the actions you write down?

---

113 Patrick Lencioni, 2002, *The Five Dysfunctions of a Team: A Leadership Fable*, John Wiley & Sons.

3.26.2 Using NLP to motivate the team

Individual commitment to a group effort – that is what makes a team work, a company work, a society work, a civilization work.

Vince Lombardi, American football player and coach

NLP has a lot to offer in terms of motivating high performing teams. When the allied forces were mustering for the push into Kuwait and Iraq during the first Gulf War in 1990, the commander of allied forces General 'Storming Norman' Schwarzkopf – a physically imposing man in his own right – called on NLP guru Anthony Robbins to deliver a motivational speech to the Special Forces who would be the first to go into hostile territory.

What motivates you? Most of us learned about the carrot and stick approach of rewarding or punishing behaviour, and unfortunately this is ingrained into our working culture of reward and discipline. Does that motivate you? Studies have repeatedly shown that, for anything other than simple manual tasks, neither carrot nor stick are effective in improving performance. Excessive rewards have even been shown to be counter-productive; history will judge whether the mega-bonuses of the 'Masters of the Universe' during the banking crisis of 2008 were a factor. What has been found to motivate professionals is:[114]

1. Purpose – mapping our identity on to a superordinate goal. You could use the chunking exercise for this.
2. Autonomy – being given the freedom to decide what you do and when to maximise your own performance. You could use the group coaching approach to facilitate this.
3. Mastery – being given the opportunity to develop yourself to become even better at what you do.

Would these motivate you? How can you give your team members even more of this? Maybe ask them if that is what they want and how it can be facilitated.

In projects there is a lot of focus on getting things done. One camp seems to be focused on doing this through task and process, while another advocates an approach of relationship management. This reflects the NLP meta-program for working organisation. A majority naturally focus on task or object, while less than 20 per cent naturally pay attention to feelings and thoughts of themselves and others. About a third sit somewhere between. Of course, that is for the general population. Do you think business analysis might filter people towards one bias?

For people-oriented people, they are likely to have a preference for stakeholder management plans and communication plans, though they might not actually like the process of creating them! If you are trying to motivate a people-oriented person then do not over-emphasise the task aspects, but rather the interactions.

---

114 Daniel H. Pink, 2011, *Drive: The Surprising Truth About What Motivates Us*, Canongate Books.

For task-oriented people, just give them the goal and let them go, but not before you have got them to acknowledge the other people that they should speak to about it and keep informed as otherwise they may forget, as it will not be their focus. For task-oriented people, RACI charts are a very useful process tool for them to follow, clearly articulating for each activity who:

- is **R**esponsible for actually doing it;
- is **A**ccountable for the results;
- needs to be **C**onsulted;
- should be **I**nformed.

As we rarely have the pleasure of getting to know groups before training starts, during NLP trainer training we are taught the SNOGA model to help pace both ends of the five main motivational meta-programs:

- **S**elf (internal frame of reference) – other (external frame);
- **N**ew (different) – build (same);
- **O**ptions – procedures;
- **G**oals (towards) – problems (away);
- **A**ctive – reflective.

Politicians use this same approach in election speeches. A generic introduction to a group coaching session might go something like this:

> This is going to be an active experience and there will be some time to sit and reflect.
>
> I hope there will be new things, and things to build on your present expertise. It will help you to achieve goals and solve issues.
>
> You will get an idea in yourself of why you do what you do, as well as feedback from others. As well as giving you some processes and procedures that will enable you to do things more easily and confidently, after the program you will have more choices in how you do things.

Use SNOGA to check whether key communications are biased only to a few of your stakeholders.

3.26.3 Working style – we all want to be in teams, right?

> The achievements of an organization are the results of the combined effort of each individual.
>
> Vince Lombardi

From most vacancy notices it would appear that, according to the preferences of the HR department, we should all aim to be team players. In a working environment, however, only about 20 per cent prefer to work as a cooperative team and have shared responsibility, according to the studies by Rodger Bailey.[115] A similar proportion want to have clear accountability and work independently. The majority prefer proximity – clear responsibility but have others involved. Hence, most people prefer well-defined responsibilities to be productive and stay motivated, and if accountability is not clear then most people will become disengaged. How would individuals in your team score on this meta-program?

> A long time ago, I captained the university's weightlifting team as reigning champions at the national championships on home soil. Loughborough, probably the best sporting college in England, fielded an Olympic medal winning athlete, but dropped him from their three-man team. When I asked the captain why, he simply replied, 'He is not a team player.'

Despite what was a financial drive into open plan offices, most people are not extroverts needing constant company either. In her hugely successful book on the power of introverts,[116] Susan Cain points out that practically all the great inventions in our history were created by introverts. She also points out that open plan offices can be a version of hell to the introverts who might otherwise be driving innovation. Look out for her TED talk to watch a deep introvert modelling public speaking.[117] What working arrangements would help you to get the most out of your team?

3.26.4 Using Team Charters to identify common values and behaviours

> The culture of any organization is shaped by the worst behaviour the leader is willing to tolerate.
>
> Gruenter and Whitaker[118]

A project kick-off meeting helps to engender identity, and many large projects have 'away days' to start to normalise behaviours. Where practical, co-location of the core team is invaluable in creating identity, especially when resources report to different functional departments, or even different organisations. Although there will be some natural norming of behaviour where there is co-location, it is best to explicitly agree some expectations with the team. I use the format in Figure 3.70 to facilitate and capture a team charter.

What are the values and behaviours of the team that you would like to be part of? Add them to the list. Rather than draft or impose these, you should facilitate the co-creation of these so that the team has maximum ownership. Only what gets enforced are the actual values and beliefs of the lead team.

---

115 Rodger Bailey, cited in S. R. Charvet, 1995, *Words That Change Minds: Mastering the Language of Influence*, Kendall Hunt.
116 Susan Cain, 2012, *Quiet: The Power of Introverts in a World that Can't Stop Talking*, Penguin.
117 http://www.ted.com/talks/susan_cain_the_power_of_introverts [accessed 13 July 2016].
118 ITIL from Experience: How to deal with a team member that disrupt project meetings http://www.itilfromexperience.com/
How+to+deal+with+a+team+member+that+disrupt+project+meetings [accessed 13 July 2016].

Figure 3.70 Team charter for values and behaviours in high performing projects

Team values	Team behaviours
<ul><li>We are a high performance team.</li><li>We achieve our goals.</li><li>We deliver value to the business.</li><li>We are true to our word.</li><li>Under promise, over deliver.</li><li>etc.</li></ul>	<ul><li>We will turn up on time for team meetings.</li><li>We will submit reports on time with no chasing.</li><li>We will meet our commitments, or ask for help if we meet challenges.</li><li>We will notify our fellow team members of changes via the project plan and change log.</li><li>etc.</li></ul>

3.27 BAS AND PMS WORK BETTER TOGETHER

> In the long history of humankind (and animal kind, too) those who learned to collaborate and improvise most effectively have prevailed.
>
> Charles Darwin

I still see major change programs being run as projects, with scope documents and milestones driving activities, with scant regard to whether or not we are making progress to a defined end state and stated benefits. A competent BA is essential to keep any change program focused on strategic objectives. Figure 3.71 indicates key activities. Does your organisation work this way?

Figure 3.71 Complementary activities of the business change manager and program manager

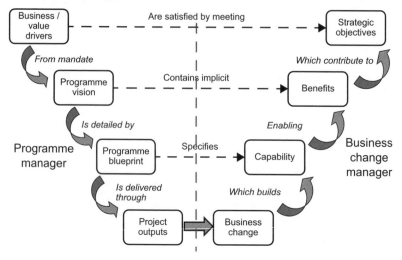

3.27.1 'The dynamic duo'

> If everyone is moving forward together, then success takes care of itself.
> Henry Ford

Perhaps catalysed by the PMI introducing a business analysis qualification, there has been a spate of papers, conference presentations and training courses aimed at helping the BA and PM appreciate how they can behave in a more complementary way rather than, as sometimes happens, a conflicting way. Not being a shrinking violet when it comes to marketing, I have also contributed to this genre, including a talk on 'working better together' at the first collaborative event in the UK between the IIBA and the PMI, of which I am a member of both. Figure 3.72 provides another perspective on how the two interact, though here it infers only to starting and finishing together, rather than ongoing coordination as in Figure 3.71.

Figure 3.72 'The dynamic duo' (adapted from Maritato 2012)[119]

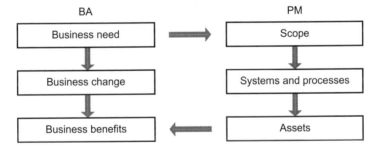

3.27.2 Sharing perspectives on the solution

> You have to get along with people, but you also have to recognize that the strength of a team is different people with different perspectives and different personalities.
> Steve Case

I expect that we will have professional respect for each other's contribution. We have complementary roles, and we are working on the same project in the same context, so we must have similar world-views, right? By now you understand that we all have unique views, and the role in which we carry them out is one factor that filters and shapes our view.

---

119 Michele Maritato, 2012, 'Project Management and Business Analysis: The Dynamic Duo', Proceedings of PMI EMEA Congress, 7–9 May, Marseilles, France http://marketplace.pmi.org/Pages/ProductDetail.aspx?GMProduct=00101371701 [accessed 23 June 2016]. http://www.pmi.org/learning/partnership-project-managers-business-analysts-9865 [accessed 23 June 2016].

You also understand that rapport is achieved by appreciating the other person's world-view and speaking to that. To realise the full potential of each partner's acumen, and the foundation of any lasting partnership for that matter, we need to understand our partner's perspective. We have explored different perspectives in public talks, and come up with the list in Figure 3.73.

What is your perspective? How do these views compare to yours? How are they different? What can you do to explore and understand each other's perspectives so that you are better able to help each other to succeed? Try Exercise 3.26 to better understand where your own biases lie.

Figure 3.73 Exploring and sharing perspectives

BA	PM
• I want to understand business drivers and needs	• I want a definite scope that I can deliver cleanly and I want it signed off early
• I need time to get scope and requirements defined and agreed	• I want to deliver cleanly in phases, like building a house from the foundations up, and prefer to use a waterfall method
• I want to gain many stakeholder perspectives	• I do not want anyone else talking to senior stakeholders and setting expectations
• I want to be more agile as business needs evolve	• I want any additional functionality to be deferred to next release
• I want to model requirements in the right way	• I want to plan activities in an efficient way
• I want to focus on what value is being created	• I want any changes to be paid for
• If things are not working, then I want to change them until they do	• I want a short, clean acceptance
• I want to focus on behaviours	• I want to focus on and measure activities
• I expect to have iteration until benefits are realised	• I do not want to do any re-work

---

Exercise 3.26 Where do 'generic' BA and program manager biases lie?
By this stage of the book, you will have come across many aspects of the different meta-programs. In the table at Figure 3.74, quickly score where you think that the two roles might naturally fall in a generic program of change. Score a low mark if more like the left column and high score if more like the right column.

Do they look more similar or different? That probably depends more on whether you naturally score as a matcher or a mis-matcher. How do you think a PM might score the two roles, the same or differently? Review your initial scores from your personal assessment in Exercise 3.2. Where do you fit in relation to the two roles? Are you an agile team, and would you be able to flex your behaviours in the partnership too in order to achieve more together?

Figure 3.74 Where do 'generic' change manager and program manager biases lie?

	Bias BA score PM		
Option			Procedure
Person			Task
Specific			Big picture
Collaborative			Accountable
Towards opportunities			Away from problems
Externally referenced			Internally referenced
Match			Mismatch
Associated with feelings			Dissociated
In time			Through time
Extrovert			Introvert
Difference			Sameness
Pro-active			Reactive
Cooperative			Independent

3.27.3 Having a mindset towards collaboration and creating a superordinate goal together

Having discussed this topic with many colleagues over the last couple of years while working on this book, we came to the conclusion that projects and partnerships work best where there is a mindset for collaboration, and the contextual system at least lets that happen, if not directly supporting it. Is your working style biased towards collaboration?

Looking back to Dilt's neurological levels for rapport (Figure 2.9), at the top of the pyramid to optimise our changes towards success, we should quickly establish a superordinate goal and a common identity and brand. This should be no surprise, as they underpin any successful commercial partnership or joint venture. Are you both in the same boat? Do you wear the same team T-shirts, or are you in team BA and team PM? Are you rowing together to the same destination? Are you 'better together'? If not, what are you going to do about it tomorrow? Would you benefit from having that discussion, perhaps as part of the team charter exercise?

3.28 SETTING GOALS AND ACHIEVING WELL-FORMED OUTCOMES

> A dream becomes a goal when action is taken toward its achievement.
> Bo Bennett, businessman and author

To effect any change, whether it be personal effectiveness, change in others or organisational change, we need to be targeting the desired outcome rather than subordinate activities. This is consistent with a programmatic approach to delivery and focus on outcomes and realisation of business benefits rather than activities. As you read in Section 2.3 on fundamentals of NLP, focus on outcomes is one of the pillars of NLP, and several techniques have been modelled to help achieve your goals.

3.28.1 Which beliefs and values motivate you?

> Happiness is that state of consciousness which proceeds from the achievement of one's values.
> Ayn Rand, author and philosopher

People who have a strong sense of what is important to them, those in tune with their values, usually have a real sense of purpose which helps to propel them towards their goals. The things that you *want* to do, rather than feel you *have* to do, will be aligned to your values. Of course, there are some things that are imposed on us, and these may conflict with our inner nature and could result in some internal sabotage, or at least a lack of enthusiasm. If this is often the case, then why keep swimming against the current rather than finding your own flow?

Exercise 3.27 Values elicitation
What is important to you in work? Do not write down the things that you put on your CV or say at interview just because you think that it is what people want to hear in order to give you the job. What do you *really* like doing?

1. Just jot them down for now.
2. What aspects of work don't you like?
3. Again, just jot them down.

4. Is there anything that would help to make these things that you don't like more palatable?

5. Jot them down too.

6. Now write each one on a sticky note and start to put them in order of preference, with most desirable at the top and least liked at the bottom, or left to right if you prefer. Here are some examples:

   - challenge;
   - recognition;
   - working with a team;
   - telling people what to do;
   - working with data;
   - solving problems;
   - managing a budget;
   - writing reports;
   - working with customers;
   - working with stakeholders;
   - coaching;
   - planning;
   - variety;
   - working up a business case;
   - negotiating;
   - working with suppliers;
   - developing specifications;
   - writing reports;
   - being home by 6pm.

7. How does this list measure up to what you are currently doing?

8. Do you know anyone who likes the things that you don't?

9. How could you do more of what motivates you and delegate more of the things that you don't like?

10. Ask people what it is that they like about the things that you do not like. (Hint: they probably have a different view of the world and different values.)

3.28.2 Do you prefer sameness or difference?

The meta-program for 'sameness or difference' will have a large influence on your own career path and goals. Only about five per cent truly prefer sameness, but of course you will meet five in a hundred on your next change project. At the other end of the spectrum, about 20 per cent like out-and-out difference – change for change sake. These are easy to get on board, but as soon as you have implemented your change they will want to keep changing it. Some of these kinds of people ran R&D in the nuclear sector in the early days, resulting in only two of the nuclear reactors in the UK being the same design, the rest all requiring different fuel production lines, and so on, at great expense. Incidentally, the only two that were the same were under the Ministry of Defence – quite a conservative bunch in comparison. Most people are in the middle and like same-with-difference or difference-with-same. Some people are comfortable doing the same kind of assignment over and over again, while others like to take on new roles, new sectors and new industries. What about you?

3.28.3 Stating goals as outcomes

For those working in change management, and particularly those working to frameworks such as Managing Successful Programs (MSP),[120] the term 'outcome' will probably have replaced the more popular 'deliverable' from the project management lexicon. The focus moves from building the asset, for example a school, to creating a capability, for example a teaching environment, all the way through to full alignment of goals with the operational outcome of 'well educated children'. Start with the outcome in mind and work backwards.

Exercise 3.28 Achieving well-formed outcomes

1. Think of an outcome that you would like to achieve.
2. State the outcome in the positive. 'Don't think of an elephant' does not work, as the subconscious brain does not process negatives. For example, rather than 'stop smoking', think of something that you want to start, for example 'start being fit and healthy'.
3. Scale the challenge. As you learned in the section on 'know yourself', some of us have a meta-program for big picture, while some are into the detail. You need to chunk up or down until you get some something that is meaningful to you. Like any project, you may want to break a big change down into a number of smaller ones and deal with them in turn. After all, even the great pyramids were built one stone at a time.
4. Be specific. What is it exactly that you want to change, and how? When you have it what will it give you? How will that make your life better?
5. Evidence – how will you know when you have it? Would others be able to tell, and if so, how?

---

120 Office of Government Commerce (OGC), 2007, *Managing Successful Programs*, TSO.

6. Is the outcome congruent with your beliefs? Do you believe that it is possible? Do you believe that you are able? If not, go back to the start (or consider the NLP belief change techniques). Do you think that you deserve it? Many people are thought to 'self-sabotage' because they have some inner conflict and a part of them that believes that they do not deserve to be successful/rich/ happy/loved and so on.

7. Is the desired outcome largely within your control? If not, think of something that you can bring under your control.

8. Resources – is it worth it? What is the opportunity cost, that is, what could you do with your time and effort instead?

9. Ecology – what might be the impact on self and others? Are we happy to give up watching football to make time to get that qualification? What effect might those extra hours have on your family? Is it who you are and congruent with your beliefs, or are you just doing what other people tell you that you should be doing? If so, do not worry, you will probably fail along the way. On the other hand, you may succeed and be unhappy.

10. Action – make a realistic plan. Pay particular attention to the first step – what, when, how. Now just do it!

The journey of a thousand miles begins with one step.

Lao Tzu

When you set your goals, reflect on the full picture and balance those of work and play. Personally, I am successful in achieving professional outcomes, but have not yet mastered the art of devoting equal resources to relaxation.

Now repeat this exercise by coaching someone else, for example one of your team, to achieve a goal. As many of you will have found, going through the process of coaching someone forces you to truly understand a topic.

3.29 MANAGING OURSELVES

Anyone can become angry – that is easy ... but to be angry with the right person, to the right degree, at the right time, for the right purpose, and in the right way – that is not easy.

Aristotle, The Nicomachean Ethics

Self-management was listed in the review of behavioural competencies in Section 1.5, particularly in the skill set required for Change Management Practitioner, and forms a whole quadrant of the standard EI framework. It is defined under EI as, 'the ability to remain in control despite our emotional state'. In the world of NLP we prefer to refer to it as 'the ability to control our emotions so that they do not control us'. The difference is that in NLP we choose to change our state once we have become aware of it being detrimental to desired outcome, rather than trying to control anger.

3.29.1 Help, I have been emotionally hijacked

We live in a space between different, and often conflicting, world-views and people who sometimes press our 'hot buttons'/emotional triggers. Have you ever sent an email response in anger, or had a heated argument in public, only to regret it on the way home? Were you emotionally hijacked; the victim of your own emotional state?

When we are stressed we tend to be overly pessimistic and risk averse, but when we are euphoric we can also make poor decisions by disregarding risk. How great would it be to be able to control our emotions so that they do not control us?

Our emotions, and hence our actions, are largely determined by the frame we put around an event. To control your emotions, constantly practice the reframing exercises demonstrated in Section 3.23.

I was employed as program director for an IT-enabled transformation project in an organisation that was going through turmoil after a scathing audit report. Most of the organisation's leadership had been removed and the posts being refilled. Morale was as low as I have seen in an organisation. To cap it all, the head of IT had been suspended for bullying, and the impact was obvious on the behaviour of the staff, who were reacting from a place of fear and anger rather than logic. I was asked to take charge of the IT function as the deputies were seen as 'uncooperative' with the new management. Fortunately, I had been offering some out of hours counselling to individuals in the organisation and, after one of the deputies (X) had another brutal run-in with the new director, I managed to persuade him to take some coaching. When we ran through the standard approach of asking, 'Is your behaviour having the desired effect, or would you like to start doing something that does?' we got some movement. The angry reactions, rather than protecting his department, were actually putting it in peril of being downsized and outsourced. His retort of, 'It's all right for you, you do not get angry' was met with my response of 'I can show you anger if you want, but only in a situation where it gets results.' We then explored behaviours that were supportive of his desired outcome of protecting the department and its services, and at the same time, his job. We used some of the techniques described in the next section. At the same time, I spoke to his director, saying that I was doing some counselling with X and he would now start to see some fundamental changes in his behaviour, including more cooperation. (You may recognise this as being a suggestion.)

At future meetings X would smile as he thought about nice things and, rather than argue with the director, would reply with remarks such as: 'Thank you for pointing that out. Good point. We will have a look at that and get a short report back to you before our next meeting.' A virtuous circle ensued, with lack of anger enabling a more cooperative relationship. X kept his job, the director got his results and I got satisfaction from seeing someone being in control of themselves rather than reacting from primordial reflex. No one wants to follow a leader who is not in control of themselves. Isn't it good to be able to choose?

> Don't panic.
>
> Douglas Adams, author of *The Hitchhiker's Guide to the Galaxy*[121]

3.29.2 Practice in choosing resourceful states

> In theory there is no difference between theory and practice. In practice there is.
>
> Yogi Berra

Sometimes, we go through days 'too busy' or too numb to be in tune with our own emotions. Fortunately, emotions have a physical manifestation in our bodies that can help us to recognise those emotions in ourselves and others. The key to successful interaction with others is to become more aware of the state you are in and take the opportunity to choose a more resourceful state (see Figure 3.75). You will make good choices and decisions when you are in a resourceful state (confident, for example), but more likely to make poor choices and decisions when you are in an un-resourceful state (angry, upset, irritated, frustrated, fearful, depressed, for example). A resourceful state is not the same as being dissociated, though that is another useful tool if not overdone.

Figure 3.75 Being in control is about choice, not power

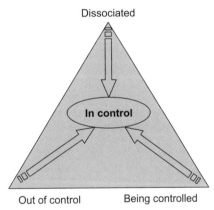

Exercise 3.29 demonstrates the principle of our mood manifesting itself in our physiology.

---

121 Douglas Adams, D. 1995, *The Hitchhiker's Guide to the Galaxy: A Trilogy in Five Parts*, William Heinemann.

Exercise 3.29 Manifesting resourceful physiology

1. Remember a sad time from recent events that you can associate with. Can you feel it as if it were happening now?

2. Accentuate the physiology. Stoop your shoulders more. Crumple your chest. Let your mouth curl down more. Let your head drop down until your chin touches your chest. Sink into your seat. How sad does that feel?

3. Now try to remember a happy recent event, but try to keep the same physiology. Go on, keep trying.

4. What happened? Did you manage to feel happy? If so, you would have had to have changed your physiology. Hence, to manage your state, manage your physiology first.

5. Now try the opposite experience, that is, imagine a happy time. What is the physiology you need to accentuate for Step 2? Remember it (or even anchor it, as described in Section 2.13). Practise it often, especially when you are feeling as you did here, but do not want to any more.

If you prefer, you can come at this from a more orthodox psychological approach. At a TED talk given in 2012, Amy Cuddy presented dramatic results of adopting 'power physiology'[122] on performance. Basically, you model the physiology of a 'winner'; stand tall, head held high, arms in the air, smile on your face, rocking on the balls of your feet. In subsequent debate, there was a view that these were artificial 'parlour tricks'. If we practise these behaviours repeatedly, however, they become innate. I want to show up as the best version of myself that I can and am happy to adopt and practise any technique that helps me to do so more of the time.

Our bodies change our minds, and our minds can change our behaviour, and our behaviour can change our outcomes.

Amy Cuddy

The following exercise proves popular on training courses, especially when people have a particular situation that they are worried about and want to rehearse it in a resourceful state.

Exercise 3.30 The circle of excellence
In this exercise we are going to be using an NLP technique known as 'The circle of excellence'. It will use sub-modalities (Section 2.12), anchors (Section 2.13) and future pacing (Section 2.16).

1. Identify what would be a useful resource as the opposite to your particular un-resourceful state (for example, if you tend to react angrily to a supplier, you might want the feeling of calm).

---

122 Amy Cuddy, 2012, 'Your Body Language Shapes Who You Are', TEDGlobal http://www.ted.com/talks/amy_cuddy_your_body_language_shapes_who_you_are [accessed 13 July 2016].

2. Imagine a spot in front of you or put a marker down such as a piece of coloured paper.

   a. Think about a time when you have had this desired resource (e.g. calm, confident).

   b. When you feel really associated into that feeling, anchor yourself by squeezing together your thumb and forefinger (for example).

   c. Step onto that spot and fully experience the emotional state for a few seconds.

3. Step out of the spot.

4. Repeat the process to add any other resource states that might be useful to manage your state. Access the resourceful state, anchor it in exactly the same way, step onto the spot each time. Fully experience it, then step out of it. Repeat with as many resourceful states as you can think of.

5. Finally, imagine a situation in the future where you might need to manage your state, then access the resourceful state. Fire your anchor as you step into the situation and notice what happens. Your state will shift. This step is known as future pacing, that is, imagining some future event and putting it to an imaginary test. You are now equipped with an anchor that you can use any time, any place, to help you manage your state from an un-resourceful one into a more resourceful one.

Any time that you think that it would be useful to have those resources, fire your anchor; for example, by squeezing your thumb and finger together if that is what you used. The more you practise using it, the stronger the anchor and the trigger will become. It can also kick start a positive/empowering belief cycle.

3.30 HANDLING STRESS AND BUILDING RESILIENCE

Sometimes life hits you in the head with a brick. Don't lose faith.

Steve Jobs, Zen Buddhist

Managing stress and building resilience were not specifically mentioned in competencies for BAs, but they do form an essential part of self-management and this topic has proven the most popular for my one-day master classes.[123]

There is a strong correlation between mental toughness, or resilience, and management seniority. The good news is that NLP can help you to remove stress at the source rather than trying to develop a thick skin, though it can help you to do that too. Indeed, there are popular authors on NLP with whole books on the subject of stress management.[124]

---

123 APM, 2012, 'Building Resilience and Managing Stress: How to Achieve More and Bend Less' http://www.apm.org.uk/news/building-resilience-and-managing-stress-how-achieve-more-and-bend-less [accessed 13 July 2016].

124 For example, P. McKenna, 2009, *Control Stress*, Bantam Press.

Sometimes, to get the job done, we work too hard, pushing our engine past the red line. For short bursts of speed, this is OK and sometimes necessary. Over long periods of time, however, it is detrimental to our wellbeing, and often to those around us. As others will be taking a lead from our behaviour, it also leads to dysfunctional behaviours across the team. Over a long period, it becomes counter-productive because our performance deteriorates. It is our duty to turn up, in life as well as work, appropriately rested and with a clear head. This means that we need to set aside time for family and friends, hobbies and interests, holidays and relaxation. It is also extremely beneficial to build a contemplative activity akin to meditation into our daily routines to help clear our mind of 'dwelling' and other negative thoughts that affect our performance.[125]

3.30.1 About stress, triggers and effects

In small doses, stress provides a useful stimulus. Stress is a natural response built in humans as a 'fight or flight' response to danger. In today's society we often involuntarily invoke this 'fight or flight' mode in response to social situations. More correctly, it is a 'freeze, flight or fight' response, and like rabbits in the headlights, quite often our response to stress is neither to fight or flee, but to remain inactive and stuck in the situation.

The problem is that, unlike the historic dangers that the response evolved to meet, these social situations can be prolonged and ongoing. The result can be chronic stress, which results in strain, that is, where we do not return to our original state after prolonged and cumulative stimulus. This is sometimes referred to as burn-out.

Long before burn-out occurs, primitive responses triggered by stress hormones result in many decisions being routed to the primordial part of our brain, rather than the higher functions more suited to social interaction. It focuses our senses on a single issue facing us, to the detriment of wider social interactions.

3.30.2 Working stress response

NLP regards response to stress as a meta-program. People with a 'feeling' pattern respond to stress at work by going into their emotions and then getting stuck there, making it difficult for them to function normally. At the opposite extreme, people with a 'thinking' style do not have a strong emotional response to stressful situations. Great for leadership, you may think, but unfortunately this means that they are not good at empathising either. These two extremes account for perhaps a fifth of the working population each, with the majority being in the continuum between and having some natural ability to choose whether to empathise or stay detached. Note the similarity to the feeling/thinking category in Myers–Briggs Type Indicators.

3.30.3 Reframing stressful situations

> How much pain have they cost us, the evils which have never happened.
>
> Thomas Jefferson

---

125 Stephan Bodian with Dean Ornish, 2012, *Meditation for Dummies*, John Wiley & Sons.

The good news is that stress is triggered by the thought of a situation, not by the situation itself. The brain processes these thoughts, equates the stimulus and context as danger, and triggers the stress response. Once the threat passes, you tell yourself that you are safe, and in response to these new thoughts your body returns to its natural state of balance. We can use NLP to reframe the context so that we avoid triggering stress. At the same time, we can choose to manage our state as practised in Exercise 3.28.

One of the most stressful constraints is time, especially when faced with complex interdependencies. Not only can we not control time, but people also have different attitudes to time, with only a few focusing on 'the now' and most living in the past or the future. But can we reframe time? Well, we can reframe our attitude to it. I used to think of time on a project as being like an egg timer, filled with sand that was running out. When a precious resource is 'running out' it is bound to cause stress. But time will never run out – it is abundant and infinite. Refresh yourself on the process of being 'in time', practised in Section 3.7.2.

In planning we are only dealing with an abstract mathematical summation of third-party estimates based on imperfect data. By the law of averages, the estimate should be under as many times as it is over, and that is making the unlikely assumption that the plan does not suffer from the well-established phenomenon of optimism bias.[126] What we can do is track progress against assumptions, monitor risks which may affect planned duration, and address mitigating actions for issues that are impacting the plan. I have yet to see anyone getting stressed over a risk log, but maybe I have not seen enough projects yet. Do not mistake this for meaning that I think that time is unimportant, just that stressing about it does not lead to a resourceful state, and reviewing risk and issues logs is likely to be more beneficial to the completion date than looking at a stopwatch.

3.30.4 Removing the source of stress

> If you are distressed by anything external, the pain is not due to the thing itself, but your estimate of it; and this is your power to revoke at any moment.
>
> Marcus Aurelius

In NLP we say that every action, emotion and behaviour has a positive intent, no matter how bad the actual consequence.

In my early career I would sometimes get stressed about project boards to the point where I felt unwell. When I 'had a chat with myself', I realised that I was coming from a place of fear as I was not in control of the board and disliked surprises. I recognised that this feeling had started after I had been 'ambushed' at one board by someone with a hidden agenda. Instead of gritting my teeth and continuing as I had done, I started to visit key stakeholders ahead of board meetings to see what issues might come up and get their views on them. As a civil servant at this time, it was not usual to arrange

---

126 B. Flyvbjerg, 2003, *Megaprojects and Risk: An Anatomy of Ambition*, Cambridge University Press.

meetings with people who were senior to you unless it was via your line manager. Individuals turned out to be quite welcoming of chats outside the floodlights, and said things that they would not have at meetings where notes were taken. This gave me the confidence to relax more at the actual project boards and operate from a state of resourcefulness. Fortunately, it got me into the excellent practice of active stakeholder management, which was not widespread at that time.

A room full of people is a room full of different perspectives and motivations, hearing and seeing different things through the filters of their own experiences, values, beliefs and behavioural meta-programs. Better to explore those perspectives one on one where practical so that you can understand the positive intent of their comments and actions. You will find that it all makes perfect sense when you stand on their map of the world.

If you are feeling stressed, then there is a positive intent within you. Is it trying to protect you from something? As in the example above, what other strategies might there be to protect you from this perceived risk so that you can adopt an alternative strategy to stress and avoidance?

Exercise 3.31 Look for the positive intent of the emotion

1. Think about the thing that you are feeling stressed about. Close your eyes and associate with the feeling.
2. What are the feelings, sounds and images attached to this stress response?
3. Ask yourself: What is the positive intention of this worry? What does it give me?
4. Notice what answers come to mind and keep asking this question until you have at least three. You may be surprised at some of the answers.
5. Now, ask the creative part of your brain to come up with at least three new ways of achieving the same positive intent as your stressful behaviour.
6. Check with yourself that you are happy with these new ways to avoid stress.
7. Visualise how it will feel to do those new behaviours instead of stressing out in the future.
8. Keep doing this until it feels like a natural response.

3.30.5 Use of dissociation to avoid stress

One of the recognised NLP meta-programs is association/dissociation. When associated, we are in touch with our feelings and this is a very resourceful state for working with people. It is also the state most sensitive to stress. Conversely, the dissociated state is useful in potentially stressful situations. The real skill is being able to switch between the two according to context.

Sometimes, we can become dissociated from our feelings. For one reason or another, some people can remain in a dissociated state (see Figure 3.76). They are not particularly happy or sad, but just go about their allocated tasks much like an automaton. Often it is the result of some trauma or depressing event in the past, but it can become a way of life. People in this state are easy to spot for NLP practitioners as their eye movements are very limited and they often adopt a slightly off-centre, out of focus look into the middle distance, making it almost impossible to determine visual sensory information and cues from their body language.

Figure 3.76 The dissociated mental state

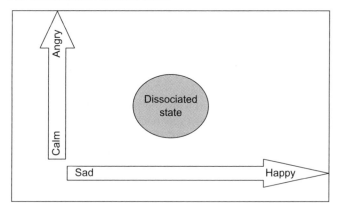

On the other hand, being able to dissociate from events in a controlled way is a very powerful technique. In another arena where mental control and calmness can be the difference on the podium, the world champion snooker player Jimmy White is attributed with the quote, 'Play like it means nothing when you know that it means everything.' He won the snooker World Cup three times playing for England and scored the maximum possible break of 147 points at the World Championship. The skill is being able to switch in and out of this state, and not living your life in it.

Exercise 3.32 Dissociating from stressful situations

This technique uses sub-modalities to affect our perception of events. Note that this exercise is very similar to one for curing phobias.

1. Think of a situation that previously made you feel stressed and notice the pictures, sounds and feelings associated with the situation.
2. Imagine stepping out of the picture and sending it, with its associated sounds and feelings, way off into the distance and watching it play out on a cinema screen far away.

3. Make the picture black and white, make it smaller and smaller and switch off any sounds and feelings.

4. While you are looking at the picture in the distance, notice if there are any new insights. Make a note if they have given you a new or different perspective on the situation.

5. Keep sending the cinema screen further and further away (ensuring there are no sounds or feelings there and that you are looking at yourself in the black and white picture) until you have no emotional response when watching the picture.

6. Think about a similar situation in the future that may have previously caused you to feel stressed and notice how you feel now. You should be feeling calm. If you do not, then repeat the exercise until you do feel calm. Alternatively, run the 'movie' backwards and add some 'keystone cops' music alongside it.

I ran this exercise as a demonstration with one person who felt herself very stressed when in the presence of one particular manager. The stress affected her performance, causing the manager to make remarks that fed back into the cycle. The exercise broke the negative feedback cycle completely. From there, she was able to explore his positive intent, and realised that he was not intentionally bullying anyone. He was just dissociated and ignorant of his impact. From then on, she could not help but giggle to herself every time she saw his face and associated it with that squeaky voice we sent all the way to Uranus. After being promoted that year, she has now left to be an NLP coach.

3.30.6 The mind–body connection and rapport with self

We never obtain peace in the outer world until we make peace with ourselves.

Dalai Lama

You may be one of the lucky ones who always seem to be in harmony with yourself. Some describe it as being 'grounded' or 'centred'. For the rest of us, there is usually some measure of internal conflict going on. This can manifest itself in self-sabotage, and in the extreme can progress towards depression, stress-related illness and worse. Some of us who work with NLP and health issues believe that this is because the conscious and unconscious mind fall out of rapport, and communication between the two breaks down. Stress is an excellent strategy for breaking down connection with ourselves, as it causes decisions to be made from the primitive part of our brain rather than our higher centres of consciousness. So, to get back into rapport with ourselves, we should first deal with stress in the moment, for example by using the techniques in Exercises 3.33, 3.34 and 3.35.

Exercise 3.33 Handling stress in the moment

We have talked about avoiding stressful situations, but what do we do if we find we are already in one? Try the following exercise to help you to get back to a calm state.

1. Breathe slower and deeper: usually we breathe fast and shallowly in the top of our lungs when we feel stressed (especially if we are visually oriented). Build-up of carbon dioxide in the lungs makes the heart race faster and can bring on a sense of panic without even trying. One of the first things to do is to slow down your rate by dropping your breathing all the way down into your diaphragm, using the whole of your lungs to breathe. Keep doing this until your breathing is deep and slow.

2. Anchor a calm state: repeat the 'circle of excellence' (Exercise 3.27 in Section 3.29.2), but use a different place to anchor states of calmness and add anything else that you think would be an antidote to your stressed state.

Tension is who you think you should be. Relaxation is who you are.

Chinese proverb

Exercise 3.34 Meditation and self-hypnosis

Invest in a calming hypnosis track to listen to before you go to sleep and listen to it regularly. I have several on my iPhone and listen to them when I am travelling by train to meetings. Paul McKenna has a hypnosis tape dedicated to controlling stress that accompanies his book of the same name.

Exercise 3.35 Get the juices flowing

NLP guru Anthony Robbins says, 'Motion is emotion';[127] that is, our physiology affects our mental state. Hence, to change your mental state over time, make big changes to your physiology, for example, through exercise. Make time in your life for regular exercise that gets your heart pumping and lungs breathing more deeply. It has these benefits:

- It will act as a 'pattern interrupt' technique to break long-lasting cycles of negative thoughts and emotions.

- It will keep you healthy (which can be a problem in relatively sedate office environments).

- It will stimulate your hormones in a natural cycle.

- The exercise itself will give you a dose of endorphins as a reward, which will counteract stress hormones.

---

127 Anthony Robbins, 1992, *Awaken the Giant Within*, Simon & Schuster.

3.30.7 Engineering happiness through daily habits

> He who lives in harmony with himself lives in harmony with the universe.
>
> Marcus Aurelius

I recommend daily journaling and reflection to anyone dedicated to ongoing personal and professional development. I reviewed a bestseller called *Happiness by Design* by Paul Dolan,[128] who was David Cameron's government advisor on wellbeing. He advocates the practice of only journaling positive experiences. The effect of this over time is to change our focus from things that have not gone as we might have liked towards even the small things that we have enjoyed or went well each day. In NLP terms, through habit, we are gradually shifting our frame, and hence managing our internal state, by repeatedly priming and anchoring those experiences. No particular surprise, then, that Paul Dolan was a doctoral student of Daniel Kahneman, the Nobel Laureate who introduced us to the effect of framing and priming on internal representation and decision making. As Dolan says, it is not what happens to us that determines how we evaluate our lives, but what we focus our attention on. When we are happy, we perform better, are more fun to be around and a better team player. Coming full circle, we become much more resilient. Of more than 100 'self-help' books I have read, the simple exercise set out in Exercise 3.36 is the one which I have personally found to achieve the biggest change in my base-line emotional state, even more than meditation, and it has helped me through some of my bleakest life events to date.

Exercise 3.36 Engineering your personal happiness

1. List things that you did well today.
2. List things that went well for you today.
3. List things that you enjoyed today.
4. List people that you enjoyed being with today.
5. List people that you would like to spend more time with.
6. List things that you would like to do more of.
7. Repeat until you have at least 10 things in your list.
8. Repeat at the end of each day in a journal. Over time they will become much easier to recall and you will be able to complete your list quickly as your focus changes.
9. Notice over time how you are doing more things you enjoy, focusing on things you enjoy, and spending more of your time feeling happy and content.
10. As your focus improves your demeanour, more people want to be around you, which causes a positive feedback loop.
11. Notice how you are becoming happier by design.

---

128 Paul Dolan, 2014, *Happiness by Design: Finding Pleasure and Purpose in Everyday Life*, Allen Lane.

So, do you want to focus on being happy, or obsess about things which probably won't happen? What are you going to do about it?

Life will bring you pain all by itself. Your responsibility is to create joy.

Milton H. Erickson

3.31 IMPROVE YOUR EMOTIONAL INTELLIGENCE THROUGH MEDITATION AND MINDFULNESS

Mindfulness has been shown to be an invaluable tool to help bolster people's resilience to psychological stress. It also boosts concentration, depth of thought, happiness and achievement.

Anthony Seldon, vice chancellor/CEO of Britain's first private university

I am an advocate of meditation, and I am not the only one. The incoming vice chancellor (CEO) of Britain's first private university has put mindfulness on the agenda for all medical students in order to help improve their emotional intelligence and to 'be calm and present in the moment and fully attentive to clients'.[129] Might it be useful to you too?

The techniques described in previous sections on stress management are most useful for managing stress in the moment, whereas the value of meditation is to gradually reset your equilibrium over time. After a session or a week of meditation you may not notice any difference, but when you make it a daily habit, and look back after a year, you will realise that your outlook and mood has changed.

At its core, meditation is about being in the present and connecting with yourself. In Section 3.7.2 I showed you how to move yourself to be 'in time' in preparation for various workplace activities that require you to be fully present. For meditation, our focus is internal rather than external. I think of it as a period of listening to what my body is telling me.

This approach might have seemed too new age for the corporate world only a few years ago, but the popularity of the approach in world leading companies at the forefront of innovation led many mainstream companies to follow suit, though the approach has been somewhat dumbed down.

At Google, they have a long elective course on mindfulness aligned to the principles of emotional intelligence, parallel to the approach taken here.[130] As a metaphor, think about your mind as being like a busy motorway junction, with lots of thoughts, ideas and concerns all rushing around you at speed. The act of mindfulness helps you to take a seat at the side of the road instead of standing in the middle of all the traffic. From our safe vantage point we can lose the emotional attachment to the traffic and let the noise quieten down. To mix metaphors, as the ripples in the pond start to dissipate, we start to get a sense of calm and a clearer reflection of who we really are. Try Exercise 3.37.

---

129 *The Sunday Times*, 3 May 2015, Education, page 9.
130 Google 'Search Inside Yourself' program https://siyli.org/ [accessed 13 July 2016].

Exercise 3.37 First steps in mindfulness

It also helps to be guided by a steady voice – you can download a soundtrack from the accompanying NLP4BAs website to get you started. Alternatively, you can download applications to your phone that will help you to practice mindfulness as well as discipline you into regular practice. For now, try these simple steps:

- Pick a regular time when you can prioritise 10 minutes for your own wellbeing and personal development. When you feel like really committing to yourself, put it in your diary as a regular appointment.

- Find a quiet place where you are not likely to be disturbed. You can make use of headphones. I regularly use my car, and have a set of noise cancelling headphones to use on train and plane journeys.

- Sit comfortably. Lying down can work if there is no risk of you falling asleep and messing up your diary.

- I like to keep my eyes just slightly open as a compromise between detachment and awareness.

- The key to this mindfulness exercise is your breathing. Focus on it and take some deep breaths. Breathe in through your nose and out through your mouth.

- Now, focus on your diaphragm and feel your stomach push out like a baby's when you breathe in.

- As you breathe out, let your shoulders drop with each breath until the tension has left your body.

- I visualise my breaths as bringing in light and energy, and exhaling black smoke as anything that is polluting my body or mind leaves my body.

- In this preparatory phase I start to register how my body feels, working down from my head to my toes. How are all the parts doing? I like to imagine that I can feel a change slowly working its way down my body.

- From the tip of your head, down your face, ears, chin, neck, shoulders, chest, sternum, spine, kidneys, liver, diaphragm, pelvis, thighs, knees, calves, ankles, feet, to the tip of your toes. Give them a wiggle. How is it all feeling, how is it working?

- Now, count 10 steady breaths in, and out, while focusing only on your breathing.

- Then let your mind drift where it wants to while you remain a passive observer to those thoughts.

- As your thoughts start to drift off, or 1–3 minutes in if you have a guide/recording, bring your focus back to your breaths and count 10 again.

- And let your mind drift again for a couple of minutes.

- And back to your breaths.

- Repeat 3–5 times.
- After your last set of 10 observable breaths, let your consciousness start to return the place you are in, and how good you feel to be alive.
- Now, with a calm mind, move forward into the rest of your day.

The key to this exercise is repetition for months, over which you are training your mind to focus and dissociate from thoughts and emotions at will. With long-term practice you will be better trained to be in charge of your thoughts and emotions rather than a hostage to them.

When you can completely control your thoughts and emotions, how might your life be different?

Mindfulness helps you go home to the present.

Nhat Hanh

3.32 THE IMPORTANCE OF ETHICS

It is true that integrity alone won't make you a leader, but without integrity you will never be one.

Zig Ziglar

Ethical behaviour is once again becoming fashionable in society and to the professions,[131] and was specifically mentioned in the review of competency frameworks in Section 1.4.2. The popular backlash to the near failure of the global banking system is likely to accelerate the pace of change.

NLP, when done well, can achieve incredible personal change. Therefore, it must be done with due care and in an ethical manner. One of the cornerstone publications to bring NLP into the domain of management in 1983 was the well-named book *Influencing with Integrity*.[132] What we refer to as 'well-formed outcomes' (Section 3.28) means that the goals we set for personal change must be in the best interests of all parties. If we are naive enough to attempt to effect change that is not in the interests of all parties, then we are not likely to succeed because we will lack 'congruence'. That is, our words and actions will not be aligned. This is evident when we see some people trained in NLP-like sales techniques subverting the process by trying to persuade potential customers to buy things that they do not need. This results in the seller coming over as desperate, and the victim suffering from buyer's remorse.

NLP *can* be used effectively for sales by using techniques to establish if the prospect has a need and is likely to buy, where they are in their buying cycle and what their buying strategy is. If they do not have a need for what we offer, then a good sales-person quickly

---

131 A. Godbold, 2009, 'Ethics in Project Management', Presentation given to the APM Annual Conference, London, October.
132 G. Z. Laborde, 1984, *Influencing with Integrity: Management Skills for Communication and Negotiation*, Crown House.

moves on to the next prospect without wasting the time of either party. NLP can also be used to model excellent behaviour from successful peers in sales.[133]

Similarly, when people try to manipulate matching and mirroring of body language in order to gain rapport for some selfish end, it comes over as creepy and can actually break rapport. In my opinion, 'mirroring' is best used as an output measure to test whether rapport has been achieved rather than as an input to effect rapport artificially. If you take an honest and active interest in people, then you will naturally achieve rapport without the need to fake it.

> Trust because you are willing to take the risk, not because it is certain or safe.
>
> Zig Ziglar

3.33 SUMMARY OF PART 3

> In my experience, popular NLP is about 10% real and 90% marketing. But the real part is very powerful.
>
> Scott Adams, Ericksonian-trained wizard, author of *Dilbert*[134]

Part 3 started by making the case for using NLP to help develop emotional intelligence and agile behaviours. We learned that, although the theory is important, it is structured practice which builds the professional.

We built on the work of Covey and other management gurus who promoted the need to 'sharpen our toolset' and maintain a thirst for continuous development. To achieve something, we must first believe that it is possible, and we introduced a process for changing limiting beliefs.

From Plato onwards, we were advised that our most fundamental requirement is for self-awareness, and we explored the use of language and behaviour profiling of our 60-plus meta-programs to understand ourselves and where we might need to flex our behaviours according to context to become more agile in our mindset. We went on to look at the basic process for modelling effective behaviours.

As a BA, sometimes you need to be able to see the big picture, while at other times you need to understand the detail. Sometimes you need to explore options, while for some activities you need to manage the process. NLP techniques to choose preferences were practised, as was matching of language to different stakeholders with different preferences.

Cross-cultural working, both in terms of nationalities and organisational and professional cultures, was explored. 'Yes' does not always mean that, and we practised using

---

133 J. O'Connor and R. Prior, 1995, *Successful Selling with NLP*, Thorsons.
134 Scott Adams, August 2015, 'Wizard Wars', Scott Adams' Blog http://blog.dilbert.com/post/126916006856/wizard-wars/ [accessed 13 July 2016].

our sensory acuity to determine what was behind it. The role of the team charter in establishing common values and behaviours was described.

Timelines are a big theme in NLP, and tools for developing flexibility in being people-focused or task-focused were introduced. We practised being 'in the moment'. Better ways to match the natural inclinations of different stakeholders using language patterns were discussed.

'Future pacing', often used by successful athletes and business people to imagine them-selves having already achieved their goals, was applied to the highly effective 'pre-mortem' technique to imagine looking back on projects to identify possible causes of failure.

Leadership means different things to different people, and the evolution of emotional intelligence in leadership, which is about influence rather than authority, was described. We explored different styles of leadership, from command and control to coaching, and contexts where they were useful and where they were not. The role of coaching and self-coaching was explored further.

Storytelling and use of metaphor have been used by all the great leaders and we mod-elled some of those patterns. We discussed when we should switch from precise lan-guage to vague language patterns to motivate diverse groups towards a common vision, and what those patterns looked like. We learned that these NLP techniques have been taught by past and present NLP 'wizards' to past and present global leaders.

We moved on to self-management; how to manage our own mental state and thoughts to present ourselves with charisma and give confidence to ourselves and our audience. Personal values, attributes and authenticity were introduced, alongside exercises to explore and develop our personal brand.

Part of the BA role is to facilitate solutions, and we practised modelling Walt Disney's strategy for creativity. We moved on to look at how we should harness the wisdom of crowds to co-create the future business through a process of facilitation.

We cannot talk about business analysis without talking about requirements. Following the words of Steve Jobs – Zen Buddhist and NLP wizard, not to mention founder of Apple – we cannot always expect the customer to know what they want. We practised several techniques for separating needs from wants using different approaches and strategies for framing better questions for better answers.

Having determined requirements, we went on to a big section on the different elements of implementing transformational change. Again, future pacing was used to co-create a common vision, and we applied language patterns to create a 'burning deck' to acceler-ate change. The key enablers of change were reinforced, and techniques for overcoming common barriers were described.

Managing key stakeholders is paramount to success, and we explored hard tools and soft skills for effective engagement. As we discussed in Part 2, we all have our own maps of the world and differing perspectives, and we focused on effective approaches and language patterns to build rapport fast.

Communicating change is required to achieve engagement, and we looked at the different ways people take on and filter information. We practised flexing delivery styles and language patterns to engage a wider audience.

We know that communication is more about listening than talking, and we explored how the NLP 'meta-model' can help us to uncover not only deletions and distortions, but also the other party's map of the world and the filters they apply.

The person who sets the frame of a discussion is at a great advantage, and we looked at how to frame and reframe conversations. Although we cannot affect those events that have already happened, we can change their effect on us by reframing how we think about them and hence their impact on our emotional state.

It is said that life is a negotiation, and we practised an array of NLP techniques to bridge the communication gap, including use of second position to explore the other party's map of the world and the way our words might make them feel. We used the process of 'chunking' to gain agreement.

Often we need to assert our position, and we modelled a simple strategy to assert ourselves early without provoking aggression.

The sum is greater than the parts, and we laid the foundation for building high performance teams. Common 'dysfunctions' usually stand in the way of effective teams, so we looked at ways of reducing those behaviours.

Although the perspectives of BAs and PMs were shown to be different through the lifecycle, they are complementary. They work best when they recognise that they are a partnership and establish a superordinate goal and collaborative working.

The relationship between motivation towards goals and common values was established, and we practised turning dreams into reality using the structure of 'well-formed outcomes'.

Having jumped from knowing our self to understanding and influencing others, we returned to what the emotional intelligence school refer to as managing ourselves. We learned that we choose our state, and practised choosing resourceful states. We also looked at a range of NLP techniques for managing stress and building resilience. While we need to be able to deal with pressure in the moment, longer term it helps to engineer our thinking to a more resilient state, and we practised some tools for 'engineering happiness'.

The approach of mindfulness is used in some organisations, including Google, to help develop emotional intelligence, and simple patterns to practise were laid down in exercises.

It has been said by influential people recently that, although popular NLP can be 90 per cent marketing, the remaining 10 per cent is highly effective and is used by captains of countries and industry to profoundly influence our decisions. Hence it is necessary to stress the role of ethics – we are bound to work for the benefit of those parties and not for self-interest. For those that stray from this path, they become incongruent and lack authenticity. Trust and rapport are lost, and without rapport you do not have anything.

So, in conclusion, as NLP is a methodology for modelling effective behaviours and language patterns, it provides a very powerful approach to increasing all aspects of emotional intelligence, from self-awareness and self-management, through social awareness to understanding what is going on around us in the heads of other people, to being able to influence those people in very elegant ways. As we read in the Introduction, these complement the procedural aspects of business analysis to build the truly professional BA. Study and practice it and you too can become even more agile. For more information of further practical study visit http://www.NLP4BA.com.

I don't think much of a man who is not wiser today than he was yesterday.

Albert Einstein

INDEX